Quicken 99

FOR BUSY PEOPLE

Blueprints for Quicken 99

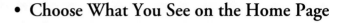

On the following pages, we provide blueprints for some of the best ways to use Quicken 99:

- Choose What You See on the Home Page

- Balance a Bank Account Quickly

- Write and Print Checks Electronically

- Get a Bank Statement Online

- Pay Your Bills Online

- Update Your Stock Portfolio Online

- Generate Reports and Graphs

- Track Your Investments

- Get a Jump Start on Your Taxes

Schedule payments so you can be reminded
to make them each time you start Quicken. You
can record these payments directly from the
Home Page (pages 142-149).

Choose for yourself what appears
on the Home Page, the first window
you see when you start
Quicken (pages 55-56).

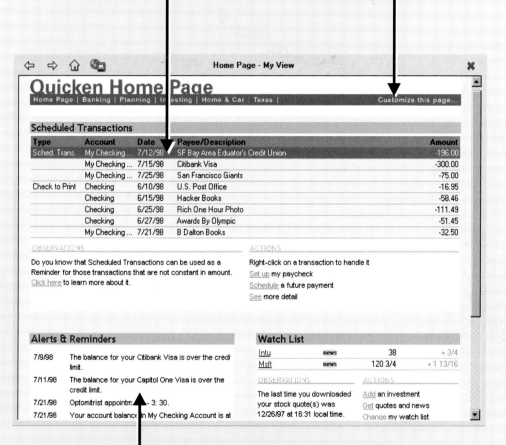

Make alerts and reminders appear on the
Home Page so you can tell when you're low
on checks or when an account drops below
a minimum balance, for example (pages 140-142).

Having trouble reconciling an account?
These buttons can help (pages 87-89).

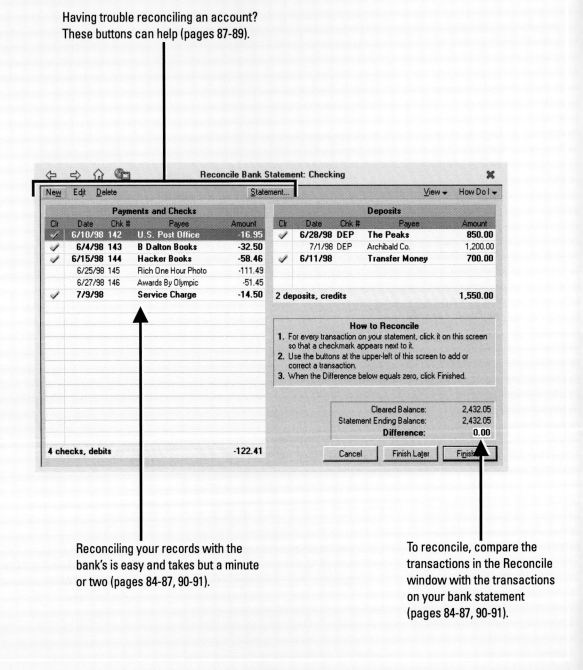

Reconciling your records with the
bank's is easy and takes but a minute
or two (pages 84-87, 90-91).

To reconcile, compare the
transactions in the Reconcile
window with the transactions
on your bank statement
(pages 84-87, 90-91).

Print your checks to establish a more professional image
with creditors and clients (pages 98-99, 107-108).

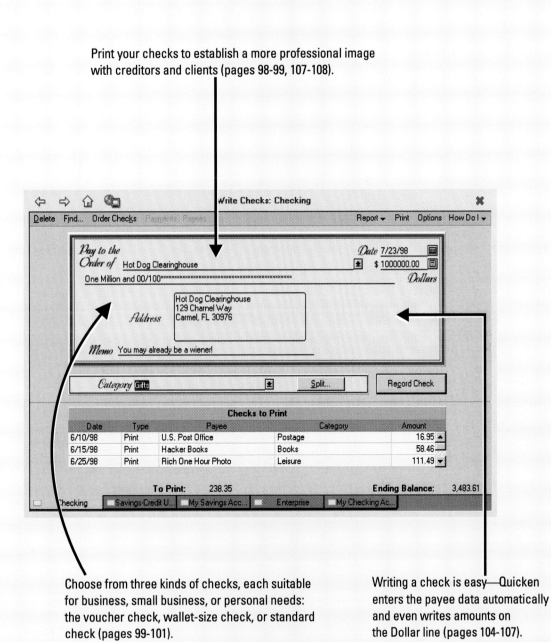

Choose from three kinds of checks, each suitable
for business, small business, or personal needs:
the voucher check, wallet-size check, or standard
check (pages 99-101).

Writing a check is easy—Quicken
enters the payee data automatically
and even writes amounts on
the Dollar line (pages 104-107).

Download a bank statement over the Internet
and find out which transactions have cleared
and what the balance in your account is (pages 122-126).

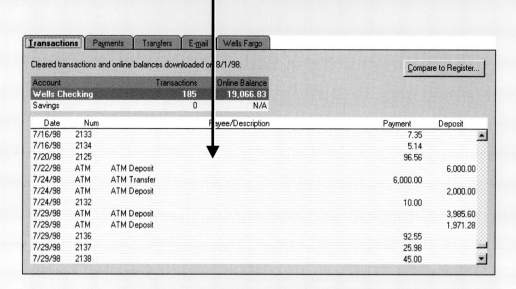

To reconcile an account online, compare the
records in your register to the bank's records
(pages 122-126).

Sign up with your bank to pay bills over the Internet. It's a little cheaper and a lot faster than paying bills by mail (pages 118-120).

Transfer money between accounts and send e-mail to your bank (pages 121-122, 126-128).

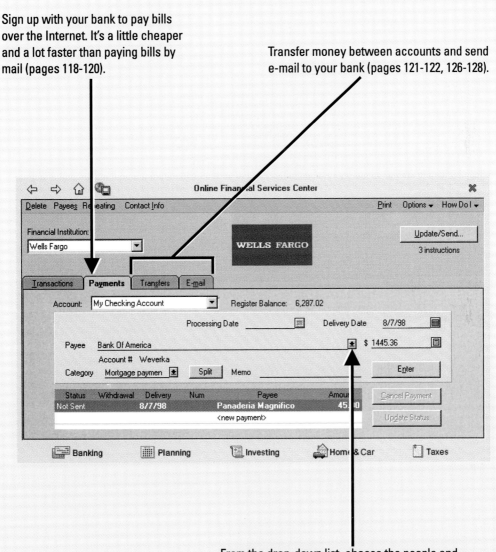

From the drop-down list, choose the people and companies you intend to pay. Payments, along with e-mail messages and electronic funds transfers, are sent when you connect to the Internet (pages 128-131).

Security prices are downloaded directly into the Portfolio View window, which lists the value of your investments (pages 258-260).

You can update the values of the securities you own instantly from the Internet—and it's free (pages 131-133, 257-258).

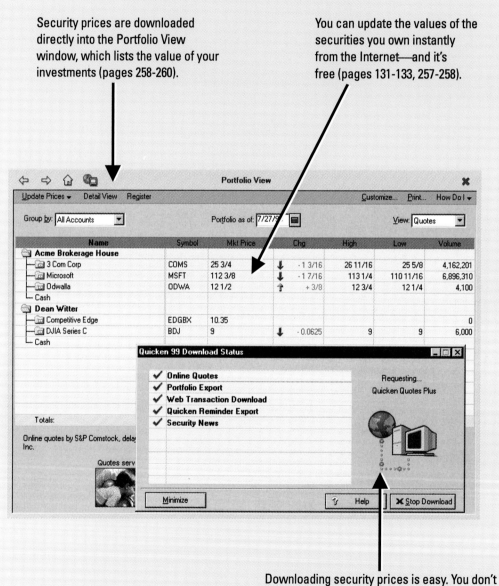

Downloading security prices is easy. You don't have to negotiate the Internet or make a lot of menu selections (pages 131-133).

Display any of Quicken's five graphs in 2-D, 3-D, black-and-white, or color (pages 164-170).

Customize a report of your own or use one of Quicken's 29 ready-made reports (pages 159-164).

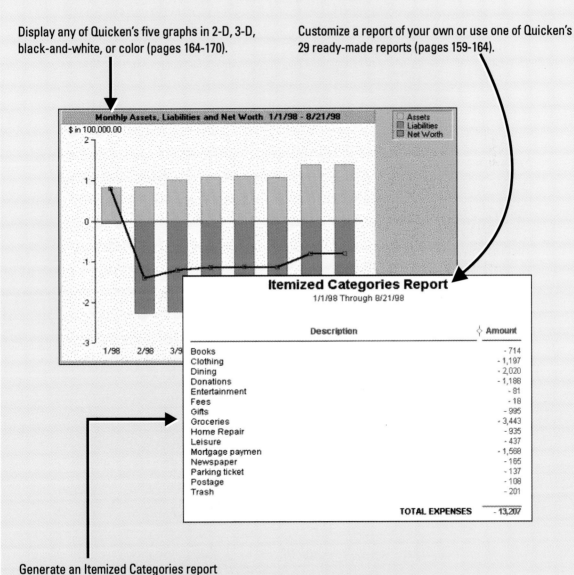

Generate an Itemized Categories report to show how much you've spent in each category and subcategory (pages 159-161).

Record the purchase or sale of shares, dividends, and stock splits, among other investment transactions, so you can track the true value of your investments (pages 263-271).

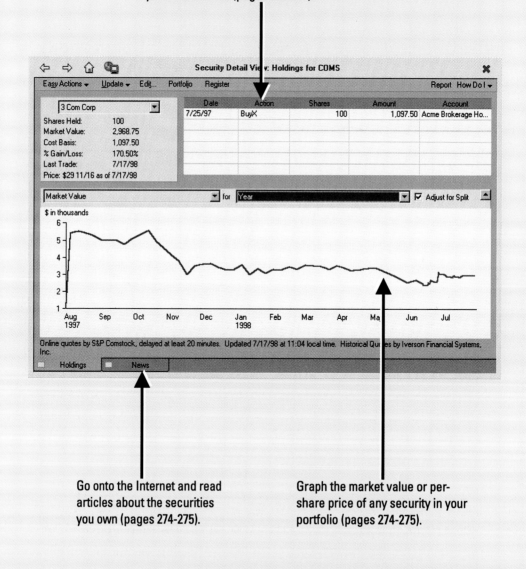

Go onto the Internet and read articles about the securities you own (pages 274-275).

Graph the market value or per-share price of any security in your portfolio (pages 274-275).

Use Quicken's Tax Planner to see how
purchasing a house or changing jobs will
affect your taxes (pages 286-289).

Import your Quicken data directly into
the TurboTax tax-preparation program
(page 291).

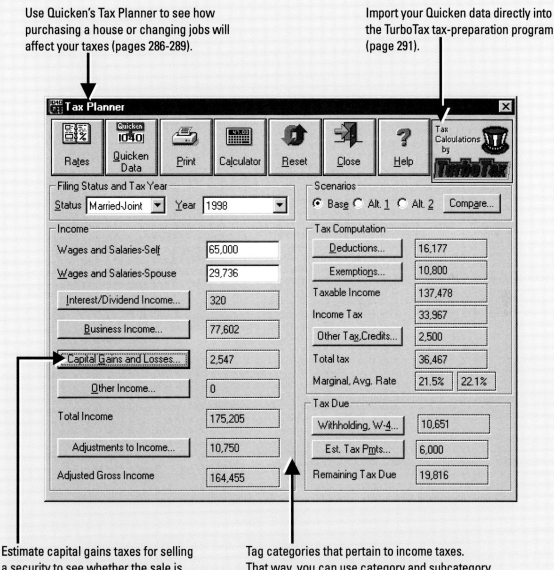

Estimate capital gains taxes for selling
a security to see whether the sale is
worthwhile (pages 289-290).

Tag categories that pertain to income taxes.
That way, you can use category and subcategory
data to calculate you income taxes (pages 281-284).

Quicken 99

FOR BUSY PEOPLE

The Book to Use When There's No Time to Lose!

Peter Weverka

OSBORNE

Osborne/**McGraw-Hill**

Berkeley / New York / St. Louis / San Francisco / Auckland / Bogotá
Hamburg / London / Madrid / Mexico City / Milan / Montreal / New Delhi
Panama City / Paris / São Paulo / Singapore / Sydney / Tokyo / Toronto

*A Division of The **McGraw·Hill** Companies*

Osborne/**McGraw-Hill**
2600 Tenth Street
Berkeley, California 94710
U.S.A.

For information on translations or book distributors outside the U.S.A., or to arrange bulk purchase discounts for sales promotions, premiums, or fund-raisers, please contact Osborne/**McGraw-Hill** at the above address.

Quicken 99 for Busy People

1234567890 DOC DOC 90198765432109

ISBN 0-07-211916-0

Publisher: Brandon A. Nordin
Editor-in-Chief: Scott Rogers
Acquisitions Editor: Joanne Cuthbertson
Project Editor: Nancy McLaughlin
Editorial Assistant: Stephane Thomas
Technical Editors: Robin Merrin, Tom Merrin
Copy Editor: Claire Splan
Proofreader: Jeff Barash
Indexer: Rebecca Plunkett
Computer Designer: Mickey Galicia, Jean Butterfield, Peter F. Hancik
Illustrator: Lance Ravella, Brian Wells
Series and Cover Design: Ted Mader Associates

For Henry, a busy lad

About the Author

Peter Weverka is the author of Osborne's *Quicken 98 for Busy People*, and co-author of *Windows 98 for Busy People* (with Ron Mansfield) and *Office 97: The Complete Reference* (with Stephen Nelson). He has edited more than 80 computer books, and he writes for various magazines, including *Harper's* and *Spy*.

Contents at a glance

Contents

ACKNOWLEDGMENTS

I would like to thank the usual suspects at Osborne/McGraw-Hill for their work on this book. My name appears on its cover, but this book is *truly* a collective effort.

My thanks go especially to copy editor Claire Splan for deftly wielding the scalpel, and to project editors Nancy McLaughlin and Cynthia Douglas for ensuring that the manuscript and artwork traveled smoothly through the production process. Special thanks to Stephane Thomas, finder of lost books, for her encouragement and for keeping this book on schedule.

Tom and Robin Merrin pored over the manuscript to make sure that all the instructions on these pages are indeed the right ones, and Jeff Barash went over the typeset pages with a currycomb to repair last-minute errors and typesetting snafus. Thanks as well go to indexer Rebecca Plunkett for her superb work.

As always, Osborne's Production team went the extra mile to make sure that this book meets the company's standards. I would like to thank Mickey Galicia, Jean Butterfield, and Peter F. Hancik for typesetting the manuscript and for their meticulous layout work.

Thanks again to all these editors who worked on the first and second editions of this book: Michelle Khazai, Mark Karmendy, Sally Engelfried, and Gordon Hurd.

Finally, thanks to Publisher Brandon Nordin, Editor-in-Chief Scott Rogers, and Acquisitions Editor Joanne Cuthbertson for their passionate support of the *Busy People* series, and to Sofia, Henry, and Addie for tolerating my vampirish working hours and strange, eerie demeanor at daybreak.

Peter Weverka
San Francisco
August, 1998

INTRODUCTION

Officially, Quicken 99 is a software program for tracking your finances, but unofficially the program is much, much more than that. By following the directions and advice in this book, you can use Quicken as a tool for making wise financial decisions—choices that will be your first steps toward financial security.

In order to make sound financial decisions, you must be conscientious of your spending habits and know how much income you really have. How can you save for a down payment on a house if you don't know how much you are capable of saving? How can you tell if your investments are doing well if you don't track them carefully? Before you can change the way you live, at least from a financial standpoint, you have to keep accurate records.

Quicken makes it very, very easy. Balancing a checkbook and doing other mundane banking chores is simple with Quicken. Quicken users can track their investments, record information about how they spend their money, draw up budgets, and even pay bills and get financial advice online. These days, with so many folks owning mutual fund shares and stocks, personal finances are more complicated than ever. Having a program like Quicken can be helpful indeed.

After you know where you stand financially, you can use the data you've collected about yourself to start refining your financial decisions. Using the techniques laid out in this book, you can find out what your net worth is, how much you spend in different areas, what your investments (if you have any) are worth, and how much you will owe in taxes next year. You will know how to print your own checks, generate reports and graphs that describe in clear terms what your spending habits are, plan for your retirement, compare mortgages and loans, analyze different types of investments, and even get a credit report about yourself from the Internet.

WHO SHOULD BUY THIS BOOK?

This book is for users of Quicken 99 and Quicken 99 Deluxe, the newest versions of Intuit's popular computer program. It is for intelligent, busy people who want to get to the heart of Quicken and its many excellent features without having to spend a lot of time doing so.

You don't need to know much about computers to make use of this book or Quicken. What you do need to know I will explain in passing. One reason Quicken is so popular is that it doesn't ask its users to know computers well. All you have to know to is how to turn the computer on and wiggle your fingers over the keyboard.

WHAT'S IN THIS BOOK, ANYWAY?

Everything that is essential and helpful in Quicken, everything that might be of use to a busy person, is explained in this book. And it is all explained in such a way that you will learn how to make Quicken serve *you*. I don't simply describe how to use Quicken in this book—I tell you how to crack the whip and make Quicken do *your* bidding.

Chapter 1 explains the basics of starting the program and setting up accounts. It tells how to find your way around the screen and use Quicken's Help program. In Chapter 2, you learn how to record financial transactions, fix entry mistakes, and print a register.

Chapter 3 presents a number of tasks that you can do right away to make your work in Quicken more productive. It explains how to set up categories so you know precisely where you spend money, how to make the Quicken Reminders screen work your way, and how to choose what you see when Quicken starts. Chapter 4 picks up where Chapter 3 left off, explaining how to use supercategories, categories, and classes to monitor your income and spending.

In Quicken, many different features work hand-in-hand to give users a comprehensive understanding of their finances. Unlike other books about Quicken, this one includes numerous cross-references so you can jump from place to place and learn how to make all of Quicken's features work for you. Watch for cross-references like this in the page margin.

Chapter 5 simplifies the onerous task of balancing, or reconciling, a bank account, and Chapter 6 explains everything you need to know about printing checks.

I hereby dedicate Chapter 7 to Flash Gordon, brave citizen of the future. Chapter 7 describes how to enter the exciting but scary world of cyberspace, where all money is digital and nobody pays cash for anything. It explains how to pay bills online, download account records, and get stock quotes.

Chapter 8 describes how to use Quicken like your very own executive secretary—it can help you schedule payments, keep important addresses, and jot down reminder notes. In Chapter 9, you'll learn how to get a fix on your finances by generating reports and graphs. Chapter 10 spells out how to back up Quicken data, copy and delete files, and put passwords on files so others can't peek at them.

In Chapter 11 you'll learn how to keep track of loans, liabilities, and assets. Chapter 12 explains how to plan for your retirement and your child's college education, and how to forecast your future income. Chapter 13 gets into financial analysis techniques, including how to shop for loans and mortgages and calculate how an investment will grow.

Chapter 14 addresses the arduous problem of tracking investments. There you'll learn how to record everything from stock splits to corporate securities spin-offs. Finally, Chapter 15 teaches you how to prepare for tax time with Quicken. You'll learn how to estimate what your income tax will be, find tax deductions, generate tax reports, and use Quicken along with TurboTax to report your income taxes.

GETTING THE MOST OUT OF THIS BOOK...

Since you, like most of us, are probably a busy person, this book was designed and written to take you straight to the instructions you need. In that spirit, you will find the following elements in this book. They point to important things you should know about in the text.

Blueprints

The blueprints at the very front of this book are like previews of coming attractions. While you are waiting for the movie to begin, look at the blueprints. The page numbers on the blueprints tell you where to turn in this book to learn more about a topic that has aroused your curiosity.

Fast Forwards

Each chapter begins with a handful of Fast Forwards. Fast Forwards are step-by-step, abbreviated instructions for doing things that are explained later on. Each Fast Forward is cross-referenced to pages in the chapter that you may turn to for all the details. However, you might not need the details. You might find that you're savvy enough to learn all you need to know from a Fast Forward!

Expert Advice

Where you see the egghead dude and the words "Expert Advice," prick up your ears and read attentively, because that is where you will find timesaving tips and techniques that will help you become a better Quicken user.

Shortcuts

In Quicken, there are often two ways to do things—the fast but dicey way, and the slow, thorough way. Whenever you see this necktie guy leaping over the fence, you'll know I'm explaining a fast but dicey technique. He is taking a shortcut. You can safely follow his lead by reading the Shortcuts carefully.

Cautions

The Quicken computer program is for tracking money, where it goes, and where it comes from. Your money is nothing to trifle with, so when I describe a task that you might regret doing later or that you should think carefully about before doing, I do so in a Caution. The imp peeking out of the manhole cover obviously did not read the Cautions!

Definitions

See this fellow? He has good muscle definition and a very small head. Where you see him, you will also find a word definition. Do you know what "amortized" means? How about "taskbar"? With the help of this aching turboguy, I define financial and computer terms throughout this book.

STEP BY STEP

Step by Step

When I describe an especially complicated or long-winded procedure, I put it in a blue "Step by Step" box, along with a picture of the relevant Quicken screen. These Step by Steps are meant to help you learn tasks quickly and thoroughly. Use them as references when you have forgotten how to perform a procedure, or when you need to brush up on a task you already know.

I'D LIKE TO HEAR FROM YOU!

If you have a comment about this book or a question about Quicken 99, or if you'd like to share one of your own shortcuts or tricks for using the program, then please send me an e-mail message. I am being held hostage at **Peter_Weverka@msn.com**. All inquiries and comments are welcome, because they help me pass the time in captivity. Best of luck with Quicken!

The Bare Essentials

INCLUDES

- Starting Quicken

- Exploring the Quicken screen

- The different kinds of accounts

- Setting up an account

- Creating a new file for recording transactions

- Exiting Quicken

- Running the Quicken Help program

FAST FORWARD

Start Quicken ➤ pp. 5-6

Quicken
Deluxe 99

- Double-click the Quicken 99 icon (or the QuickEntry 99 icon if you only want to enter a few account transactions).
- Click the Start button on the taskbar, choose Programs | Quicken (and Quicken Deluxe 99 as well, if you are running Quicken Deluxe).

Choose a Command from a Menu ➤ p. 8

1. Open the menu by clicking on it or by pressing ALT and the key that is underlined in the menu name.
2. When the menu appears, click a command or else press the underlined letter in the command name.

Remove (or View) the Iconbar or Activity Bar ➤ p. 8

1. Right-click on the empty, right side of the screen to see the shortcut menu.
2. Click Show Top Iconbar to remove (or add) the check mark.
3. Choose Show Activity Bar to remove (or add) the check mark.

Set Up a Savings or Checking Account ➤ pp. 11-16

1. Choose Features | Banking | Create New Account. In the Create New Account dialog box, click the Checking or Savings button.
2. Click Next, and, on the EasyStep tab, enter an account name and description. Then click the Next button.
3. If you have your last bank statement, make sure the Yes option button is selected, click Next, enter the statement date and ending balance, and click Next again. However, it isn't necessary to enter the account balance information now. You can simply

click the No option button, click Next, and click Next again after you've read the "That's Okay" screen.

4. Click No if this isn't an online account. Otherwise, click Yes and refer to Chapter 7, which explains online banking. Click Next to move ahead to the following screen.

5. Read the Summary tab and make sure that the information you entered is indeed accurate. You can make changes on this screen if you want.

6. Click the Info button and, on the Additional Account Information screen, jot down intimate details about the account, and click OK.

7. Click Done.

Exit Quicken ➤ *pp. 17-18*

- Choose File | Exit.
- Click the Close button (the X) in the upper-right corner of the Quicken screen.

Take Advantage of Quicken's Help Program ➤ *pp. 18-19*

- Press F1 or click the Help button on the iconbar to get information about the screen you are currently looking at.
- Choose Help | Index to get to the Help Topics dialog box; from there you can go to the Index tab and look up subjects in alphabetical order, to the Contents tab and search for help by topic, or to the Find tab to run a keyword search of the Help files.
- Click the How Do I button and then choose a question.
- Click the Help button in dialog boxes.

This chapter gives you the lay of the land. It describes which buttons to click and which commands to choose to get around in Quicken. In this chapter, I tell you the one or two things you should know right off the bat if you want to get the most out of Quicken. I also explain how to start and close the program and how to open an account and a new file. Last of all, this chapter describes the Quicken Help commands in case you want to seek advice from Quicken itself.

A WORD TO THE WISE

Quicken makes it very, very easy to record financial transactions. When you want to balance a savings or checking account, you don't have to punch calculator keys or scribble numbers in the margin of a checkbook, because Quicken does the math for you. To find your net worth, all you have to do is click one or two buttons. You can keep track of where you spend money. If you want to know how much you spent on groceries, federal income taxes, pet grooming, tattoos, or another spending category, you only have to give a command.

That is the good news. The bad news is that you have to enter financial data carefully for Quicken to do its job well. To see why getting the numbers right is important, look at the graphs in Figure 1.1 (Chapter 9 explains how to create graphs like this one). For the Monthly Income and Expenses bar graph to be accurate, you must faithfully record paychecks and investment income. For the Expense Comparison pie chart to be accurate, you must categorize expenses carefully.

If all you want to do is balance your checking and savings accounts, you've got it made. The program gives you lots of opportunities to double-check the accuracy of checking and savings account transactions. But if you are using

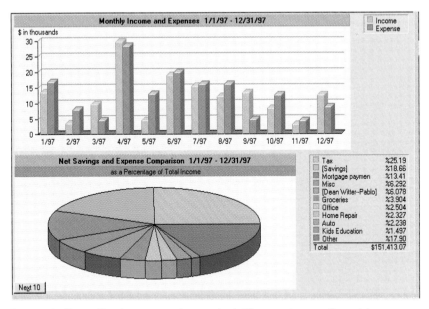

Figure 1.1   Charts like these are only meaningful if you enter your financial data correctly.

Quicken to track investments, to budget, to compare investments, or to do anything that falls on the far side of complexity, you have to be careful when entering your data.

STARTING QUICKEN

Starting Quicken is as easy as falling off a log. As shown in Figure 1.2, all you have to do to start the program is click the Start button on the left side of the *taskbar* (the stripe along the bottom of the Windows screen), click Programs to see the Programs menu, and click Quicken. If you are a user of Quicken Deluxe, you also have to choose Quicken Deluxe 99 on the submenu.

Quicken
Deluxe 99

An even faster way to start Quicken is to double-click one of the Quicken shortcut icons on the desktop, the Quicken icon or the QuickEntry icon. When you installed Quicken, the program created these shortcut icons for you. The shortcut icon is the big dollar sign that says "Quicken 99" or "Quicken Deluxe 99" underneath it. Double-click it to start Quicken.

QuickEntry 99

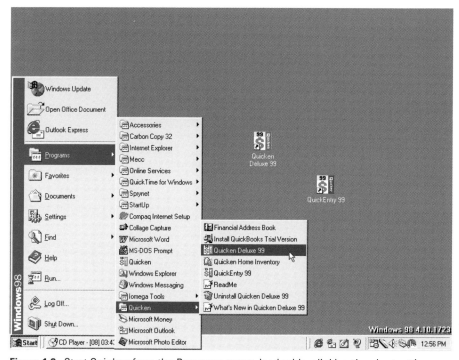

Figure 1.2 Start Quicken from the Programs menu, by double-clicking the shortcut icon, or by double-clicking the QuickEntry icon.

"QuickEntry: The Fast Way to Enter Transactions" in Chapter 2 explains how the QuickEntry screen works.

Double-clicking the QuickEntry icon opens the QuickEntry screen, where you can enter one or two transactions. When you start Quicken in earnest, you see a list of the transactions you entered in the QuickEntry screen. From there, you can enter your transactions into Quicken by clicking a button.

A FAST TRIP AROUND THE QUICKEN SCREEN

The Quicken screen looks intimidating at first. Why all the buttons, pictures, doodads, and menus? With this much clutter, you could be watching MTV. The screen is so cluttered because much of it is redundant. In other words, a lot of these buttons and whatnots activate the same commands. To create a report, for example, you can choose Reports | EasyAnswer Reports, click the Reports icon on the iconbar, or click the Planning button on the activity bar and choose Report on my spending from the pop-up menu.

Figure 1.3 shows the main ingredients of the Quicken screen. Don't let the screen intimidate you. Soon you will know your way around the screen as well as the fastest and best way to get from place to place. To help you get off on the right foot, the following pages describe the Quicken screen in detail.

Chapter 3, "Stuff to Do Once to Make Your Life Easier," shows how to tweak the Quicken screen and make it work better for you.

Figure 1.3 The Quicken screen with a register on top. Five windows are open; their Quick Tabs appear on the right side of the screen.

The Menu Bar

Quicken's *menu bar*, found along the top of the screen, offers eight menus. To open a menu and see its commands, either click on its name or press the ALT key and the letter that is underlined in its name. To open the File menu, for example, either click File on the menu bar or press ALT-F. To choose a command from an open menu, either click its name or press the letter that is underlined in its name.

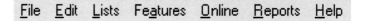

The Iconbar

Below the menu bar is a long string of icons called the *iconbar*. Click an icon to give a command. The icons are very useful and are the fastest way to give commands. I explain what the icons do throughout this book.

Direction Buttons

The *direction buttons*—Go Back, Go Forward, and Go to my Quicken Home Page—work much like the Back, Forward, and Home buttons on a Web browser:

- **Go Back**   Returns you to a screen you were viewing before. Quicken remembers the screens you have visited. Click the Go Back button to retrace your footsteps across several screens.

- **Go Forward**   Takes you to a screen that you retreated from.

- **Go to my Quicken Home Page**   Takes you to the Home Page, your home base and the first screen you see when you start Quicken.

EXPERT ADVICE

Throughout the Quicken program, but especially on the Home Page and "Center" screens—Banking, Planning, Investing, Home & Car, and Tax—are hyperlinks that you can click to get from place to place. These hyperlinks work like the hyperlinks on a Web site: Click one and you land in a new location. You can tell where the hyperlinks are because the pointer changes into a gloved hand when you move it over a link.

Account Buttons

Along the top of the register are the *account buttons*, which are explained throughout this book. For now, all you need to know is that clicking an account button is one of the fastest ways to give a command in Quicken.

Close Button

Click the *Close button* (the X) in the upper-right corner of a Quicken window when you get tired of looking at it. Clicking the Close button snaps the window shut and removes its Quick Tab from the right side of the screen as well.

Quick Tabs for Turning Quicken's "Pages"

On the right side of the screen are the *Quick Tabs*, one each for the register, window, report, and whatnot that you have opened or created in Quicken. Click a Quick Tab to go to another open window. In the illustration shown here, a grand total of five tabs appears. By clicking one, you could move to the Account List window, a register, the Home Page, the Tax Center, or an Account Balances report.

Registers, Registers, and More Registers

If you've ever had a job as a bookkeeper or accountant, you know that a *register* is a book for recording expenditures and revenue. For each account you set up, Quicken creates a register. You can see a credit card register in Figure 1.3.

Registers look different depending on the kind of account you are dealing with, but all have places for entering transaction dates and transaction amounts. Here is a checking account register:

Date	Num	PayeeCategory		Payment	Clr	Deposit	Balance
4/24/98	2000	Rooftop PTA		8 00	R		4,574 31
		Donations					
4/26/98	2001	NCTC		25 00			4,549 31
		Kids Education	Application fee				
4/27/98	2002	PG & E		47 76	R		4,501 55

Account Tabs for Switching Between Accounts

In Chapter 3, "Rearrange the Account Tabs" demonstrates how to line up the buttons the way you want them to line up.

Along the bottom of each register is a row of *account tabs*. You will find one color-coded tab for each account you set up. Account tabs make it easy to open account registers. Rather than go to the trouble of opening an account register by going to the Account List window, all you have to do is click an account tab. If you track more than six accounts, arrows appear on the left and right sides of the account tabs. Click an arrow to slide the tabs over and get to the one you are looking for.

The Activity Buttons

Yet another way to give commands is to click one of the *activity buttons* along the bottom of the screen. (If you don't see the buttons, right-click on the empty area below the Quick Tabs and choose Show Activity Bar from the shortcut menu.) Click one of these buttons and a small menu appears. I mention the activity buttons and menus throughout this book. For now, all you need to know is that the activity buttons present yet another way to give commands in Quicken:

SETTING UP AN ACCOUNT

When most people hear the word "account," they think of bank accounts—checking accounts, savings accounts, and the like. In Quicken, an "account" is simply a way to track the value of something. There are nine kinds of accounts: checking, savings, credit card, cash, money market, investment, asset, liability, and 401(k).

Whatever the account you want to set up, the basic procedure is the same. The following few pages explain the different kinds of accounts and how to set them up.

The Different Kinds of Accounts

Figure 1.4 shows the dialog box for choosing which kind of account type to set up. I trust you know already what the Checking, Savings, and Credit Card buttons are for. What about the others?

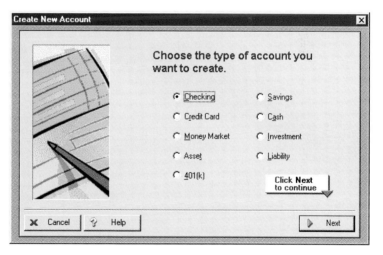

Figure 1.4 Choose which kind of account to set up in the Create New Account dialog box.

This short list explains what the nine accounts are:

Account	What It Is For
Checking	Recording activity in a checking account.
Savings	Recording activity in a savings account.
Credit Card	Recording credit card transactions, finance charges, and credit card payments. See "Recording Transactions in Credit Card Accounts" in Chapter 2 for details.
Cash	Recording old-fashioned cash payments and tracking petty cash accounts. See "Managing a Cash Account" in Chapter 2.
Money Market	Tracking the value of money market funds that you can write checks against (if you can't write checks against the money market fund, create an investment account). See Chapter 14.
Investment	Tracking the value of something you bought with the idea of selling it later at a profit—mutual funds, stocks, bonds, securities, IRAs, Keoghs, CDs, treasury bills, annuities, precious metals, collectibles, REITs, and unit trusts. See Chapter 14.
Asset	Tracking the value of things that you own—real estate, a truck, a collection of Staffordshire porcelain figurines. See "Keeping Track of Assets" in Chapter 11.
Liability	Tracking debt—a mortgage, car loan, or income taxes owed, for example. See Chapter 11.
401(k)	Tracking the value of as well as contributions to a 401(k) retirement plan. See Chapter 14.

An Account's Starting Date and Opening Balance

When you set up a new account, Quicken asks for an opening balance, the amount of money in the account as of the day you want to start tracking it. It isn't necessary to give this information right away, because you can always go back and enter the opening balance later. Still, at some point in the life of your account you have to give some thought to its starting date and opening balance.

If you intend to use Quicken to help with taxes, you need to record transactions as of January 1. Obviously, it doesn't do any good to track itemized deductions as of July 31 or October 16, because the IRS wants to know the full story of what you did all year. An account's starting date doesn't matter if you intend to use Quicken only for balancing a checking and savings account, but it does matter for tax purposes and for some kinds of financial analysis.

As for the opening balance, knowing that is easy if you just opened the account. You know exactly how much money is in a new bank account because no checks have been written, no deposits or withdrawals have been made, and no interest has been earned. All you have to do is tell Quicken how much your initial deposit was if you just opened the account.

DEFINITION

Balance: How much money is in a bank account. Or, in the case of asset, liability, and investment accounts, what the thing being tracked in the account is worth.

But if you want to start tracking an account you've had for a while, or if you need to know what your account balance was on January 1, you have some detective work to do. You have to find out how much money was in the account as of the official starting date at the top of the account register in Quicken. If you kept careful records—if you balanced your checkbook each time you wrote a check, for example—knowing the balance as of a certain date is easy. But if, like me, you didn't balance your checkbook until you started using Quicken, you have to do some careful backtracking. You have to find out what your account balance was on the date you have chosen for your starting date. That might mean going to the first entry in the register and changing the opening balance the first time you reconcile the account.

For detailed instructions on reconciling an account, see Chapter 5.

Setting Up a New Account

To set up a new account, you have to start from the dialog box shown in Figure 1.5. Whichever kind of account you set up, the procedure is nearly the same. Follow these steps to get to the Create New Account dialog box and set up a new account:

1. Choose Features | Banking | Create New Account or click Accts on the iconbar and then click the New button in the Account List window.

2. In the Create New Account dialog box (see Figure 1.4), click one of the nine account buttons and then click Next to go to the Account Setup dialog box, shown in Figure 1.5.

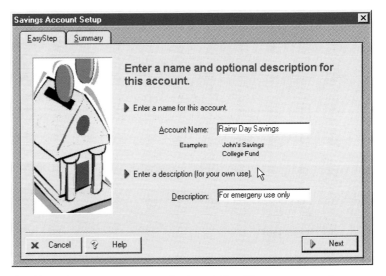

Figure 1.5 Enter the account name and a description. The name you enter appears on account tabs in register windows.

3. Type a name for your account. The name you type appears on account tabs at the bottom of registers and in the Account List window.

4. In the Description text box, type a few words that describe the account you are setting up. The words you type will appear in the Account List

window as well. If you have, say, two checking accounts and three savings accounts, this is a good place to write a few words that help explain which account is which.

5. When you click Next, Quicken asks if you have the last statement for this account:

   - **Yes**   If you have a statement or you know how much money is in the account because you just opened it, you can click Yes and then click Next. In the following dialog box, enter the statement date and ending balance listed on the statement (or enter **0** of you just opened the account), and click Next again.

   - **No**   No big deal if you don't have a statement. You can change the starting balance by changing the first entry in the register later on. If you choose the No option button and click Next, Quicken consoles you with a screen that says it's okay not to know the account's value.

6. If you are setting up a checking, savings, credit card, investment, or money market account, the next screen asks if you intend to track your account online. Online banking is explained in Chapter 7, where I also tell you how to come back to the Account Setup dialog box and click the Yes option here. Skip ahead to Chapter 7 if you must; otherwise, click the Next button.

7. Click the Next button to go to the Summary tab. It gives you an opportunity to double-check the information you entered and change anything, if necessary. Make changes if you wish on this tab.

8. Click Done. You're finished—and not a moment too soon.

Click the Info button on the Summary tab to get to the Additional Account Information dialog box. As Figure 1.6 shows, this is a good place to keep phone numbers, contact names, and the like. To get back to this screen later, click Accts on the iconbar, click the account in the Account List, and click the Info button.

In the case of an investment account, Quicken asks whether you can write checks or use a debit card against the account. Chapter 14 has instructions for setting up investment accounts, including 401(k)s.

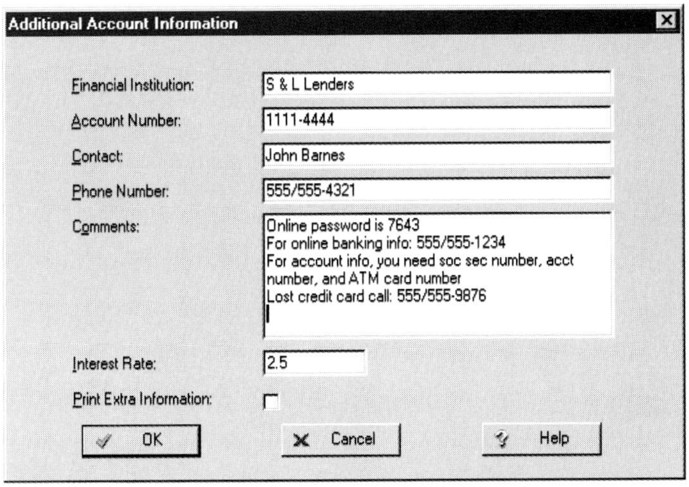

Figure 1.6 Keep vital statistics about an account on the Additional Account Information screen where you can get to it in a hurry.

CREATING A NEW FILE FOR A BUSINESS OR A SECOND PARTY

No matter how many accounts you open, all the information you keep about your finances is kept in a file called Qdata. (Actually, it's kept in seven files, each called Qdata but with a different three-letter ending. That doesn't matter, though, because the seven files are kept in one bundle to make things easier on you.) Most users of Quicken do not need to create a second file. However, you need another file under these circumstances:

- You use the program to track your business as well as your personal finances and you want to keep the two separate.
- You track someone else's finances as well as your own.
- Someone besides you uses Quicken on your computer to track his or her finances.

Follow these steps to create another Quicken file:

1. Choose File | New. A meek dialog box called "Creating a new file: Are you sure?" appears.
2. The New Quicken File option button is already selected, so click OK.
3. In the Create Quicken File dialog box, type a name in the File name box.
4. Click the Categories button and, in the Quicken Categories dialog box, choose the set of generic categories that best describes what you want to track with Quicken, and then click OK.
5. Click OK to leave the Create Quicken File dialog box. Quicken opens the new file, and you find yourself staring at the dialog box for creating an account (see Figure 1.4).

Now that you have two (or more) files, how do you get from one to the next? To do that, choose File | Open to see the Open Quicken File dialog box, click the name of the file you want to open, and click the OK button.

SHORTCUT

The fastest way to open another Quicken file is to choose its name on the bottom of the File menu. If the file is one of the last four that you opened, its name is on the File menu, ready to be clicked.

SHUTTING DOWN QUICKEN  IMPORTANT

 When you want to stop using Quicken and go on to bigger and better things, either choose File | Exit or click the Close button (the X) in the upper-right corner of the Quicken screen.

People who use computers are accustomed to saving their files before exiting a computer program, but you don't have to do that in Quicken. Each time you enter a transaction in a register, the data is stored on the hard disk, so you don't have to choose a Save command or click a Save button. In fact, if you look for a Save button or command in Quicken you will look in vain—there isn't one.

CAUTION

Back up your Quicken data whenever you finish using the program. "Backing Up Financial Data" in Chapter 10 explains how.

GETTING HELP WHEN YOU NEED IT

Dare I say it, but this book does not explain every nook and cranny of Quicken. I would need two or three hundred extra pages to do that. If you, however, are the type who explores nooks and crannies, if you are a supersonic Quicken user who needs the official word about every feature in Quicken, you might need to seek help from Quicken. This part of the book explains how to do that.

Quicken offers many different ways to seek help:

- Click the Help button on the iconbar or press F1 (or choose Help | Current Window) to learn about the Quicken screen you are staring at.
- Click the How Do I button and click a question:

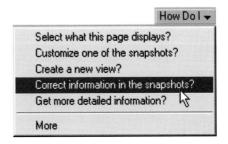

- Click the Help button in a dialog box to learn about the options in the dialog box.
- Choose Help | Index to open the Help program and search for topics on your own.

When you choose Help | Index, the Help program opens, as you can see in Figure 1.7. Now you can seek help in one of three ways:

- **Contents tab**   A list of general topics with book icons next to them. Double-click a book, it opens, and you see either more books or

Search for help on a topic.

Find a topic in Quicken's help files.

Search for general advice.

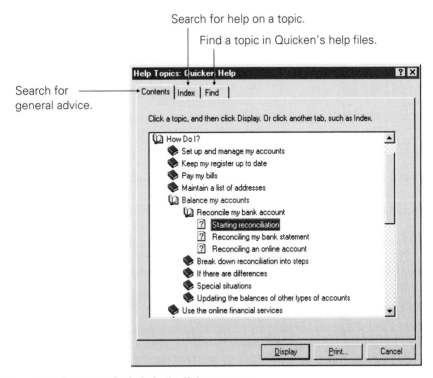

Figure 1.7 Rummage for help in the Help program.

subtopics with question marks next to their names. Double-click the question mark next to the subtopic that piques your interest and you see an advice screen for doing a task.

- **Index tab** A list of topics in alphabetical order, similar to a book index. Choose Help | Index if you know by name what you need help with. Type the name of the topic in box number 1. If you're lucky, the alphabetical list of topics in box number 2 scrolls down to the topic name you entered. Either click the Display button, or else click a subtopic under the topic you want, and then click Display. A help screen appears.

- **Find tab** Type the name of a topic you need help with, and then double-click a topic heading in box 3.

2

Recording Your Financial Activity

FAST FORWARD

Open an Account Register ➤ *pp. 25-26*

Account Balances

Business Checking	1,004.46
Savings	20,158.05
Savings-Credit Union	1,326.35
Wells Checking	9,167.59
Capitol One Visa	0.00
Citibank Visa	-596.93
Dean Witter--Addie	2,883.97
Dean Witter--Pablo	23,309.65

- Click the Accts button and then double-click an account name in the Account List window.
- In the Home Page or Banking Center window, click the hyperlink named after the account you want to open.

Enter a Transaction in a Register ➤ *pp. 26-30*

6/20/98	2045	Canned Foods		
		Cala Foods	-52.94	Groceries
		California Casualty	-969.00	Insurance:Homeo...
		Canned Foods	-22.73	Groceries
		Capitol One	-409.98	[Capitol One Visa]
		Cash-Business	-600.00	Expense-Bus
		Chevron	-9.34	Auto:Fuel
		Chow	-47.00	Dining
		Citibank Visa	-644.81	[Citibank Visa]

1. Fill in the rows. Press TAB or click in the next box to move from box to box.
2. Enter a date in the Date box by typing it in or by clicking the calendar and then clicking on the month and the day.
3. Press TAB or click in the Num box and choose an option that identifies the transaction.
4. If you are writing a check or making a deposit, enter a name in the Payee box. You can do that by typing the first few letters of the name if you've paid to or received money from the named person or party before.
5. Type the amount of the transaction in either the Payment or Deposit box.
6. Optionally, enter a description of the transaction in the Memo box.
7. If necessary, click the arrow in the Category box and choose an expense or income category for the payment or deposit.
8. Click the Enter button.

Move from One Register to Another ➤ *p. 29*

<	Citibank Visa	Capitol One Visa	Business Checking

1. Click one of the rectangular account tabs along the bottom of the register. Each tab has the name of an account on it.
2. If necessary, click an arrow at either end of the row of account tabs to slide the buttons over so you can get to the one you want.

Split a Transaction to
Categorize It in More Than One Category ➤ pp. 31-33

1. Fill in the register as you normally would, and then click the Split button.

2. In the Split Transaction window, click the arrow on line 1, choose a category from the drop-down menu, enter a dollar figure in the Amount box, and click Next.

3. Do the same on line 2 and on as many lines as necessary to divide the transaction across different categories.

4. When the Split Total equals the Transaction Total, click OK.

Split Transaction Window

Use this window to itemize the transaction, and get more detail.

	Category	Memo
1.	Auto:Fuel	
2.	Books	
3.	Clothing	
4.		
5.		

Transfer Money from One Account to Another ➤ pp. 33-35

1. Open the register of the account from which you want to transfer money and click the Transfer button.

2. In the Transfer dialog box, enter the transfer date, if necessary. In the Amount box, enter the amount of money you are transferring. In the To Account box, click the arrow and choose the account the money is to be transferred to.

3. Click OK.

Transfer

Record a Transfer betweer

Transfer Money From: To Account:

Wells Checking   Savings

Description

Transfer Money

Void a Transaction ➤ p. 37

1. Put the cursor in the transaction you want to void.

2. Either press CTRL-V or click the Edit button on the register and choose Void Transaction. A fat **VOID** appears in the Payee box.

2045	**VOID**Entropy Inc.
	Home Repair

The last chapter explained how to get rolling with Quicken. In this chapter, you get down to brass tacks. This is where you learn how to enter financial transactions in a register. Here, you learn how to track where the money that comes into your accounts comes from and where the money that goes out of your accounts goes to. I hope more money is coming in than going out, but if that isn't so, you will soon learn why.

This chapter explains how to open an account register. It tells how to record transactions and how to change, void, and delete them. It spells out how to transfer money between accounts, fix mistakes in account registers, and get around in long registers with hundreds and hundreds of transactions in them. For people who like to leave paper trails, this chapter also explains how to print an account register.

WHAT IS A REGISTER, ANYWAY?

Chapter 1 explained how to set up an account in Quicken. For each account you set up, Quicken creates an *account register*. Figure 2.1 shows an account register for a savings account. Registers differ slightly from account type to account type, but all have a place for entering transaction dates and amounts. The Balance column shows the running balance in the account and below the Balance column is the ending balance. There is also the Clr column, which tells whether the transaction has been cleared with a bank or brokerage house.

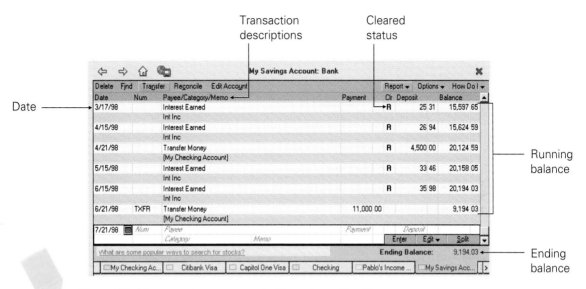

Figure 2.1 All transactions are recorded in registers like this one.

OPENING AN ACCOUNT REGISTER

The first step to entering transactions is to open the register that the transaction is to be entered in. As I mentioned in Chapter 1, you can skip merrily from one account register to another by clicking account tabs along the bottom of the register. Here are two other ways to open an account register:

- Click a hyperlink named after the account whose register you want to see. You can find these hyperlinks on the Home Page and the Banking Center (choose Features | Centers to get there).

- Click the Accts button on the iconbar (or press CTRL-A) to open the Account List window, and then double-click the name of the account whose register you want to open.

By the way, the Balance Total figure in the Account List window shows your net worth, the sum of your assets and liabilities. If the Account List window intrigues you, turn to "Decide How to Handle Closed Accounts in the Account List" in Chapter 3.

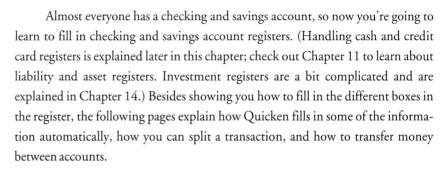

ENTERING TRANSACTIONS IN SAVINGS AND CHECKING ACCOUNT REGISTERS

Almost everyone has a checking and savings account, so now you're going to learn to fill in checking and savings account registers. (Handling cash and credit card registers is explained later in this chapter; check out Chapter 11 to learn about liability and asset registers. Investment registers are a bit complicated and are explained in Chapter 14.) Besides showing you how to fill in the different boxes in the register, the following pages explain how Quicken fills in some of the information automatically, how you can split a transaction, and how to transfer money between accounts.

Filling in a Register

When you open a register, Quicken takes you to the first empty row at the bottom. This is where you record the transaction. Even if you are recording a transaction that occurred months ago, you can enter it on the last line because Quicken arranges transactions in date order in registers.

Follow these steps to record a transaction in a register:

1. In the Date box, enter the transaction date.

   Today's date appears in the Date box, but you can change that either by typing in another date or by clicking the baby calendar. When you click it, a full-fledged calendar appears. Click the arrows on either side of the month name to advance or go backward month by month, and when you've found the right month, click the day the transaction was or will be made.

2. Either press the TAB key or click in the Num box to move the cursor there.

3. Click the down arrow and choose an option that describes the transaction you are about to enter.

Table 2.1 describes the options. Options with asterisks beside their names appear on the list only if you have signed up to use Quicken's online banking services. Chapter 7 describes the online services.

Num Option	What It Means
Next Check Num	The transaction is a check; enter the next check number in my checkbook. (If Quicken enters the wrong number, type in the correct one.)
ATM	The transaction is a cash withdrawal made at an automated teller machine.
Deposit	The transaction is a deposit to this account.
Print Check	The transaction is a check that you intend to print.
Send Online Payment*	The transaction is an electronic payment made to a company or an individual.
Online Transfer*	The transaction is a money transfer made online from one account to another.
Transfer	The transaction is a money transfer from one account to another.
EFT*	The transaction is a payment made to a company that is set up to receive electronic fund transfers (EFT stands for *electronic funds transfer,* not *electro-funk therapy*).
Edit List	Click this button to get to the Edit Num List dialog box, where you can click the New button to create a Num option of your own.

Next Check Num
ATM
Deposit
Print Check
Transfer
EFT

Edit List

* Available only if you have signed up to use Quicken's online services.

Table 2.1 Num Menu Options for Describing Transactions

4. Press TAB or click in the Payee box to move there.

A list appears with the names of parties you have paid money to and received money from in the past. So that you don't have to enter the same data over and over again, Quicken "memorizes" the names and transaction statistics of all parties you have paid or received money from.

5. Either type in the first few letters of the name of the party you are paying or receiving money from, or scroll to and click the party's name on the list. Don't bother pressing the SHIFT key to capitalize the first letter—Quicken does that for you.

	Redwing Shoes	-149.39 Clothing
142	Redwing Shoes	

"Make QuickFill Work Your Way" in Chapter 3 explains QuickFill in more detail.

If you've entered the name before, a box with the party's name appears above the Payee box. Not only does the party's name appear, but a cash amount and an expense or income category appears as well. What you are seeing is a very handy feature called *QuickFill.* By pressing TAB, you can fill in an amount and category name instantly.

6. Press TAB or click in the Payment or Deposit box to move there, and then enter an amount.

To enter an amount, you don't need to enter any commas or dollar signs. All you have to do is enter the numbers themselves. As for a decimal point, enter it only if the amount includes cents as well as dollars. In other words, if your payment or deposit is $25.00, all you have to enter is **25**, but if it is $25.99, you have to enter **25.99**.

On the right side of both the Payment and Deposit boxes is a baby calculator. Click it and a significantly larger calculator comes to life on your screen. You can click its buttons to add, subtract, divide, and multiply figures. Click the Enter button (it has an equal sign on it) and the sum or product of your calculation—the amount of several checks you are depositing, for example—is entered in the register.

7. Press TAB or click in the Category box and either type the first few letters of a category or subcategory name to enter it, or scroll to and choose a category name from the pop-up menu.

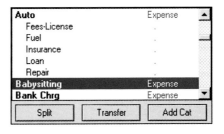

It might not be necessary to enter a category name because QuickFill may have entered the right one for you. At the top of the pop-up menu are income categories; then come expense categories; and last come transfer categories (which you can use to transfer money between accounts).

So important are categories, I devote many pages to them in "Make Your Own Categories and Subcategories" in Chapter 3. To get the most out of Quicken, you have to create meaningful income and expense categories that work for you.

8. Optionally, click in the Memo box and enter a few words if, for any reason, this transaction might look odd and mysterious when you review your finances months from now.

Enter

9. Click the Enter button or press the ENTER key to record the transaction in the register.

You hear a chime like the noise made by an old-fashioned cash register and the transaction is saved to the hard disk in your computer. The cursor moves down the register and the next row is highlighted so you can enter another transaction there.

QuickEntry: The Fast Way to Enter Transactions

QuickEntry 99

Suppose one or two checks or deposits need recording and you're in a hurry or you don't care to negotiate the Quicken windows. For times like those, Quicken offers the QuickEntry screen, a bare-bones register that you can enter transactions in. After you enter transactions in the bare-bones register, you simply close the QuickEntry window. Next time you start the program, you get the opportunity to record the transactions that you were in such a hurry to enter in your Quicken registers.

To record transactions this way, click the QuickEntry icon. As shown at the top of Figure 2.2, you shortly see the QuickEntry window, where you can enter transactions to your heart's content. Click an account button along the bottom of the screen if you need to get to a different register. When you're done entering

Enter your transactions here.

Click an account button to move to a different register.

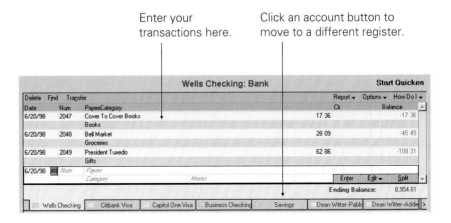

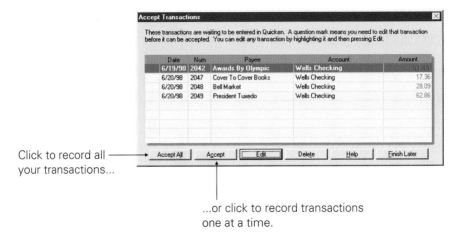

Click to record all your transactions...

...or click to record transactions one at a time.

Figure 2.2 When you're in a hurry, enter transactions in the QuickEntry window (top). Next time you start Quicken, you are given the opportunity to record the transactions in account registers (bottom).

transactions, click the Close button (the X) to close the QuickEntry window or click the Start Quicken button to start the Quicken program in earnest.

Next time you start Quicken, you see the Accept Transactions dialog box shown at the bottom of Figure 2.2. Click the Accept All button to record all the transactions in the list in your account registers, or else click a transaction and then click the Accept button to record transactions one at a time. Click the Edit button if a transaction needs changing before you record it. Even if you click the Finish Later button, you can always choose Features | Banking | Accept Transactions while you're working in Quicken to see the Accept Transactions dialog box.

Splitting a Deposit or a Payment Across Different Categories

When you categorize a transaction as part of entering it in a register, sometimes the transaction doesn't fit neatly into one category. For example, if you were to deposit two checks, one from your place of work and one from your Aunt Enid (a birthday present), the deposit wouldn't fit into a single category. It would fall into two categories: Income and Gift Received. Likewise, if you wrote a check to the All & Sundries General Store to pay for a submarine sandwich, stamps, and a hat, the payment wouldn't fall into a single category, but into three: Groceries, Postage, and Clothing.

To categorize a transaction, you can split it and record it two, three, four, or four hundred different ways. Registers offer the Split button for that very purpose. Follow these steps to split a transaction:

Split

1. Record the transaction in the usual way, by entering the date, a choice from the Num menu, a payee name, and a payment or deposit amount.

2. Click the Split button on the register (it's to the right of the Enter and Edit buttons). You see the Split Transaction window shown in Figure 2.3.

3. In the Category box, either type a few letters to enter a category or click the arrow and choose one from the list.

4. Press TAB twice or click to go to the Amount box, and then enter a figure.

5. Click the Next button. Quicken puts the remainder of the transaction on line 2 in case you have only one more category to enter.

6. Repeat steps 3 through 5 for each item you want to categorize.

    If you have to delete a line, click on it, click the Edit button, and choose Delete from the drop-down menu. Choose the Insert command on the drop-down menu to insert a line above the line that the cursor is in. Click the Adjust button as a last resort if you can't

A single payment can be split
into numerous categories.

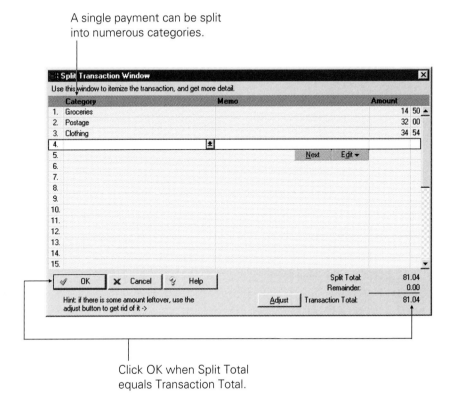

Click OK when Split Total
equals Transaction Total.

Figure 2.3 Split transactions to record payments that don't fit in a single category or checks from different payees.

account for some of the money. Quicken will calculate the difference for you.

When you are done, the Split Total and Transaction Total in the lower-right corner of the screen should be equal, and the Remainder should be 0.00.

7. Click OK.

Back in the register, the word "Split," a check mark, and an X appear in the Category box:

6/20/98	143	All & Sundries Store			81 04	*Deposit*	960 46
		--Split--	✓ X *Memo*			Enter Edit ▾	Split

When you deposit several checks at once, you can use the Split Transaction window (see Figure 2.3) to total the checks in the deposit. To do so, do not enter a deposit amount before you click the Split button. Then, in the Split Transaction window, record the check amounts. When you're done, the Transaction total shows the amount of the deposit.

To review a split transaction in a register, click the Split button or the check mark. Quicken opens the Split Transaction window so you can have a look at the transaction and perhaps make changes. Click the red X and click Yes in the Clear all split lines? dialog box if you decide that this shouldn't be a split transaction after all. The Category box is rendered empty so you can choose a single category and abandon the idea of splitting the transaction.

Transferring Money Between Accounts

Sometimes not enough money is in the checking account, so you have to bolster it by transferring a few dollars from savings to checking. And sometimes, thanks to hard work or good fortune, you end up with more money in checking than you need, in which case you transfer money from checking to a savings, a 401(k), or an investment account. The Step by Step box just ahead explains how to transfer money between Quicken registers.

Transfer money between Quicken accounts when you transfer money between real-life bank accounts; when you purchase stock, buy a CD, or make another kind of investment; or when you contribute to an asset that you are tracking in a Quicken register. It seems odd to transfer money when you are buying something like stock, but look at it this way: The stock is yours. You are really transferring wealth—*your* wealth—from one place to another.

STEP BY STEP Transferring Money Between Accounts

1 Click the Transfer button. You see the Transfer dialog box.

3 Click the down arrow in the To Account box and choose the account that will receive the money.

4 Change the date, if necessary.

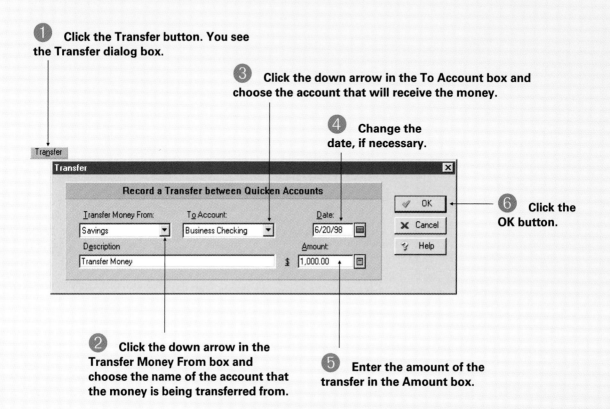

6 Click the OK button.

2 Click the down arrow in the Transfer Money From box and choose the name of the account that the money is being transferred from.

5 Enter the amount of the transfer in the Amount box.

When the transfer is complete, the letters TXFR (for transfer) appear in the Num box of the transaction, the words "Transfer Money" appear in the Payee box, and the name of the account you transferred the money to appears, in brackets, in the Category box. The date and the amount you entered appear, too:

6/20/98	TXFR	Transfer Money		1,000 00		4 46
		[Savings]				

Meanwhile, in the register that received the money, the words "Transfer Money" appear in the Payee box, the amount of the transfer is entered in the Deposit box, the balance is increased, and the name of the account you transferred money from appears in brackets in the Category box. To see what I mean, press CTRL-X or click the Edit button (it's next to the Enter button), and choose Go to Transfer from the menu to get to the other register:

6/20/98	*Num*	Transfer Money		⬆ *Payment*	1,000 00	22,008 05
		[Business Checking]	*Memo*		Enter Edit ▾	Split

MOVING AROUND
IN A REGISTER WINDOW

The longer you work with Quicken, the longer your account registers grow, and the harder it is to get from place to place. What if you are staring at a transaction line dated December 12 and you need to see a transaction that you made in June? You can get there with the scroll bar or by pressing keys. The *scroll bar* is the stripe along the right side of registers (and some menus) that resembles an elevator shaft. Use these techniques for moving around with the scroll bar:

- Click the up or down arrow on the top or bottom of the scroll bar. Each time you click, the screen moves up or down by one transaction.

- Click on the scroll bar itself, not on either of the arrows or on the scroll box. Each time you click, you see a new screenful of transactions.

- Drag the scroll box up or down. The *scroll box* is the elevator-like box in the scroll bar. As you drag, a white box appears to show you the date (and whatever is in the Num column) of the transactions you are moving to.

To navigate your register with the keyboard, use these techniques:

Press	To Move
↑ or ↓	Up or down by one transaction
PGUP or PGDN	Up or down an entire screenful of transactions
CTRL-PGUP or CTRL-PGDN	To the first or the last transaction in the month
CTRL-HOME or CTRL-END	To the first or last transaction in the register

SHORTCUT

To go to a transaction that you recorded on a particular date, click the Edit button (it's beside the Enter button) and choose Go to A Specific Date. Then enter the date in the dialog box and click OK.

CORRECTING MISTAKES IN REGISTERS

Inevitably, everyone makes mistakes when they enter transactions in registers. Most people do not have the nimble fingers of an expert typist or shoplifter. Therefore, these pages explain how to fix entries in registers, delete and void transactions, find errors, and fix errors *en masse*.

Changing Part of a Register Entry

If you botch a transaction and want to start all over, click the Edit button (next to the Enter button) and choose Restore Transaction from the menu to erase all of the data you've entered so far.

Even if you've clicked the Enter button, heard the chime and sent financial data to the hard disk, you can still alter it. To do that, click where you made the mistake, press the BACKSPACE or DEL key to erase it, type in the correct data, and click the Enter button.

Voiding and Deleting Transactions

Deleting and voiding a transaction are two very different things. A deleted transaction is erased from your financial records; it might just as well never have happened. A voided transaction remains in your data records (along with the word VOID and a few asterisks) so you know that you made the transaction, but later voided it. If you write a check by hand and have to tear it up because you accidentally entered the wrong name in the Payee line, void the transaction instead of deleting it. That way, you have a record of what happened to the check.

Here is how to delete and void a transaction:

- **Deleting** Put the cursor in the register row where the transaction is and do one of the following: press CTRL-D, click the Edit button and choose Delete Transaction from the menu, or choose Edit | Transaction | Delete. Then click Yes in the Delete the Current Transaction? dialog box. The entire transaction is deleted as though you never made it.

VOIDVortex Plumbers
Home Repair

- **Voiding** Put the cursor in the transaction and do one of the following: press CTRL-V, click the Edit button and choose Void Transaction, or choose Edit | Transaction | Void Transaction. A fat **VOID** appears in the Payee box.

Finding and Fixing Entry Errors in Registers

Suppose you made a blunder somewhere in a register but you aren't sure where you made it. You misspelled somebody's name or put an income transaction in the wrong category. Worse, suppose you made the same error many times. How can you fix your errors without wasting an afternoon?

You can use two commands: Edit | Find & Replace | Find and Edit | Find & Replace | Find/Replace. The first one locates transactions in a register. The second locates transactions and gives you the opportunity to fix them *en masse*. As the upcoming Step by Step box explains, you can also look for transactions by changing the order in which they appear. Normally, Quicken arranges transaction by date, but you can also arrange them in other ways.

STEP BY STEP Finding Transactions by Rearranging the Register

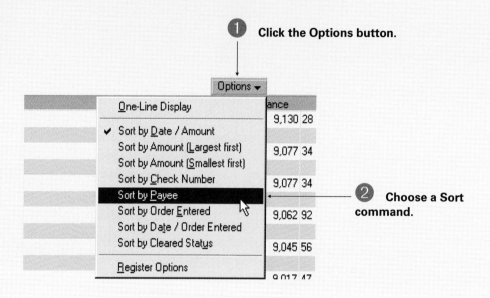

① Click the Options button.

② Choose a Sort command.

Finding Errors in Registers

Follow these steps to find a single entry in a register or all the entries of a certain kind in all your registers:

1. Open the register and click the Find button (it's below the Go Forward button), press CTRL-F, or choose Edit | Find & Replace | Find. The Quicken Find dialog box shown in Figure 2.4 appears.

2. Click the arrow in the Search box and choose an option from the drop-down menu to help narrow the search. For example, if you believe that the item you are searching for is in the Payee box, choose Payee.

3. Click in the Find box and either enter what you are looking for or click the arrow and choose it from the drop-down list. Type a number if you are looking for an amount.

Enter the search item.

Choose the column where the search
item is found on the register.

Finds transactions
one at a time

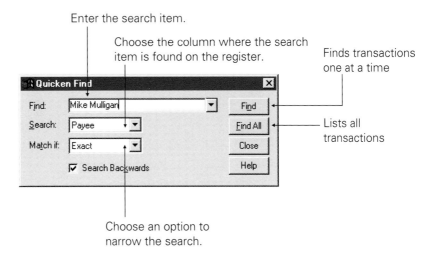

Lists all
transactions

Choose an option to
narrow the search.

Figure 2.4 Click the Find button to find the most recent transaction; click Find All to
see a list of all transactions.

4. Click the arrow in the Match if box and make a choice if you don't
know precisely what the name or number you are looking for is.
Choose Contains if you want to find transactions that include the
criterion you entered in the Find box; choose Exact to find the
transactions that contain your criterion and nothing else. For example,
a search for "Waldorf" with the Contains option finds "Waldorf
School," "Waldorf-Astoria," and "Waldorf," but the same search with
the Exact option only finds "Waldorf." Use the Starts With or Ends
With option when you don't quite know what you are looking for but
vaguely remember how its name begins or ends. Use the last four
options on the Match if menu to search for dollar amounts.

5. Tell Quicken how to conduct the search by clicking a button:

- **Find button** Climbs up the register to the first transaction that
satisfies your search criteria (if you want to climb down the register
and search from top to bottom, click the Search Backwards check
box). From there, you can either click in the register, alter the

transaction and click Enter, or click the Find button again (or press SHIFT-CTRL-F) to see if Quicken finds another instance of the thing you so desperately seek.

- **Find All button** Opens the Quicken Find window with a list of all the transactions in all your registers that satisfy the search criteria, as shown in Figure 2.5. From the list, you can zero in on a single transaction by double-clicking it. You will be taken to a register displaying the transaction you selected. To get back to the Quicken Find window, click the Find Quick Tab on the right side of your screen.

Date	Acct	Num	Payee	Cat	Memo	Clr	Amount
11/25/96	My Checking Acc...	ATM	Rainbow Grocery	Groceries		R	-49.27
7/8/96	My Checking Acc...	1444	Rainbow Grocery	Groceries		R	-58.76
6/23/96	My Checking Acc...	1429	Rainbow Grocery	Groceries		R	-54.61
5/28/96	My Checking Acc...	1398	Rainbow Grocery	Groceries		R	-44.84
4/26/96	My Checking Acc...	1372	Rainbow Grocery	Groceries		R	-62.70
3/26/96	My Checking Acc...	1339	Rainbow Grocery	Groceries		R	-38.94
3/5/96	My Checking Acc...	1326	Rainbow Grocery	Groceries		R	-59.35
2/18/96	My Checking Acc...	1320	Rainbow Grocery	Groceries		R	-62.82
2/18/96	My Checking Acc...	1319	Rainbow Grocery	Groceries		R	-16.98
1/23/96	My Checking Acc...	1297	Rainbow Grocery	Groceries		R	-49.67
3/22/98	Capitol One Visa		Rainbow Grocery	Groceries		R	-42.40
3/10/98	Capitol One Visa		Rainbow Grocery	Groceries		R	-58.34
12/14/97	Capitol One Visa		Rainbow Grocery	Groceries		R	-52.49
7/30/97	Capitol One Visa		Rainbow Grocery	Groceries		R	-79.55
7/14/97	Capitol One Visa		Rainbow Grocery	Groceries		R	-82.16

☑ Show Matches in Split   Item Found in 41 Transactions

Figure 2.5 Double-click any transaction in the Quicken Find window to see that item displayed in a register.

SHORTCUT

To find a transaction more easily, you can rearrange the transactions in the Quicken Find window. Click the Sort by button and choose an option.

Finding and Fixing Errors *En Masse*

Now that you know how to find data in a register, you can learn how to find data and replace it *en masse* with new data. To do that, you use the very powerful and sometimes mischievous Edit | Find & Replace | Find/Replace command. Finding transactions with this command is done the same way as finding transactions with the Edit | Find & Replace | Find command. The difference is that, once the data is found, you can replace it with new data.

CAUTION

You never quite know what Edit | Find & Replace | Find/Replace will do to your data. Back up your data before you use the command, and if your financial records get mangled, restore your records from a backup file. Chapter 10 explains how.

Follow these steps to find and replace data in registers:

1. Choose Edit | Find & Replace | Find/Replace. You see the Find and Replace dialog box shown in Figure 2.6. (This one has been filled out already, and the search has been conducted.)

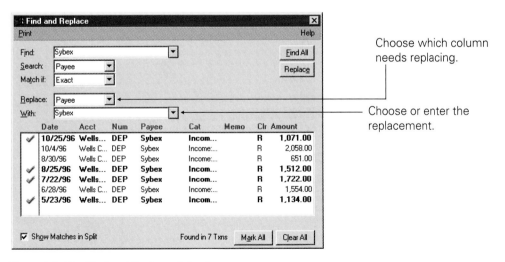

Choose which column needs replacing.

Choose or enter the replacement.

Figure 2.6 The Find and Replace dialog box

Quicken offers a special command for reassigning transactions to different categories. See "Fixing Mistakes in the Way Transactions Are Categorized" in Chapter 4.

The top of this dialog box is nearly identical to the Quicken Find dialog box that the previous handful of pages explained how to fill out. The only thing missing is the Find button, because to conduct a Find and Replace operation you click the Find All button, get a list of all the transactions that meet your criteria, and then pick and choose which ones to replace with new data.

2. Starting with the Search box, use the Find, Search, and Match if boxes to pinpoint the data that you want to replace (the last handful of pages, including Figure 2.4, explain how to do this).

3. Click the Find All button. A list on the bottom half of the dialog box shows all the transactions that were found that match the criteria.

4. Click the arrow in the Replace box to choose which part of the transactions needs replacing.

    The option you choose from the Replace drop-down menu determines which options, if any, become available in the With drop-down list. If you choose Category/Class from the Replace list, for example, you see a list of categories on the With list. If you choose Amount, enter an amount yourself in the With box.

5. Tell Quicken which transactions to replace:

    • **All of them**   Click the Mark All button at the bottom of the dialog box.

    • **Some of them**   Click in the narrow column to the left of the transactions you want to replace. As you click, check marks appear. If you have to, click the Clear All button to remove all the check marks and start over.

6. Click the Replace button. A dialog box tells you how many replacements are about to be made and asks whether you have the guts to go through with it.

7. Click OK. Another dialog box tells you how many replacements were made.

8. Click OK again.

MANAGING A CASH ACCOUNT

Chapter 1 explained how to set up an account and mentioned the different kinds of accounts you can create, including the cash account. To create a cash account if you do need one, follow the standard procedure for creating an account and choose Cash in the Account Setup dialog box. Then, each time you withdraw cash for your business from a checking or savings account, record it as a transfer from the savings or checking account to the cash account. When you spend cash, record it in the register's Spend column and describe and categorize it as you would a check payment. After you've made a few entries in a cash account register, it looks something like Figure 2.7. How do you like the lavender stripes?

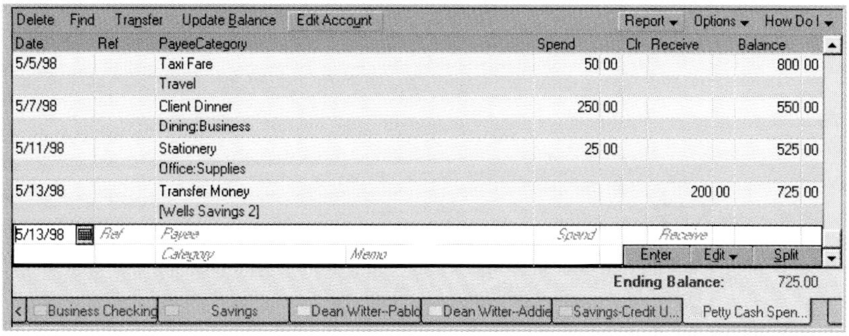

Figure 2.7 One way to track cash spending: a cash account

Cash accounts are not for everybody. A cash account might better be called a "petty cash account," because it is chiefly of use to small businesses for tracking day-to-day cash spending. Rather than set up a cash account, home users can simply track cash spending from a checking account. I'll show you how.

To track cash spending from a checking or savings account, record cash withdrawals as split transactions and use the Split Transaction window to categorize and describe how the money was spent. Earlier in this chapter, "Splitting a Deposit or Payment Across Different Categories" explains how to split a transaction. It isn't absolutely necessary to track how you spend each dime of the $20,

$40, or $100 that you withdraw from an ATM machine, because you can always categorize it in the Misc (Miscellaneous) category. But if you are a stickler for finding out exactly where the money goes, use the Split Transaction window to record how you spend the $200 withdrawals that you take out of checking and savings accounts:

	Category	Memo	Amount
1.	Groceries		40 00
2.	Books		80 00
3.	Dining		60 00
4.	School Supplies		20 00

RECORDING TRANSACTIONS IN CREDIT CARD ACCOUNTS

Under "Credit Card Analysis" on the Home Page and Banking Center you can find a startling statistic: how much you've spent this year so far with credit cards. See "Choose for Yourself What Appears on the Home Page" in Chapter 3 to learn about the Home Page.

These days, when the mail always includes at least one invitation to get a new credit card, almost everybody has plastic. And everybody who has plastic and uses Quicken needs to set up a credit card account. Create two, three, or four, if necessary—one for each credit card you own. The process of opening an account is explained in "Setting Up an Account" in Chapter 1.

The only difference between a credit card account and most other Quicken accounts is that a credit card account tracks what you owe, not what you have. Each time you charge something and record the transaction in your credit card account, Quicken deducts the amount you charge, so the account balance almost always shows a negative number (in red, no less!), as shown in Figure 2.8.

Credit card charges are entered like other register transactions. The Payee box is for recording whom the purchase was made from. The amount of the charge goes in the Charge box. The Category box is for classifying the transaction. When you make a payment to the card issuer, it is recorded in the Payment box. To make a payment, you transfer money into your credit card account from the checking account that you are using to pay the bill. In Chapter 5, I explain how to do this, as well as how to record a credit that the credit card company gives you (perhaps because you returned an item), and how to reconcile a credit card account.

Date	Ref	Payee/Category/Memo	Charge	Clr	Payment	Balance
6/5/98		Strand Bookstore Books	48 80			1,126 24
6/6/98		Val's Redwood Room Dining:Business	93 20			1,219 44
6/6/98		Stacey's Books Books	67 25			1,286 69
6/6/98		Virgin Megastore Gifts	36 87			1,323 56
7/9/98		Canned Foods Groceries	4,587 94			5,911 50
7/11/98		Shell Auto:Fuel	101 00			6,012 50

Capitol One Visa: Credit

Delete   Find   Transfer   Reconcile   Edit Account   Report ▾   Options ▾   How Do I ▾

7/21/98 ▦ Ref   Payee   Charge   Payment
                Category   Memo   Enter   Edit ▾   Split ▾

Is it about time to begin estate planning?   **Credit Remaining:** -1,012.50   **Ending Balance:** 6,012.50

☐My Checking Ac... ☐ Citibank Visa ☐ Capitol One Visa ☐ Checking ☐Pablo's Income ... ☐My Savings Acc... ▷

Figure 2.8   Each time you charge something, record it in a credit card register and watch the red balance—what you owe—increase.

EXPERT ADVICE

To keep credit card spending under control, diligently record your charges as you make them. As you see the amount that you owe in the credit card register get bigger and bigger, you might be discouraged from spending so much with your credit card.

On the subject of uncontrolled spending, you can have Quicken warn you when a card is about to reach its credit limit. See "Being Alerted to Financial Events" in Chapter 8. You can also devise a plan for getting out of debt. (See Chapter 12.)

PRINTING AN ACCOUNT REGISTER

'Round about April 15, when your income taxes are filed and you are putting away your receipts, check stubs, and other financial papers, print a copy of your account registers for the past year and file them away, too. That way you leave behind a wider, deeper, more distinguishable paper trail for others to follow. Here are instructions for printing all or part of a register:

1. Open the register and press CTRL-P or choose File | Print Register. You see the Print Register dialog box.

2. Type a descriptive name in the Title box. The name you type will appear at the top of the report.

3. In the Print Transactions From and To boxes, enter a range of dates that describes which transactions to print. For example, to print all of 1998's transactions, enter **1/1/98** and **12/31/98**.

4. Click the Print Split Transactions check box to make split transactions appear in their entirety on the report.

5. Click the Print button. You see the Print dialog box, whose fancy gizmos you can ignore, unless you want to change fonts or print to a disk file.

6. Click the OK button.

3

Stuff to Do Once to Make Your Life Easier

INCLUDES

- Creating new categories and subcategories

- Deciding what goes on the Quicken Home Page

- Telling Quicken what you want to see when you start the program

- Rearranging the account tabs so you can open registers quickly

- Hiding accounts on the Account list

- Using QuickFill to enter transactions quickly

- Changing your view of a register

FAST FORWARD

Create a New Category or Subcategory
for Categorizing Register Transactions ➤ pp. 50-53

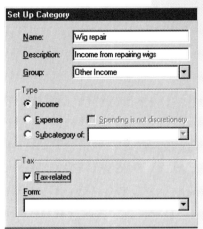

1. Choose Lists | Category/Transfer to open the Category & Transfer list.
2. Click the New button.
3. In the Set Up Category dialog box, enter a name and a short description of the category or subcategory.
4. From the Group drop-down menu, choose a supercategory.
5. Choose whether the category is an Income category, an Expense category, or a subcategory of a known category. If you are creating a subcategory, click the down arrow in the Subcategory of box and choose the parent category.
6. Click the Tax-related check box if you want this category's data to be included in tax summary reports.
7. Click OK.

Customize the Home Page ➤ pp. 56-57

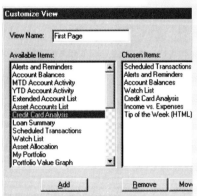

1. If necessary, click the Go to my Quicken Home Page button to open the Home Page window.
2. Either click the Customize this page hyperlink or right-click a header ("Alerts & Reminders," for example) and choose Customize this view from the shortcut menu.
3. In the Available Items list, click the items you want to place in the window and click the Add button.
4. To remove an item from the window, click it in the Chosen Items list and then click the Remove button. To move an item higher or lower in the window, click the Move Up or Move Down button.

Arrange Account Tabs So You
Can Find and Click Them Easily ➤ *pp. 58-59*

1. Open an account register.

2. Drag an account tab left or right. As you do so, a white box appears below the pointer. Release the mouse button when the account tab is in the right position.

"Lock" Memorized Transactions
So That They Stay the Same ➤ *p. 61*

1. Choose List | Memorized Transaction (or press CTRL-T).
2. Click a transaction that you want to lock and then click in the Lck column.

Cat	Lck	Cal
School Supplies	🔒	🗐
For Kids	🔒	🗐
Kids Education	🔒	🗐
Books	🔒	🗐
[4127 -23rd Street]		🗐

Pack More Transactions onto a Register Window ➤ *pp. 61-62*

1. Click the Options button in the register window.
2. From the drop-down menu, choose One-Line Display.
3. Do the same to get the two-line view of the register back.

> ✔ One-Line Display
>
> ✔ Sort by Date / Amount
> Sort by Amount (Largest first)
> Sort by Amount (Smallest first)
> Sort by Check Number
> Sort by Payee
> Sort by Order Entered
> Sort by Date / Order Entered
> Sort by Cleared Status
>
> Register Options

Remove or View the Iconbar or
Activity Buttons Onscreen ➤ *p. 63*

1. Right-click on the right side of the screen below the Quick Tabs and choose Show Top Iconbar or Show Activity Bar from the shortcut menu.

2. To view or remove the iconbar or activity buttons, right-click again and choose Show Top Iconbar or Show Activity Bar.

In every computer program, you can put your best foot forward by learning how to do two or three or four important things right from the start. Learn the handful of important things and you can save hours and hours of work in the long run.

This short chapter explains the four or five things you can do in Quicken to make yourself more productive. It describes how to make categories and subcategories that accurately track your finances, choose what appears on the Home Page, and decide for yourself which window appears when you start the program. You also learn how to rearrange the account tabs so you can find them faster, make the excellent QuickFill feature even better by pruning the memorized transaction list, and get more room to work onscreen.

MAKE YOUR OWN
CATEGORIES AND SUBCATEGORIES

Chapter 4 describes how you can also use supercategories and classes to categorize transactions.

Categories are the basic elements for tracking income and expenses. When you record a transaction, Quicken gives you the chance to categorize it. If you want, you can rely on the generic list of categories that Quicken provides when you install the program, but sooner or later you have to create categories of your own. If you are self-employed, creating categorizes for all tax-deductible expenses is essential. If you run a small business, creating the right categories is the first step in finding out where you make the most money and where you merely spin your wheels. If you want to find out where the money goes so that you can put yourself on a budget, you need to create categories that clearly show what your spending habits are.

"Tagging Categories for Tax Purposes" in Chapter 15 explains how to tag categories so that you can use them to generate tax reports and estimate your income tax payments. Chapter 15 also explains how to assign each category to a line on a specific income tax form (1040, Schedule A, Schedule C, and so on) so you can export tax data to TurboTax, an income tax preparation program.

Figure 3.1 shows an income and expense graph. It compares income and expenses in a bar graph, and, in a pie chart, shows how much was spent in the ten largest expense categories. By carefully creating and choosing categories, you can generate meaningful graphs like these.

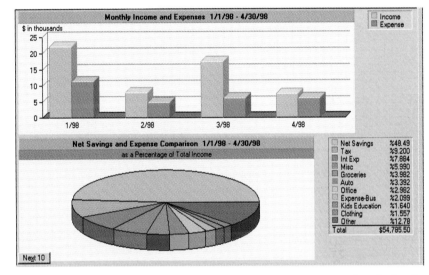

Figure 3.1 An income and expense graph. As the legend shows, the slices in the pie chart represent expense categories.

The following pages explain how to create your own categories and subcategories. You also learn how to delete categories and change their names. And if you want to borrow category lists from Quicken, you can do that as well. Besides the standard list, the program offers tailor-made category lists for married people, homeowners, small businesses, children, and investors. Read on.

EXPERT ADVICE

You can make Quicken display a message box if you try to record a transaction without categorizing it. Choose Edit | Options | Register, click the Miscellaneous tab, and click the When Recording Uncategorized Transactions check box.

Adding Categories and Subcategories to the Category & Transfer List

Follow these steps to create a new category from scratch:

1. Choose Lists | Category/Transfer (or press CTRL-C) to see the Category & Transfer List. If you are creating an income or expense category, you might click the Options button and choose Display Income Categories or Display Expense Categories tab to see which categories are already there.

2. Click the New button. You see the Set Up Category dialog box:

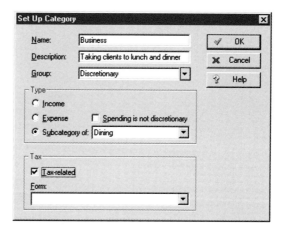

You'll learn all about budgeting in Chapter 12.

3. Enter a name for the category or subcategory.

4. Enter a short description. Your description will appear on the Category & Transfer list.

5. If you intend to draw a budget with Quicken, choose a category group from the Group list. Category groups are used for budgeting purposes.

6. Under Type, choose whether the category is an Income or Expense category. If you are creating a subcategory, click the Subcategory of

radio button, click the arrow, and choose which category on the list your new subcategory is to be subordinate to. For expense categories, click the Spending is not discretionary check box if the category describes expenses that you cannot do without.

7. Click the Tax-related check box if the category has anything remotely to do with taxes.

8. Click OK.

Starting with Generic Categories from Quicken

The other way to create a category is to pluck one from the generic category lists that Quicken offers—Standard, Married, Homeowner, Business, Children, or Investment. To borrow categories from Quicken, choose Lists | Category/Transfer or press CTRL-C to open the Category & Transfer list, click the Options button, and choose Add Categories from the menu. You see the Add Categories dialog box. Choose a set of categories from the Available Categories drop-down list. In the category list that appears, click beside all the categories that you want to create, and then click the Add button. The categories appear in the Categories to Add box on the right. Click the OK button to drop the categories into the Category & Transfer list.

Deleting the Categories and Subcategories You Don't Need

After you have worked with Quicken for a while, you know which categories you need and which categories merely take up space in the numerous Categories menus that appear throughout the Quicken program. Go ahead and delete categories that you have not assigned to any transactions. Here's how:

1. Choose Lists | Category/Transfer or press CTRL-C. You see the Category & Transfer list, which is shown in Figure 3.2.

2. Find the category or subcategory you want to delete and click it. If finding the category proves difficult, click the Options button and choose a display option from the menu.

Click the Delete button.

Choose a category
or subcategory.

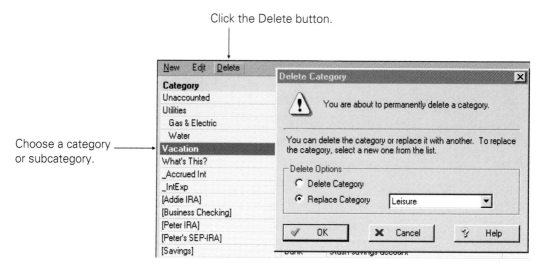

Figure 3.2 To delete a category or subcategory, select it on the Category & Transfer
List and click the Delete button.

3. Click the Delete button. A dialog box asks if you want to replace the
   category you are deleting with another category.
4. Click OK to delete the category, or else click the Replace category
   option button, choose a category from the drop-down list, and click
   OK. Throughout your registers, transactions that had been assigned
   the category you deleted are assigned the replacement category instead.

Changing the Names of Categories and Subcategories

Few things could be easier than changing the name of a category or
subcategory. All you have to do is choose Lists | Category/Transfer, find the
category or subcategory whose name you want to change, and select it. Then click
the Edit button to see the Edit Category dialog box. From there, enter the new
name in the Name box and click OK. Transactions in your registers that were
assigned the old name are given the new one automatically.

CAUTION

After you delete a category, transactions in registers that were assigned the category you deleted have no category assignments, and having empty Category boxes defeats the purpose of categorizing transactions in the first place. Before you delete a category that you've assigned to transactions in registers, use the Edit | Find & Replace | Recategorize command to find all transactions that were assigned the category you are about to delete and assign those transactions to new categories. "Fixing Mistakes in the Way Transactions Are Categorized" in Chapter 4 explains how.

To delete a category that has subcategories, you must first move the subcategories to another category or else promote the subcategories and make them full-fledged categories.

When a subcategory is deleted, all transactions that were assigned the subcategory are assigned the parent category instead. For example, if you delete the Property:Park Place subcategory, transactions that were assigned the Park Place subcategory are assigned the Property category.

CHOOSE FOR YOURSELF WHAT APPEARS ON THE HOME PAGE

Unless you tinker with the startup settings (the next topic in this chapter), you see the Quicken Home Page whenever you start Quicken. And when you click the Go to my Quicken Home Page button (the little house), you go straight to the Home Page as well. Fair enough—the Home Page is a good place to survey your financial picture. Click a hyperlink on the Home Page to open an account register or visit a Web site or learn about a Quicken feature. Click a hyperlink along the top of the page to go to the Banking Center, Planning Center, Investing Center, and so on.

As good as the Home Page is, it can be made better. You can choose for yourself what appears on the Home Page and even invent a "view" of your own—a

"Letting the Billminder Tell You What Needs Doing" in Chapter 8 explains how you can make the Billminder appear whenever you start your computer. The Billminder lists all checks that need printing, scheduled transactions, online transactions, and Calendar

second Home Page with information about a certain aspect of your finances, for example. Read on.

Customizing the Home Page

Follow these steps to choose for yourself what appears on the Home Page when you start Quicken:

1. Starting from the Home Page, either click the Customize this page hyperlink or right-click a header ("Alerts & Reminders," for example) and choose Customize this view from the shortcut menu. You see the Customize View dialog box shown in Figure 3.3

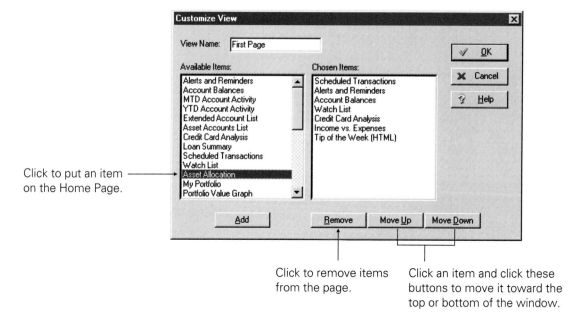

Click to put an item on the Home Page.

Click to remove items from the page.

Click an item and click these buttons to move it toward the top or bottom of the window.

Figure 3.3 To choose what goes on the Home Page, click a feature in the Available Items list and then click the Add button.

2. To put what Quicken calls an "item" on the Home Page, click it in the Available Items list and then click the Add button. To select several items at once, CTRL-click them.

Sometimes it's hard to tell by reading their names what the items are. You have to experiment, and if an item doesn't belong on the Home Page, remove it later by returning to this dialog box and completing step 3. Be sure to scroll to the bottom of the list. There are 30 items in all.

3. To remove a so-called item from the window, click it in the Chosen Items list and then click the Remove button.

4. Click an item in the Chosen Items list and then click the Move Up or Move Down button to move it toward the top or bottom of the Home Page.

5. Click OK.

Creating a New "View" from the Window

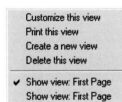

Suppose you want to gather information about a certain part of your finances—your investments, your debt, your income this year. To do that, either click the Customize this page hyperlink or right-click a heading on the Home Page and choose Create a new view from the shortcut menu. Then, in the Customize View dialog box, enter a name for your so-called view, CTRL-click items in the Available Items list, and click the Add button until you have assembled all the parts of your "view."

When you want to see your new view, right-click a heading on the Home Page and choose the name of your view from the shortcut menu. Choose Show view: First Page to return to the standard Home Page.

CHOOSE WHAT YOU SEE WHEN YOU START QUICKEN

When you start Quicken, you see the Quicken Home Page. What's more, a Quick Tab for every window that was open when you closed Quicken last time also appears. For example, if you close the program while the Account List window and a register window are open, you see the Accounts Quick Tab and Register Quick Tab next time you start Quicken. You can, however, decide for yourself what appears onscreen when you start the program.

Here are the four strategies for getting down to work:

- **No Home Page**   Don't care for the Home Page? To keep it from appearing whenever you start Quicken, choose Edit | Options | Quicken Program. In the General Options dialog box, click the Startup tab. Then uncheck the Home Page when starting Quicken option button.

- **Reminders Window at Startup**   Instead of the Home Page, you can see the Reminders window when you start Quicken (Chapter 8 explains the Reminders window). It lists scheduled transactions, alerts, calendar notes, and checks that need printing. To see the Reminders window when you start Quicken, choose Edit | Options | Quicken Program, click the Startup tab in the General Options dialog box, and click the Reminders when starting Quicken option button.

- **Same Quick Tabs Each Time**   Suppose you do most of your work in the same four or five windows. To make their Quick Tabs appear onscreen each time you start the program, open your favorite windows. Then choose Edit | Options | Desktop, click the Save Desktop on Exit option button, and click OK.

- **Pick Up Where You Left Off**   To display the same stuff that was onscreen last time you shut down Quicken, choose Edit | Options | Desktop and click the Save Current Desktop option button.

REARRANGE THE ACCOUNT TABS

The account tabs are mighty convenient. To switch from one account register to another, all you have to do is click an account tab. However, only six account tabs can appear at once. If you track more than six accounts, you sometimes have to click an arrow button to slide the account tabs over and get to the one you want.

To keep from having to click the arrow buttons very often, you can rearrange the account tabs so that the ones you click most often appear on the left side where you can find them easily. To rearrange the account tabs, drag them to new places.

A white box appears as you drag a tab. Release the mouse button when the white box is where you want the account tab to be:

DECIDE HOW TO HANDLE CLOSED ACCOUNTS IN THE ACCOUNT LIST

When you click the Accts button or press CTRL-A, you see the Account List window shown in Figure 3.4. This window lists account balances, tells whether checks need printing, and lists your net worth—your net worth as a financial entity, not as a human being, of course. By choosing an option on the Options menu, you can see accounts of a certain type, as well as view (or hide) hidden accounts. You can double-click an account name to open its register.

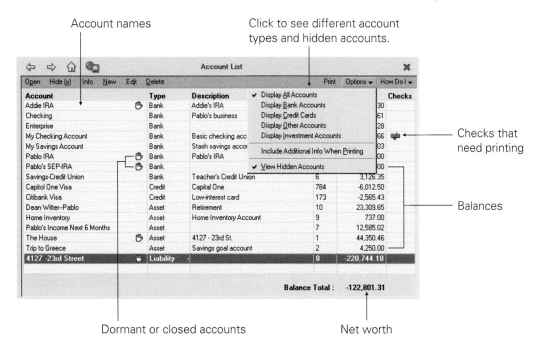

Figure 3.4 The Account List window lists accounts, their balances, and your net worth as a financial persona.

In Figure 3.4, I chose the View Hidden Accounts option to display hidden accounts—accounts that I have closed, that I don't care to see on the list, or that I don't won't to figure into my net worth. As "Renaming, Updating, and Deleting Accounts" in Chapter 10 explains, you can delete accounts you have closed, but by doing so you lose all the financial records in those accounts. Those records do not figure into reports and charts. Better to hide those accounts on the Account List. By hiding them, you retain their records, but you don't have to see them. Another reason for hiding accounts is to keep their records from figuring into the Balance Total, your net worth, which is listed on the bottom of the Account List window.

To hide an account, select it in the list and click the Hide (x) button. A hand appears beside the name of hidden accounts. Click the Hide (x) button again to "unhide" an account.

MAKE QUICKFILL WORK YOUR WAY

Whenever you record a transaction, Quicken "remembers" it and puts it on the Memorized Transaction List (to see the list, press CTRL-T or choose Lists | Memorized Transaction). Quicken remembers the payee name, the amount of the transaction, and the category you put it under so you don't have to enter this information all over again whenever you record a transaction to the same party. Instead of entering full names in registers or in the Write Checks window, you only have to type the first three or four letters. Quicken fills in the name of the payee as well as the last amount you paid or received. It even categorizes the transaction for you.

QuickFill, as good as it is, can be made even better. And that is the subject of this part of the chapter.

EXPERT ADVICE

If Quicken isn't memorizing transactions automatically, choose Edit | Options | Register, click the QuickFill tab in the Register Options dialog box, click the Auto Memorize New Transactions check box, and click OK.

"Locking" Transactions
So They Stay the Same

QuickFill "remembers" how much you paid or deposited last time around and enters the same amount in the Payment or Deposit box next time you record a transaction that involves the same person or party. Suppose, however, that you want QuickFill to keep putting the same amount in the Payment or Deposit box of the register, no matter how much you entered last time. You can do that by "locking" the transaction on the Memorized Transaction list.

To "lock" a transaction this way, open the Memorized Transaction list by choosing List | Memorized Transaction (or by pressing CTRL-T), click the transaction you want to lock, and either click the Lock icon in the lower-right corner of the screen or click in the Lck column. Transactions that have been locked show a picture of a padlock in the Lck column. To "unlock" a transaction on the list, click its lock icon to remove it.

Description	Amount	Type	Memo	Cat	Lck	Cal
Albert Lanier	90.00	Dep	Montly income from rental unit	Rental	🔒	🗐
B Dalton Books	-32.50	Pmt		Rental		🗐
Bank Of America	-2,083.69	Spl	Mortgage payment	[444 Main Street]	🔒	🗐

Pruning the Memorized Transaction List

The longer you use Quicken, the longer the Memorized Transaction list becomes. To make QuickFill work better, get out your pruning shears and cut the Memorized Transaction list down to size every few months. When you delete a memorized transaction from the list, nothing happens to it in the register. The transaction in the register stays the same, but the name under which it was entered stops appearing in the Payee box when you type the first few letters.

To delete a memorized transaction, choose Lists | Memorized Transaction or press CTRL-T. In the Memorized Transaction list, scroll to find the transaction you want to delete, click it, and click the Delete button. Click OK when Quicken asks if you want to go through with it.

EXPERT ADVICE

Another way to keep the list of QuickFill transactions from growing too long is to tell Quicken to remove transactions from the Memorized Transaction List after a certain number of months have elapsed. To do that, choose Edit | Options | Quicken Program, and click the General tab in the General Options dialog box. Then click the Remove Memorized Transactions Not Used in Last Months check box and enter the number of months that memorized transactions should stand before they are dropped from the list.

GET MORE ROOM TO WORK ONSCREEN

The Quicken screen is claustrophobic. When you have to enter a lot of transactions at once, the buttons, menus, and whatnots get in the way. What can you do about that?

After you've been around Quicken for a while and you know how to fill in a register, you might try working with a single-line display instead of a double-line display. As Figure 3.5 shows, each transaction in a single-line display occupies one

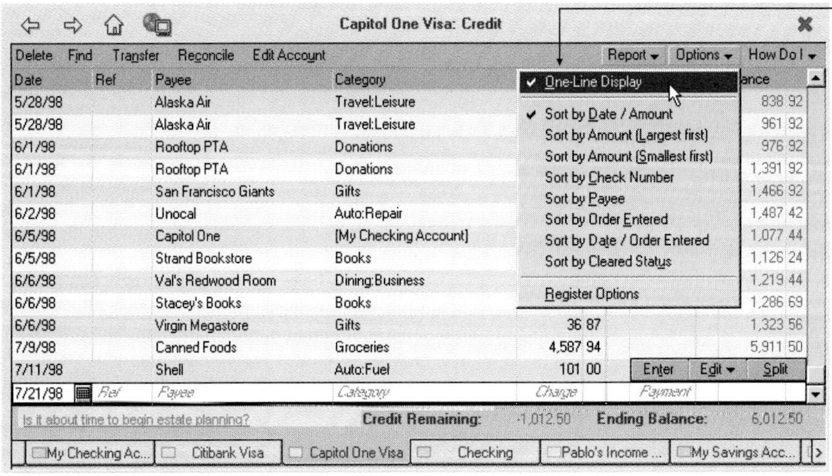

Click to switch between a single-line and double-line view.

Figure 3.5 To get a single-line view of a register, click the One-Line Display option on the View drop-down menu.

line in the register instead of two. To get a one-line display, click the Options button and choose One-Line Display from the drop-down menu. Do the same when you want to see two lines again.

The iconbar is convenient because all the important commands are there and lined up like ducks in a shooting gallery. Nevertheless, the iconbar does take up a lot of space onscreen. To remove it or remove the activity bar, right-click on the right side of the screen below the Quick Tabs. On the shortcut menu that appears, click Show Top Iconbar or Show Activity Bar. Do the same to see the iconbar or Activity bar again.

More than one Quicken user has wondered whether removing the Quick Tabs might be a good idea. To experiment with removing the Quick Tabs, right-click and choose the Show Quick Tabs option on the shortcut menu.

However, most Quicken users who take this drastic step want immediately to have the Quick Tabs back. But how do you get the Quick Tabs back, seeing as you can't right-click anymore to see the shortcut menu? Don't panic! To see the Quick Tabs again, choose Edit | Options | Quicken Program and click the Show QuickTabs check box in the General Options dialog box.

You can still move from open window to open window without the Quick Tabs. To do so, select Names from the Windows menu.

Tracking Where the Money Goes...and Where It Comes From

INCLUDES

- Recategorizing transactions in registers

- The differences between categories, classes, and category groups

- Creating a class

- Assigning a class to a register transaction

- Deleting and renaming classes

- Creating a category group

- Reorganizing, deleting, and renaming category groups

FAST FORWARD

Recategorize Transactions That You Have Already Entered ➤ pp. 68-70

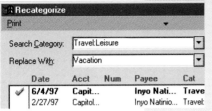

1. Choose Edit | Find & Replace | Recategorize.
2. In the Recategorize dialog box, click the arrow in the Search Category box and select a category or subcategory.
3. Click the Find All button. A list of transactions with the category or subcategory you chose appears.
4. Click to put a check mark beside each transaction that should be categorized differently, or click the Mark All button to select all the transactions.
5. Choose a new category or subcategory from the Replace With drop-down list.
6. Click the Replace button.
7. Click OK in the message box that tells you how many items are being replaced.

Use Categories, Classes, and Category Groups to Monitor Your Income and Spending ➤ pp. 70-72

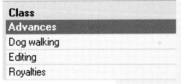

- A category (or subcategory) is a label that identifies why a transaction was made.
- A class is a label under which you can group transactions that were assigned to several different income and expense categories.
- A category group is a group of categories that have been bound together for the purpose of budgeting.

Create a New Class ➤ p. 73

1. Choose Lists | Class or press CTRL-L.
2. Click the New button in the Class List window.
3. In the Set Up Class dialog box, enter a name and a description.
4. Click OK.

Assign a Class to a Transaction in a Register ➤ pp. 73-74

1. Fill in the register as usual, and when you get to the Category box, enter a category and then choose Lists | Class (or press CTRL-L).

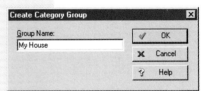

2. In the Class List window, double-click a class. In the Category box, a slash and the class name appear after the category assignment. (You can also type a slash after you enter the category and then type the first couple of letters of the class name to assign a class to a transaction.)

Create a New Category Group ➤ pp. 75-76

1. Choose Lists | Category/Transfer or press CTRL-C.
2. Click the Options button and choose Assign Category Groups.
3. In the Assign Category Groups dialog box, click the New button.
4. In the Create Category Group dialog box, enter a name and click OK.
5. Back in the Assign Category Groups dialog box, select the category group you just created by clicking on it.
6. Hold down the CTRL key and click the categories for the new category group in the Category Name box.
7. Click the Assign Category to Group button and click OK.

"Where did the money go?" is the most-asked question in American households. When you withdraw money from an ATM machine and notice the balance dwindling, when the money in the checking account runs low, you ask yourself, "Where did I spend it all, anyway?"

With Quicken, you can find out very quickly what your spending habits are. All you have to do is generate a report or graph to see the naked truth. And you can find out exactly where the money comes from, too. Quicken keeps close tabs on income and expenses. Whenever you record a transaction, you are given the opportunity to categorize it, and as long as you categorize transactions thoughtfully, you can learn a lot about your spending habits and sources of income.

This chapter picks up where "Make Your Own Categories and Subcategories" in Chapter 3 left off. Chapter 3 explained categories, the chief means of learning about your income and spending. In this short chapter, you learn about category groups and classes, the two other ways to monitor income and spending with Quicken. Not everyone needs classes and category groups, but they can come in handy for making tax projections, budgeting, and examining your finances in different ways. This chapter also shows how to fix transactions that you categorized incorrectly.

FIXING MISTAKES IN THE WAY TRANSACTIONS ARE CATEGORIZED

All is not lost if you categorized transactions incorrectly, because you can use the Edit | Find & Replace | Recategorize command to fix the problem. With this command, you find all transactions that were assigned a category or subcategory, you mark the ones that should be given a new category assignment, and then you tell Quicken which category or subcategory assignment to give the transactions that you marked.

EXPERT ADVICE

The Edit | Find & Replace | Recategorize command is for picking and choosing which transactions need recategorizing. If all the transactions to which you assigned a certain category need to be recategorized in the same way, simply change the category's name to the name of a category that is already on the Category & Transfer List. See "Changing the Names of Categories and Subcategories" in Chapter 3.

Follow these steps to recategorize transactions throughout your registers:

1. Choose Edit | Find & Replace | Recategorize. You see the Recategorize dialog box shown in Figure 4.1 (the dialog box in the figure has been filled out).

Original category
or subcategory

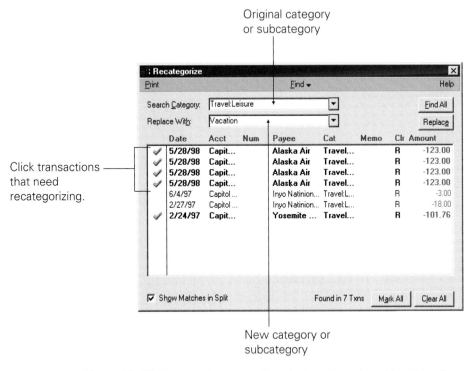

Click transactions
that need
recategorizing.

New category or
subcategory

Figure 4.1 Click next to the transactions that need recategorizing, then choose a new category or subcategory from the Replace With menu.

2. Click the arrow in the Search Category box and choose the category or subcategory that you assigned to the transactions you want to recategorize.

   To recategorize memorized or scheduled transactions, click the Find button in the Recategorize dialog box and choose Memorized Transactions or Scheduled Transactions.

3. Click the Find All button. A list of transactions appears in the dialog box.

4. Click in the left-hand column beside the transactions that should be recategorized. As you click, check marks appear beside the transactions.

5. Click the arrow in the Replace With box and choose the right category or subcategory for the transactions you selected in step 4.

6. Take a deep breath and click the Replace button.

7. Click OK in the dialog box that tells you how many replacements were made.

8. Click the close button (the X) in the upper-right corner of the Recategorize dialog box.

THE BIG PICTURE: CATEGORIES, CLASSES, AND CATEGORY GROUPS

Quicken offers three means (four, if you count the tax-related identification explained in Chapter 15) of tracking income and expenses: categories (including subcategories), category groups, and classes. At the same time that you assign a category or subcategory to a transaction, you can also assign a class or category group. You don't necessarily need classes and category groups, but they can be helpful for seeing your financial picture. Table 4.1 explains the difference between categories, category groups, and classes.

"Make Your Own Categories and Subcategories" in Chapter 3 explains how to create new categories, as well as how to delete and edit their names.

Type	Description	Use
Categories and Subcategories	Provide useful information about your finances. Using categories and subcategories in Quicken is a must.	For finding out how much you spent, what you spent it on, how much you earned, and where you earned it.
Category Groups	A collection of categories that have been bundled into a single category. For example, suppose you record the money you spend on a house in three categories: House Repair, Mortgage Payment, and Homeowner's Insurance. Besides knowing how much you spent in each category, you could find out how much you spent altogether on the house by creating a My Home category group.	Chiefly for preparing budgets, as Chapter 12 explains.
Classes	A label under which transactions are organized. Both income and expenses can be recorded in the same class. To see the advantage of using classes, suppose you manage a building. As the rents come in, you record them in the Building class; and as you pay for repairs, they are also recorded in the Building class. At the end of the year, you can generate a report for the Building class that clearly shows income from the building as well as the costs of maintaining it.	For tracking income and expenses that pertain to the same financial endeavor.

Table 4.1 Understanding Categories, Category Groups, and Classes

EXPERT ADVICE

Classes are especially useful for self-employed people who record their business as well as personal transactions in the same accounts. A transaction made for the business can be recorded in the Business class, for example, and one made for personal reasons can be recorded in the Personal class or not be recorded in any class at all. This way, you can generate reports and graphs for the Business class and see how well your business is doing.

WORKING WITH CLASSES

Classes are helpful for examining your finances in different ways. This part of the chapter explains how to create a class, assign a transaction to a class in a register, and delete and rename classes.

The report in Figure 4.2 shows a cash flow report of income in three classes—Lecturing, Teaching, and Writing. Besides categorizing payments, this person also classified them. The report clearly shows how much money was earned in different income categories for lecturing, consulting, and writing. By the looks of it, the person who generated this report should stick to lecturing and teaching. Writing doesn't pay.

Cash Flow Report
1/1/98 Through 5/31/98

Class Description	1/1/98- 5/31/98
Lecturing	7,000
Teaching	16,833
Writing	2,176
OVERALL TOTAL	26,009

Figure 4.2 The data in this report was gathered from three classes. Classes add another dimension to financial tracking.

CAUTION

Classes are not recorded automatically as part of the QuickFill feature. If you intend to use classes, you must be diligent about it. Quicken displays a message box if you forget to categorize a transaction, but it is as silent as the grave if you forget to assign a class to a transaction.

Creating a Class

Creating a class is pretty simple: Choose Lists | Class (or press CTRL-L) to see the Class List window, and then click the New button. In the Set Up Class dialog box, enter a name and a few words that describe your new class eloquently. (The Copy Number box is for businesses that receive more than one copy of tax forms—see the Help program if that pertains to you.) When you click OK, the class name and description appear in the Class List window.

SHORTCUT

To generate a report concerning a class, click a class name in the Class List window and then click the Report button. Chapter 9 describes reports in detail.

Assigning a Class to a Register Transaction

Assigning a class to a transaction is done as part of assigning a category. Follow these steps to assign a class to a transaction:

1. Fill in the register as you usually do.
2. When you get to the Category box, make a category assignment.
3. With the cursor still in the Category box, choose Lists | Class or press CTRL-L. You see the Class List window.

| Mt. San Jacinto Junior College |
| Income/Lecturing |

4. Double-click the name of the class that you want to assign to the transaction. The Class List window disappears and you see the register again, where a slash and the class name appear after the category in the Category box.

Deleting and Renaming Classes

To delete or rename a class, start by choosing Lists | Class or pressing CTRL-L to open the Class List window. Then click the class you want to delete or rename and do the following:

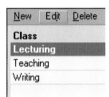

- **To Delete** Click the Delete button. A dialog box tells you that the class will be permanently deleted. Click OK. Transactions in your registers that were assigned to the class you deleted are no longer assigned a class. (You could say that those transactions no longer have class.)

- **To Rename** Click the Edit button. In the Edit Class dialog box, enter a new name and click OK. Transactions in your registers that were classified under the old name are classified automatically under the new one.

SETTING UP AND MANAGING CATEGORY GROUPS

Budgeting is explained in Chapter 12.

Unless you intend to budget with Quicken, you can ignore category groups. Category groups make budgeting easier because you can project income and expenses for groups of categories instead of individual categories and subcategories. Figure 4.3 shows the Category Group view of the Budget window. Here, you only have to budget for five category groups; if you were to budget by category and subcategory, you might have to make budget projections for 30 or 40 different line items instead of five.

To begin with, Quicken offers the four default category groups shown in Figure 4.3: Other Income, Salary Income, Discretionary Income, and Non-Dis-

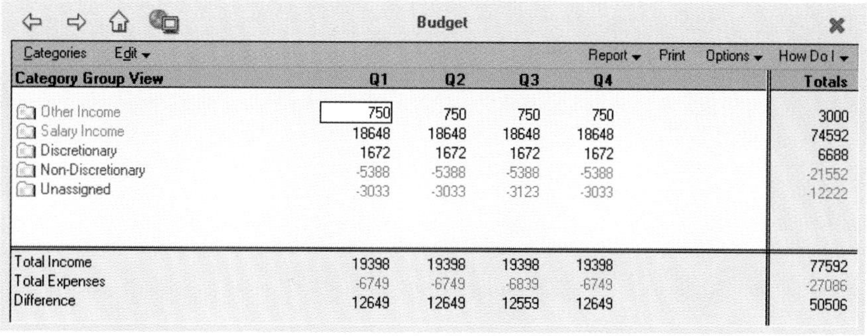

Figure 4.3 Category groups make it easier to formulate budgets.

cretionary Income. When you create a new category, you are given the chance to choose a category group. However, you can invent your own category groups or alter the default category group assignments. Following are instructions for creating a category group, putting categories in a category group, deleting a category group, and renaming one.

Creating a New Category Group

Follow these steps to create a new category group and assign categories and subcategories to it:

1. Choose Lists | Category/Transfer or press CTRL-C. You see the Category & Transfer List window.
2. Click the Options button and choose Assign Category Groups. The Assign Category Groups dialog box shown in Figure 4.4 appears. Categories and subcategories are listed in the Category Name column on the left side of the dialog box. In the Category Group column are category group assignments that have already been made. Each category can belong to only one category group.
3. Click the New button (next to the Edit and Del buttons). The Create Category Group dialog box shown in Figure 4.4 appears.
4. Enter a name for the category group and click OK.

   In the Assign Category Groups dialog box, the name you entered appears with the other category group names in the right-hand

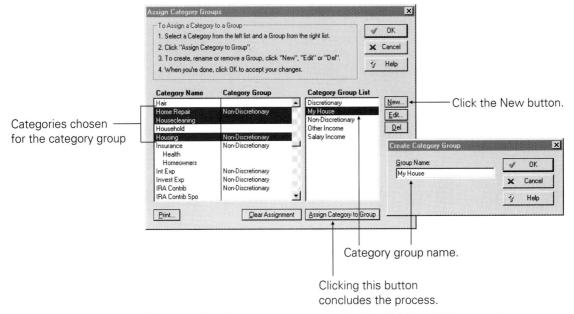

Categories chosen for the category group

Click the New button.

Category group name.

Clicking this button concludes the process.

Figure 4.4 Creating a category group and telling Quicken which categories to include in it

column. Now you tell Quicken which categories to include in your new category group.

5. In the Category Group List box, click the name of the category group you want to assign categories to.

6. Select the categories and subcategories you want for your category group. To do that, hold down the CTRL key and click on category and subcategory names in the Category Name column. As long as you hold the CTRL key down, you can click as many categories as you want.

7. Click the Assign Category to Group button.

8. Click OK to close the Assign Category Groups dialog box.

Now when you categorize a transaction in a register and assign it to the categories you chose in step 6, the income or expense you record will be recorded in your new category group as well.

Reorganizing a Category Group

If you attach the wrong categories to a category group, choose Lists | Category/Transfer (or press CTRL-C) to open the Category & Transfer List window, and then click the Options button and choose Assign Category Groups. On the right side of the Assign Category Groups dialog box (see Figure 4.4), click the name of the category group that needs reorganizing. Then hold down the CTRL key as you click in the Category Name box on the categories that shouldn't belong to the category group, and click the Clear Assignment button when you are done. Follow the directions in the previous section of this chapter to assign categories to the correct category group.

Deleting and Renaming Category Groups

Whether you want to delete or rename a category group, start by choosing Lists | Category/Transfer, clicking the Options button in the Category & Transfer List window, and choosing Assign Category Groups. Then, in the Assign Category Groups dialog box (see Figure 4.4), follow these steps:

1. In the Category Group List box, click the name of the category group you want to delete or rename.

2. Either delete or rename the category group:

   - **To Delete** Click the Del button.
   - **To Rename** Click the Edit button, enter a new name in the Edit Category Group dialog box, and click OK.

Reconciling a Bank or Credit Card Account

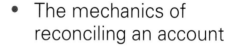

INCLUDES

- The mechanics of reconciling an account

- Recording information from the bank statement

- Clearing deposits, withdrawals, payments, and transfers in the Reconcile Bank Statement dialog box

- What to do if the account doesn't balance

- Changing a transaction in the register

- Reconciling a credit card account

- Paying a credit card bill

FAST FORWARD

Reconcile a Checking or Savings Account ➤ pp. 84-87

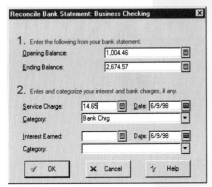

1. Open the register of the account you want to reconcile and either click the Recon button on the iconbar or click the Reconcile button in the register window.
2. In the Reconcile Bank Statement dialog box, take note of the number in the Opening Balance box—it shows the amount of money in the account as of the last time you reconciled it. Change the number, if necessary, and enter the closing balance that is shown on your bank statement in the Ending Balance box.
3. Enter a service charge (if one appears on the statement) in the Service Charge box, enter the date of the charge (probably the statement date), and categorize this charge. Do the same if you earned interest on the account by filling in the Interest Earned information from your statement.
4. Click the OK button to get to the Reconcile Bank Statement window.
5. While studying your bank statement and looking in the window, click in the Clr column next to each transaction in the window that also appears on the bank statement.
6. When the Cleared Balance and Statement Ending balance in the lower-right corner of the dialog box are the same and the Difference is 0.00, click the Finished button.
7. Click Yes or No on the Congratulations screen to say whether you want to print a Reconciliation report.

Do the Following
If an Account Won't Reconcile ➤ pp. 87-89

- Click the New button to enter a transaction from the bank statement that you forgot to record in the register.
- Click the Edit button to go back to the register and fix a transaction. Quicken takes you to the transaction that is highlighted in the Reconcile Bank Statement window.

- Click the Delete button to delete the highlighted transaction in the Reconcile Bank Statement window. Delete a transaction if you entered it twice by accident.

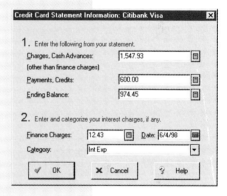

- Click the Statement button to go back to the Reconcile Bank Statement dialog box and adjust the information there if you entered it incorrectly.

Reconcile a Credit Card Account ➤ *pp. 90-91*

1. Open the credit card register and either click the Recon button on the iconbar or click the Reconcile button in the register window.

2. In the Credit Card Statement Information dialog box, enter the total for the purchases and cash advances on your statement in the Charges, Cash Advances box.

3. Enter the total of the payments you made to the credit card company and any credits the company owes you in the Payments, Credits box.

4. In the Ending Balance box, enter what the credit card statement says you owe.

5. If you were late in paying last month or you carry a credit card debt from month to month, go to part 2 of the dialog box, enter the date, and categorize the finance charges you must pay for being late. Then click OK.

6. On the Charges side of the Pay Credit Card Bill window, click off the transactions that also show on your monthly statement. As you click, the Cleared Balance and Statement Ending Balance should come into agreement. When the difference between the two numbers is 0.00, click the Finished button.

7. Fill in the Make Credit Card Payment dialog box and click OK if you want to pay all or part of the credit card bill now.

One of the best things about Quicken is being able to reconcile your accounts in a snap. What used to take an hour or more to accomplish—comparing your records to the bank's monthly statement, punching keys on a calculator—can now be done in a couple of minutes.

You can also reconcile an account by going online and downloading a bank statement. See "Getting Accurate, Up-to-Date Account Information" in Chapter 7.

This short chapter explains how to reconcile checking accounts, savings accounts, and credit card accounts. I'll show you tried-and-true techniques for making this tedious chore go as quickly as possible. This chapter also shows you what to do when an account doesn't balance.

WHAT DOES "RECONCILE" MEAN?

In financial terms, "reconcile" means to compare one set of records against another for the sake of accuracy. When you reconcile a bank account, you compare the bank's records against your records. In other words, you compare what it says on the bank statement with what you recorded in a Quicken register. If the numbers are different, you have to reconcile them somehow. Almost always, that means changing a transaction in the Quicken register to make it match what is on the bank statement. Often it means recording transactions in the register that you forgot to record. Banks *are* good at record-keeping, even though they aren't good at making lines move faster.

THE MECHANICS OF RECONCILING

The job of reconciling a checking, savings, or credit card account is done in the Reconcile window. Figure 5.1 shows a Reconcile window for a checking account. When you open this window, you see all transactions in the register that have not cleared the bank. Payments, checks, withdrawals, charges, and money

You check transactions that also
appear on the statement.

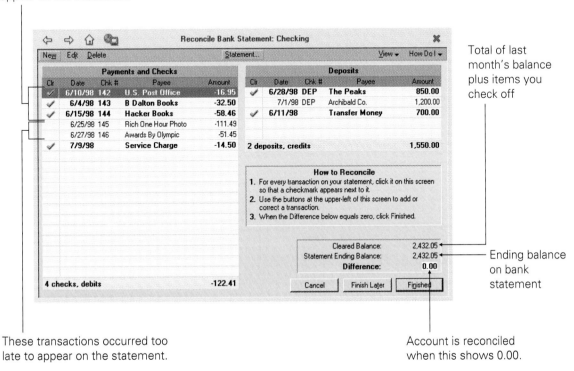

Total of last
month's balance
plus items you
check off

Ending balance
on bank
statement

These transactions occurred too
late to appear on the statement.

Account is reconciled
when this shows 0.00.

Figure 5.1 How reconciling works

transfers *out of* the account appear on the left side of the window. Deposits and transfers of money *into* the account appear on the right side. Notice that the numbers on the left side are negative and the numbers on the right side are positive.

Comparing the transactions in the Reconcile window with the transactions on your bank statement, you click the Clr (Clear) column next to each transaction that appears in both places. As you click, check marks appear and transactions are highlighted onscreen. Meanwhile, the numbers in the lower-right corner of the window change:

Cleared Balance:	1,677.42
Statement Ending Balance:	1,677.42
Difference:	**0.00**

• **Cleared Balance** This number decreases when you click the negative numbers on the left side of the window and increases when you click the positive numbers on the right side. When the account is reconciled, this number equals the Statement Ending Balance—the ending balance on your current bank statement.

- **Statement Ending Balance** This is the ending balance you got from your bank statement (you tell Quicken what it is before you open the Reconcile window—don't worry, I'll explain how to do that shortly). This number doesn't change. When you have cleared all the transactions in the Quicken register that also appear on the bank statement, this number equals the Cleared Balance number.

- **Difference** This number is the difference between the Cleared Balance and the Statement Ending Balance. As you click off transactions in the Reconcile window, this number shrinks. When it reaches zero, you have reconciled the account.

Transactions that have cleared the bank and been reconciled show an "R" in the Clr column of the register:

10/27/97	129	Walgreen's	Office:Supplies	10 45	R		2,233 67
10/31/97	130	Cash-Business	Expense-Bus	581 00	R		1,652 67
10/31/97	131	Heekin Foundation Group	Fees	25 00	R		1,627 67
11/3/97	132	U.S. Post Office	Postage	33 93	R		1,593 74

RECONCILING A CHECKING OR SAVINGS ACCOUNT

Before you reconcile an account, spread the bank statement across your desk and note what the bank says your ending balance is. Then follow these steps to reconcile a checking or savings account:

1. Either click the Recon button on the iconbar or click the Reconcile button in the register window. You see the Reconcile Bank Statement dialog box shown in Figure 5.2.

   The amount of money in the account as of the last time you reconciled it (or the account's opening balance) appears in the Opening Balance box.

1. Click the Recon button
to open dialog box.

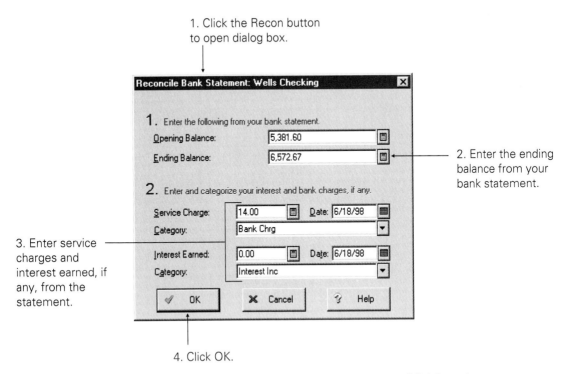

2. Enter the ending
balance from your
bank statement.

3. Enter service
charges and
interest earned, if
any, from the
statement.

4. Click OK.

Figure 5.2 The Reconcile Bank Statement dialog box is where you tell Quicken what
the ending balance on your current bank statement is.

2. In the Ending Balance box, enter the closing balance that is shown on
your bank statement. In other words, enter the amount of money that
the bank says is currently in your account.

3. If necessary, fill in the Service Charge and Interest Earned boxes along
with their dates and categories in part 2 of the dialog box.

If you ordered more checks, for example, the charge shows up on your
bank statement. Enter the amount you were charged in the Service
Charge box and, for a category, choose Office Supplies or simply
Bank Charge.

The Interest Earned box is for savings and checking accounts that
earn interest. Your bank statement tells how much you earned. Enter

the amount in the Interest Earned box and choose Interest Income as the category.

4. Click OK to move ahead to the Reconcile Bank Statement window. It is shown in Figure 5.3.

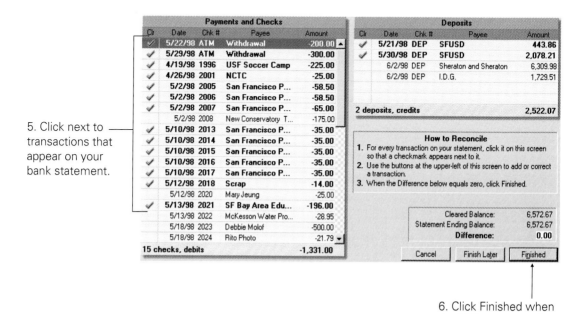

5. Click next to transactions that appear on your bank statement.

6. Click Finished when the Difference number equals 0.00.

Figure 5.3 In the Reconcile Bank Statement window, click the Clr column of transactions that show on your bank statement.

By the way, when you click OK in the Reconcile Bank Statement dialog box and move on to the Reconcile window, any service charges or interest payments you recorded in the dialog box appear in the window. Not only that, they already have check marks next to their names and are highlighted.

The Reconcile window shows all transactions—including money transfers, deposits, and withdrawals—that have not yet cleared the bank. In the left-hand column are payments, checks, withdrawals, charges, and money transfers out of the account; in the right-hand column are deposits and money transfers into the account.

5. Comparing the bank statement and the Reconcile window (and the checks, deposit slips and so on, if necessary), click the Clr column next to each transaction in the window that also appears on the bank statement.

EXPERT ADVICE

Besides matching transactions in the Reconcile window with transactions on the bank statement, you might make sure that dollar amounts match as well. This is a good time to see whether you recorded transaction amounts correctly. If an amount in the Reconcile window is incorrect, select the transaction and click the Edit button in the Reconcile window. Quicken takes you to the register so you can fix the transaction amount.

Just ahead, "Recognizing and Fixing Reconciliation Problems" explains how to recognize a reconciliation error and fix it from the Reconcile window.

Each time you click, a check mark appears in the Clr column. Meanwhile, the Difference number in the lower-right corner that expresses the difference between the Statement Ending Balance and the Cleared Balance gets smaller and smaller. When the Difference number reaches 0.00 and the Cleared Balance and Statement Ending Balance are the same, the account is reconciled.

6. Click the Finished button. A happy-looking Congratulations screen asks if you want to print a reconciliation report.

7. Click No (unless you are keeping the books for someone else—then click Yes).

Recognizing and Fixing Reconciliation Problems

When an account doesn't balance and you can't reconcile your records with the bank's, a bunch of different things could be wrong. The following checklist explains how to diagnose reconciliation problems. Meanwhile, Quicken offers four buttons—New, Edit, Delete, and Statement—along the top of the Reconcile window so you can fix errors when you find them.

- **Incorrect Amount Entry** You may have entered an amount incorrectly in the register. Compare the bank statement, paperwork, and register transactions carefully to find the error. Look for transposed numbers and numbers entered backwards. For example, $21.23 and $22.13 look very much alike at a glance, but there is a difference of 90 cents between the numbers.

  Edit

  Remedy: Either click the transaction with the incorrect amount and then click the Edit button or double-click the transaction. Quicken takes you to the transaction in the register so you can fix it. Click the Return to Reconcile button or the Reconcile Quick Tab to return to the Reconcile window.

- **Deposit Entered as Payment or Vice-Versa** Sometimes an account doesn't reconcile because you accidentally entered a payment when you should have entered a deposit or vice-versa. To spot this problem, look at payments and deposits on your bank statement and compare them to transactions on the Payments and Deposits side of the Reconcile window.

  Remedy: Click the transaction that was entered incorrectly, click the Edit button, and enter the amount either in the Payment or Deposit column of the register where it belongs. Then click the Return to Reconcile button or the Reconcile Quick Tab.

- **Transaction Wasn't Entered** Another common reason accounts don't reconcile is because a transaction or two didn't get entered. Look for a transaction on the bank statement that is equal to the difference between the Cleared Balance and Statement Ending Balance. For example, if the Difference number is $22.43, look for a transaction of that amount.

  New

  Remedy: Click the New button to enter the transaction in the register. To return to the Reconcile window, click the Return to Reconcile button or the Reconcile Quick Tab.

- **Transactions Entered Twice**   Look for transactions that were entered twice, perhaps a few days apart.

  Remedy: In the Reconcile window, click the transaction that was entered in error and then click the Delete button.

- **Ending Balance Entered Incorrectly**   Sometimes an account doesn't balance because you entered the ending balance, a service charge, or an interest payment incorrectly to begin with in the Reconcile Bank Statement dialog box.

  Remedy: Click the Statement button and enter the information correctly in the Reconcile Bank Statement dialog box. Click OK to return to the Reconcile window.

- **Opening Account Balance Is Incorrect**   If you recently started tracking this account with Quicken and this is the first time you have tried to reconcile this account, you might not be able to balance it because the opening balance—the opening balance listed in the first register entry—is incorrect.

  Remedy: Click the Register Quick Tab to return to the register, press CTRL-HOME to go to the first entry, change the opening balance in the first entry, and click the Enter button.

Finally, if worse comes to worst, you can always force a reconciliation by clicking the Finished button even though there is still a difference between the cleared and bank ending balances. Only do this as a last, drastic measure if you can't find the error. Quicken displays the Adjusting Register to Agree with Statement dialog box when you click Finished. Enter a missing amount and assign it a category. Then click the Adjust button.

EXPERT ADVICE

If your account is a new one or you started using Quicken recently, chances are you can't balance your account because the opening balance was entered incorrectly. When you start tracking an account, Quicken asks for its opening balance. Try going back to the first entry in the account register and changing it to make your account balance.

"An Account's Starting Date and Opening Balance" in Chapter 1 explains the nuances of entering the opening account balance.

RECONCILING A CREDIT CARD ACCOUNT

Reconciling a credit card account is a little different from reconciling a checking or savings account. The following pages explain how to reconcile a credit card account and record a payment to the bank or card issuer who gave you your credit card.

EXPERT ADVICE

Suppose you return an item that you bought with your credit card and receive a credit from your bank or credit card issuer. To record the credit, enter the amount of the credit in the Payment column instead of the Charge column in the credit card register. And when you record the payment, be sure to choose for a category the same expense category that you chose when you recorded the charge in the first place. Using an expense category to categorize a payment seems odd, but by doing so you make sure that your expense totals on reports remain accurate. To see what I mean, suppose you record a charge of $50 for office supplies and record it using the Office expense category. If you return the $50 worth of office supplies and receive a $50 credit, record the $50 dollar payment in the Office expense category so that your $50 initial expense is offset by the $50 that is credited you.

Entering the Statement Information

The first step in reconciling a credit card account is to open the Credit Card Statement Information dialog box shown in Figure 5.4 and enter information from the statement. Lay the credit card statement flat on your desk, open the credit card account in Quicken, and follow these steps to start reconciling:

1. Click the Recon button on the iconbar or click the Reconcile button in the register. You see the Credit Card Statement Information dialog box shown in Figure 5.4.

Enter total of purchases and cash
advances from statement.

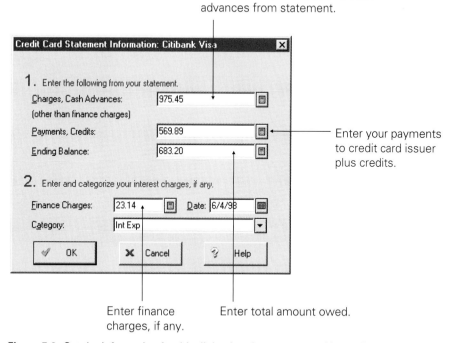

Enter your payments
to credit card issuer
plus credits.

Enter finance
charges, if any.

Enter total amount owed.

Figure 5.4 Get the information for this dialog box from your monthly credit
card statement.

You can get all the information for the dialog box directly from
your statement.

2. In the Charges, Cash Advances box, enter the total for the purchases
and cash advances on your statement, but not the finance charges. (If
this is the first time you have reconciled this account and you owe
from previous monthly statements, add the previous month's balance
to the total.)

3. In the Payments, Credits box, enter the total of the payments you
made to the credit card issuer last month as well as credits that the
issuer bestows upon you, if any. For example, if the statement says you
made a payment last month of $500, enter it now.

4. In the Ending Balance box, enter the total new balance. This number
is the easiest to find on the credit card statement. It is the total amount

that you owe and is probably located in the lower-right corner of the statement, on the "bottom line." It includes the finance charges, if any. You will enter those charges next.

5. In the Finance Charges box, enter the total finance charges from your statement. I hope they are not too high. Enter the date of the credit card statement in the Date box. In the Category box, click the arrow and choose an expense category (most likely Interest Expense or Usury).

6. Click OK.

See "Reconciling a Checking or Savings Account" and Figure 5.3 earlier in this chapter to learn how to clear transactions in the Reconcile Credit Statement window.

You see the Reconcile Credit Statement window. It looks like and works exactly like the Reconcile Bank Statement window (see Figure 5.3). Click in the Clr column next to transactions that appear on your statement. When the Cleared Balance equals the Statement Ending Balance, click the Finished button. If you can't get the account to reconcile, turn to "Recognizing and Fixing Reconciliation Problems" earlier in this chapter.

Paying the Credit Card Bill

After you finish reconciling a credit card and click the Finished button, you see the Make Credit Card Payment dialog box. It isn't necessary to pay the credit card bill right away. In fact, you might as well wait a couple of weeks until the bill is due. You can click the No button in the dialog box and pay the bill later. But if you want to pay the entire bill now, choose the bank account from which you will pay it, choose a payment method, and click Yes.

To pay part of the bill or pay later, record the transaction as a money transfer from the checking account from which you pay the bill to the credit card account. You can find account names at the bottom of the Category drop-down list. Whether you pay the bill in the Make Credit Card Payment dialog box or pay directly from a checking account register, the transaction looks something like this after it is recorded:

6/28/98	2053	Citibank Visa	607	93		8,255	68
		[Citibank Visa]					

6

Writing and Printing Checks

FAST FORWARD

Make Sure Your Checks Print Correctly ➤ pp. 101-104

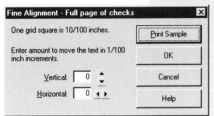

1. Choose File | Printer Setup | For Printing Checks and adjust the settings in the Check Printer Setup dialog box.
2. Click the Align button to see the Align Checks dialog box.
3. Click the Full Page of Checks button.
4. In the Fine Alignment dialog box, click the Print Sample button.
5. Depending on how your sample check printed, click the Vertical or Horizontal arrow to adjust by increments where text is printed on checks.
6. Click the Print Sample button in the Fine Alignment dialog box and see if the check printed correctly this time.

Record a Check You Want to Print Directly in a Register ➤ pp. 104-105

1. Open the register of the account you want to write the check against.
2. Choose Print Check in the Num box and record the transaction.

Write a Check in the Write Checks Window ➤ pp. 105-107

1. Open your checking account register and choose Features | Bills | Write Checks or click the Banking activity button and choose Write a check to print.
2. Fill in the Write Checks window. Enter the date, payee, amount, memo, and category, the same way you do in a checking register. Quicken writes out the amount for you. You can type an address in the Address box.
3. Click the Record Check button.
4. To review checks you've written, press the PGUP or PGDN key or double-click a check in the Checks to Print box.

Print Your Checks ➤ *pp. 107-109*

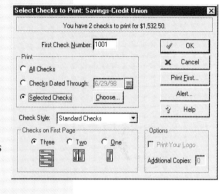

1. Open the checking account register and click the Print button in the Write Checks window or choose File | Print Checks.

2. In the Select Checks to Print dialog box, enter the number of the first check on the check sheet in the First Check Number box.

3. Choose All Checks to print all the checks, Checks Dated Through to print checks to a certain date, or Selected Checks and click the Choose button to open the Select Checks to Print dialog box and select checks.

4. If you are using a laser printer, under Checks on First Page choose the option that describes how many checks are on the first check sheet loaded in your printer.

5. Click OK to print your checks.

Reprint Checks That Don't Print Correctly ➤ *p. 109*

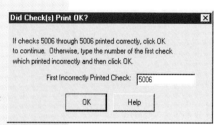

1. Find the first check that didn't print correctly and enter its number in the Did Check(s) Print OK? dialog box.

2. Click OK.

3. In the Select Checks to Print dialog box, make sure that the number in the First Check Number box is the number on the first check that is loaded in your printer.

4. If yours is a laser printer, under Checks on First Page choose the option button that describes how many checks are on the first page loaded in your printer.

5. Click OK in the Select Checks to Print dialog box.

This chapter explains how to print checks. Printed checks are consistently neat and clean, and they make a good impression on creditors and clients. They are easy to read and understand, too. I suppose you are obliged to print checks if nobody can read your handwriting.

The following pages examine the pros and cons of printing checks. They tell how check printing works, how to order checks, how to write a check, and how to void or delete one. Last but not least, this chapter explains how to print checks and reprint them if they didn't print correctly.

ALL ABOUT CHECK PRINTING

The literature that comes with Quicken claims that printing checks saves enormous amounts of time since you don't have to record checks twice, once when you write them by hand and once when you enter them in the checking register. I'm not sure how much time is saved by printing checks, unless you intend to mail them in window envelopes, because the Write Checks window has a place for printing the addresses of the people or parties to whom you write checks.

The best reason for printing checks has nothing to do with saving time—it has to do with appearances. Printed checks increase your standing with clients and creditors. A printed check says, "I'm a very serious, prosperous individual and you should regard me as such," whereas a handwritten check with spidery lettering says, "God bless you, kind sir or madam, for honoring my little check." Anyone who is in a profession where appearances count—supermodels, for example—ought to consider printing checks.

If you want to print checks, the first thing to do is order them. After the new checks arrive, you tell Quicken how to print checks, what kind of printer you have, and what size check you ordered. Quicken can't print checks correctly until it has this information. By the way, it isn't necessary for your bank to know where your checks come from. As long as the information about your bank and the checking account number are accurate, the bank will honor the checks, no matter where you got them.

WHAT KIND OF CHECKS CAN I ORDER?

"Splitting a Deposit or Payment Across Different Categories" in Chapter 2 explains the Split Transaction window.

Quicken offers three kinds of checks: standard, voucher, and wallet. See Figure 6.1 to check out the differences among the three check styles. Voucher and wallet checks include a stub. In the case of wallet checks, information from the register—the date, payee, amount, and so on—appears on a small stub on the side of the check. You can print or accounts receivable information on voucher checks. The information, which comes from the Split Transaction window, is printed on the lower two-thirds of the page.

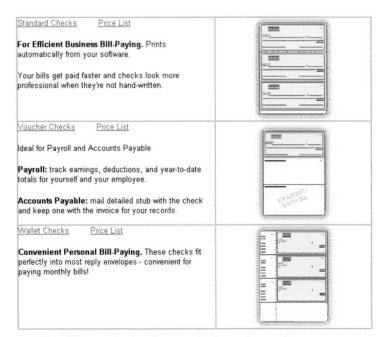

Figure 6.1 The different check styles: standard, voucher, and wallet (source: www.intuitmarketplace.com/supplies)

ORDERING THE CHECKS

Checks are not cheap. My bank charges about 5 cents per check, whereas Intuit, the maker of Quicken, charges 14 to 18 cents per check, depending on which style check you order. (When you purchase plain checks in 500 amounts from Intuit, standard checks cost 15 cents apiece, voucher checks cost 18 cents apiece, and wallet checks cost 14 cents apiece.)

Fortunately, Intuit isn't the only company that offers checks for the Quicken computer program. You can also order checks from third parties, some of which are listed in Table 6.1. Most of these companies also sell window envelopes that fit Quicken checks. If you are impatient to get your hands on the checks and you own a modem, you can order checks online from Intuit by choosing Features | Bills | Order Checks (or Online | Quicken on the Web | Quicken Store to check out all the products that Intuit offers). But I recommend shopping around. Most companies charge less for checks than Intuit does.

You will be asked for your name, address, checking account number, and other insider information when you order checks. You also need to know:

- Your bank's name, the city in which it is located, and the correct zip code.

Company	Internet Address	Telephone
American Check Printers	www.amcheck.com	800/262-4325
Checks Supplies	www.pcchecks.com	800/322-5317
Checks-R-Us	www.checks-r-us.com	800/473-3270
Designer Checks	www.hotnew.com	800/239-4087
Form Systems	www.checksforless.com	800/325-5568
Forms Solutions	www.fastchecks.com	800/749-0383
Intuit Marketplace	www.intuitmarketplace.com	none
Sensible Solutions	www.sensible-solutions.com	888/852-4325

Table 6.1 Companies That Sell Quicken-Compatible Checks

- Your bank's *fractional number*. The fractional number looks something like this: 11-22/3456. When you deposit a check, you usually list the first four numbers of the fractional number on the deposit slip.
- The size of the checks—standard, voucher, or wallet.
- The starting check number.

CAUTION

When you choose a starting check number, be sure to give a number that doesn't conflict with the numbers on checks you've already written by hand or intend to write by hand. In fact, choose a starting number that is far different from the numbers on your handwritten checks so you don't run the risk of writing two checks with the same number. It's okay to print checks and write them by hand from the same checking account, but you must be careful not to get the numbers crossed.

TELLING THE PRINTER HOW TO HANDLE CHECKS

When the checks arrive, the first thing to do is tell your printer how to handle them. Checks are expensive. You could hurt yourself in the pocketbook if you waste a check. The following pages explain how to make sure your printer can handle checks correctly and how to do a test run. By the way, you only have to do this once, so suffer patiently and in silence.

Load the sample checks that came in the Quicken box into your printer before you run the test. If your copy of Quicken didn't come with sample checks, load a thin sheet of paper in the printer. When you are done with the test, hold the sheet of paper against a real check to see if text lands in the right places and your checks can print correctly.

Follow these steps to introduce Quicken to your printer and find out if checks print correctly:

1. Choose File | Printer Setup | For Printing Checks. You see the dialog box in Figure 6.2.

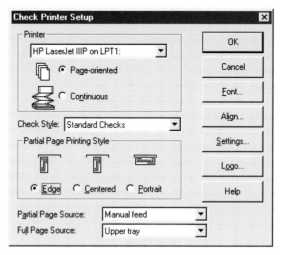

Figure 6.2 In the Check Printer Setup dialog box your new checks and your printer are formally introduced to one another.

Most of the information in this dialog box should be correct already, but if it isn't, now is the time to change the settings.

2. If necessary, click the arrow in the Printer box and choose the printer with which you will print checks.

3. If yours is a pinwheel printer that is fed paper "continuously," click the Continuous option button.

4. Click the arrow in the Check Style box and tell Quicken which kind of checks you ordered—standard, voucher, or wallet.

    If your printer is a page-oriented laser printer, you have to choose Partial Page Printing Style options at the bottom of the dialog box to tell Quicken how to print standard and wallet-sized checks that print three to a page. You very likely won't print wallet or standard-sized checks in sets of three, and when you print one or two checks at a time, you will be left with a "partial" page of blank checks that is one-third or two-thirds of a page long. So as not to waste the leftover checks, you can feed the shortened check sheet back into your printer. To do that, however, you need to tell Quicken how paper is fed to your printer.

5. Click the Partial Page Printing Style option that describes how your printer takes paper (Edge, Centered, or Portrait). (I'm sorry to say it, but you may have to burrow through the dreary manual that came with your printer to find some of the information you'll need in this section.)

6. From the Partial Page Source drop-down list, choose the option that describes how partial pages such as envelopes are fed to your printer.

7. Click the Align button. You see the Align Checks dialog box.

   The Align Checks dialog box is for running tests and making adjustments, if necessary, to where text lands on the checks you print. The three buttons are for making adjustments to check sheets with three checks on them, with two checks, and with only one check. (People printing voucher checks bypass this dialog box and go straight to the Fine Alignment dialog box.)

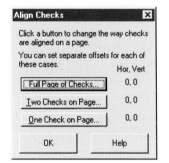

8. Click the Full Page of Checks button. You see the Fine Alignment dialog box shown in Figure 6.3.

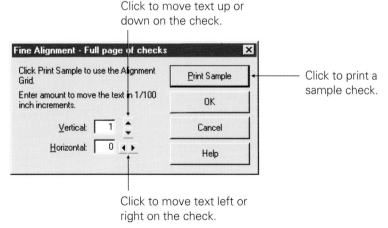

Figure 6.3 In the Fine Alignment dialog box, click Vertical and Horizontal arrows, if necessary, to move the printed text on the checks a little to the east, west, north, or south.

9. Click the Print Sample button. Quicken prints a check made out to Jane Doe of Anytown, USA.

   Examine the check to see if the text landed in all the right places. (If you printed on a piece of paper instead of on a practice check, lay the sheet of paper over a sheet of real checks and hold both sheets to the light to see where the text fell.)

10. If text didn't land where it was supposed to land, click the Vertical and Horizontal arrows in the Fine Alignment dialog box (see Figure 6.3). In the upper-right corner of the sample check you printed is a small grid. With each click, you move the text ever so slightly upward, downward, left, or right by one square on the grid. Click the Print Sample button to run the test again, and if text still doesn't land correctly on the check, click the Horizontal or Vertical arrow until the checks come out right.

11. Click OK to close the Fine Alignment dialog box.

    Back in the Align Checks dialog box, new Hor and Vert settings appear beside the Full Page of Checks button if you had to make adjustments. Chances are partial pages of checks will also print correctly, but if they don't, come back to the Align Checks dialog box and click either the Two Checks on Page or One Check on Page button and run the test on a partial sheet of checks.

12. Click OK in the Align Checks dialog box.

13. Click OK in the Check Printer Setup dialog box.

14. Stroll to the kitchen, make a cup of tea, and congratulate yourself on never having to suffer though this check alignment torture again.

WRITING A CHECK

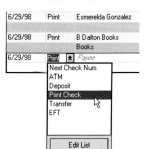

The first thing you should know about writing a check is that Quicken provides a special window for doing it, but you don't need to visit the Write Checks window unless you intend to print addresses on your checks. Instead of going to the Write Checks window, you can simply choose Print Check on the Num menu in a checking account register, as the following shortcut explains. Only use the Write Checks window if you like the window or you are writing checks with addresses on them.

If you came here to learn how to record a check in a checking account register, you came to the wrong place. See "Filling in a Register" in Chapter 2.

Filling In the Write Checks Window

Open the register for the checking account you are going to write the check against and follow these steps to write a check that you intend to print:

1. Press CTRL-W, choose Features | Bills | Write Checks, or click the Banking activity button and choose Write a check to print. You see the Write Checks window shown in Figure 6.4.

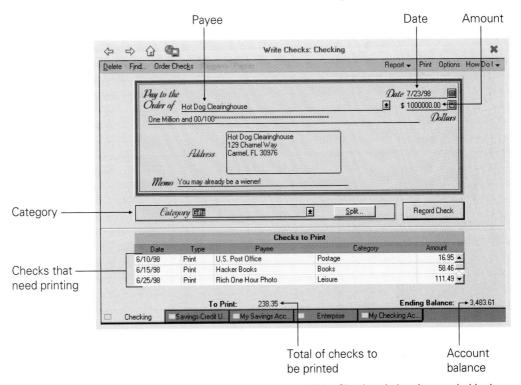

Figure 6.4 The information you enter in the Write Checks window is recorded in the checking register as well.

If you've been entering checks in the register, the buttons and menus on the Write Checks window ought to look very familiar. Everything you do to enter a check in a checking register can also be done in the Write Checks window. In the window are the same drop-down menus, a baby calendar, and a baby calculator. QuickFill works the same way in this window, too. There is even a Split button for splitting transactions. Press the TAB key or click to move from place to place. All the data you enter in this window is recorded as one transaction in the checking register.

2. Enter the date on the Date line, the payee on the Pay to the Order of line, and the amount next to the dollar sign. When you press TAB after entering the amount, Quicken writes out the amount for you on the Dollars line.

EXPERT ADVICE

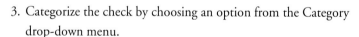

If you want to enter an address in order to send the check by mail, write the name and address of the party you are writing the check to in the Address box. When you enter an address, Quicken remembers it. Next time you write a check to the same party, the address appears in the Address box without your having to type it there.

"Keeping Track of Addresses and Phone Numbers" in Chapter 8 explains how to store addresses with Quicken.

3. Categorize the check by choosing an option from the Category drop-down menu.
4. Click the Record Check button.

A blank check appears in case you want to write another one. Write as many checks as you want. To review the ones you wrote earlier, press PGUP or PGDN, use the scroll bar, or double-click a check in the Checks to Print list. A figure showing the sum of the checks you've written appears at the bottom of the Write Checks window. The ending balance in the account appears in the lower-right corner.

Missing from the Write Checks window is a check number. That seems odd because all checks have check numbers, don't they? The check number, however, comes from the blank checks that you ordered. As part of printing a check, you tell Quicken the number on the blank check that is fed to the printer. Quicken records the number in the register when the check is printed. Meanwhile, the word "Print" appears beside unprinted checks in the checking account register:

6/29/98	Print	Gunne Sax	Clothing	138 88		8,101 80
6/29/98	Print	Last Gasp	Books	21 65		8,080 15
6/29/98	Print	French Tulip	Gifts	35 77		8,044 38
6/29/98	Print	President Tuxedo	Gifts	62 86	Enter Edit ▾ Split	

PRINTING THE CHECKS

At last—you've written the checks, and now you can print them. It isn't necessary to print all of them at once. This part of the chapter explains how to choose which checks to print, print on an incomplete check sheet, print the checks, and reprint them if they don't come out right.

Printing Checks You Have Written

Follow these steps to print the checks you have written:

1. In the Write Checks window, click the Print button; if you are starting from a checking account register, choose File | Print Checks. You see the Select Checks to Print dialog box shown in Figure 6.5. The top of the dialog box tells you how many checks need printing and the sum of those checks.

2. Glance at the checks as you load them in your printer, take note of the number on the first check, and enter that number in the First Check Number text box.

3. Tell Quicken which checks to print:

   - **All Checks**   Make sure this option button is selected if you want to print all the checks.
   - **Checks Dated Through**   Click this option button and enter a date to print checks up to and including those written on a particular day.
   - **Selected Checks**   Click this option button and click the Choose button if you want to pick and choose which checks to print. In the Print column of the Select Checks to Print dialog box, make sure a check mark appears next to the checks you want to print, and then

Enter the number of the first
check on the check sheet.

Choose which
checks to print.

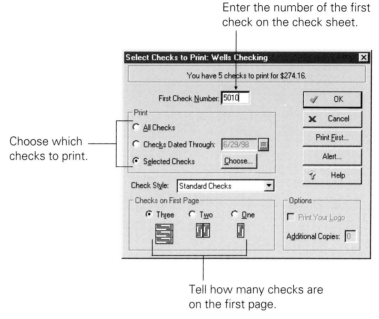

Tell how many checks are
on the first page.

Figure 6.5 Printing the checks you entered in the checking account register

click the Done button. To remove or add a check mark, click in the
Print column.

4. Glance in the Check Style box to make sure Quicken knows which
   kind of check you are printing—standard, wallet, or voucher.

5. If you are printing wallet or standard checks on a laser printer and
   only one or two checks remain on the sheet, click the Two or One

option button under Checks on First Page. Make sure that the partial sheet of checks is loaded correctly in your printer.

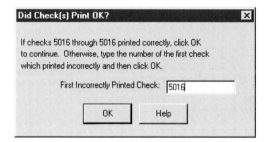

EXPERT ADVICE

If you aren't confident that checks will print correctly, click the Print First button in the Select Checks to Print dialog box to print only the first check in the batch. That way, if the checks come out wrong, you will waste only one check, not several.

6. Click the OK button. As the checks are printing, Quicken displays the Did Check(s) Print OK? dialog box:

7. Click OK in the dialog box if the checks printed correctly. Otherwise, read on.

If Your Checks Don't Print Correctly

Follow these steps if the checks don't come out right:

1. Examine the checks, find the first one that didn't print correctly, and enter its number in the Did Check(s) Print OK? dialog box.
2. Click OK. Quicken takes you to the Select Checks to Print dialog box (see Figure 6.5). Notice that the number in the First Check Number box has advanced a notch or two. Assuming that you want to try again, Quicken has entered what it believes is the next number in the check sheet.
3. Fill out the dialog box and click OK.

DELETING AND VOIDING PRINTED CHECKS

"Voiding and Deleting Transactions" in Chapter 2 explains how to void and delete checks in a register.

Until you actually print a check, it has a sort of limbo status in the register. In the transaction line where the check is recorded, the word "Print" appears in the Num box. When the check is printed, however, a check number appears where "Print" used to be.

Suppose you regret writing a check in the Write Checks window. Should you delete it or void it? If the check has been run through the printer and been assigned a number, void it. Only by voiding it can you account for the missing check number in the register. However, an unprinted check can merely be deleted because it hasn't been assigned a number yet.

Going Online with Quicken

INCLUDES

- Applying for the online services

- Setting up a modem and connecting to the Internet

- Getting an online bank statement

- Transferring money between accounts

- Paying bills online

- Updating a portfolio with online stock quotes

- Running a credit check

- Researching investments, markets, and companies online

111

FAST FORWARD

Send Payments, Bank Statement Requests, and Money Transfers Online ➤ pp. 120-122, 126-128

1. Click the Online icon on the iconbar or choose Online | Online Center.
2. On the Transactions, Payments, and Transfers tab of the Online Financial Services Center window, tell Quicken what you want to do online.
3. Click the Update/Send button.
4. In the Instructions to Send dialog box, click next to each instruction you *do not* want to send to remove the check mark, or leave the check marks as-is to send all the instructions.
5. Enter your PIN number in the Instructions to Send dialog box.
6. Click the Send button.
7. In the Connect to dialog box (if it appears), enter your password and user name, and click the Connect button.
8. After a minute or two, you see the Online Transmission Summary box. After you have read what you sent and what, if anything, was retrieved, click OK.

Get an Up-to-Date Bank Statement Online ➤ pp. 122-126

1. In the Instructions to Send dialog box, make sure a check mark appears beside the instruction to Download your latest cleared transactions and balances.
2. After the transactions have been downloaded, look at the online statement to see what the balance is and which transactions have cleared.
3. Click the Compare to Register button if you want to compare your records to the bank's.
4. Find and examine each transaction in the downloaded statement that shows "New" in the Status column. For each new transaction, click Accept to enter the transaction in the register, click Delete to ignore the transaction for the time being, or go into the register and change a transaction, if necessary.

5. Click the Accept All button to accept all the transactions with "Match" status.

6. Click the Done button.

Pay Your Bills Online ➤ *pp. 128-131*

1. Click the Online icon on the iconbar.

2. Click the Payments tab.

3. From the Payee drop-down list, choose a payee name. (The names on this list come from the Online Payees list, which you construct by choosing Lists | Online Payees.)

4. Enter the amount of the payment and categorize the payment as you would if you were filling in the Write Checks window or an account register.

5. Click the Enter button and enter another online payee and amount, if you wish.

6. Click the Update/Send button when you are ready to make the payment.

Get Stock Quotes and Mutual Fund Prices Online from Quicken ➤ *pp. 131-135*

1. Click the Port icon on the iconbar to get to the Portfolio View window.

2. Click the Update Prices button and choose Get Online Quotes & News.

3. Click the Update Now button in the Download Selection dialog box.

4. Click Done in the Download Summary dialog box.

5. If necessary, choose Online | Disconnect to disconnect from the Internet.

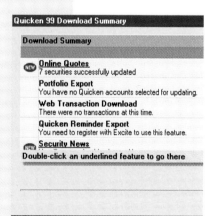

This chapter delves into the futuristic and sometimes unnerving world of Quicken's online services. It explains how to monitor a bank account by going online, pay bills electronically over the Internet, transfer money electronically between accounts, and update an investment portfolio by downloading stock quotes from the Internet.

This chapter describes the most useful online services that Quicken offers. You have to do a little setup work before you can reach out to Quicken's corner of cyberspace, and this chapter explains how to do that, too.

A SURVEY OF QUICKEN'S ONLINE SERVICES

Quicken offers a bunch of different online services:

- **Banking Online** Gives you an electronic bank statement with up-to-date information about a bank account. After you have downloaded the statement, you can learn the account's balance and see which transactions have cleared. You can also transfer the downloaded data into an account register (which saves you the trouble of entering it yourself) and send e-mail to a bank. Some banks allow money to be transferred between accounts within the same bank. To use this service, you must sign up with a bank.
  Cost: Varies from bank to bank, with the average price ranging from $3 to $5 per month.

- **Paying Bills Online**   Lets you pay bills electronically. To use this service, you must sign up with a bank.
  Cost: Varies from bank to bank. My bank charges $5 per month for the first 25 payments (that's 20 cents apiece), after which the payments cost 40 cents apiece.
- **Stock Quotes**   Lets you download stock and mutual fund quotes from **Quicken.com** into the Portfolio View window and thereby update the value of the stocks and securities you own.
  Cost: Free as long as you are using Quicken 99, the most up-to-date version of Quicken.
- **Researching**   From inside the Quicken program, you can go to the **Quicken.com** Web site, where you can get information about companies, stocks, and financial markets.
  Cost: Free.
- **Credit Report**   Lets you run a credit check on yourself. Choose Online | Quicken on the Web | Credit Check.
  Cost: Free if you print out the application and mail it in. If you get the results of the credit check online, the cost is $6.95.

ARE THE ONLINE SERVICES FOR YOU?

Intuit and others are betting that, in the same way that people rely on ATM machines to do most of their banking today, they will soon rely on home computers to pay bills and get bank statements. However, sending hard-earned money across cyberspace is a bit disconcerting, especially if you are not comfortable with computers. And when you make an online payment, you don't have a paper record to show for it. To dispute a bill, you can't wave a check in front of the merchant and say, "See, I paid for this—and here's the check to prove it."

On the other hand, paying bills online is a bit cheaper than paying them by check, and being able to download a bank statement is mighty convenient. If you are a stock market maven, getting stock quotes (and mutual fund share prices) makes updating a stock portfolio very, very easy.

MAKING THE INTERNET CONNECTIONS

Before you can begin using the online services or climb aboard the Internet with Quicken, you have to tell the program how to connect to the Internet. Quicken can use an existing Internet connection, if you have one. You also have to tell Quicken what to do after you finish banking online. You can stay on the Internet or have Quicken close the connection immediately.

Telling Quicken How to Connect to the Internet

To access Quicken's online services, you can do it either through an Internet provider you subscribe to already or through the browser that comes with the Quicken program. Follow these steps to choose the browser with which you will bank online and tell Quicken which Internet service provider (ISP) you use:

1. Choose Online | Internet Connection | Setup. As shown in Figure 7.1, you see the Internet Connection Setup dialog box with its three option buttons for establishing the connection.

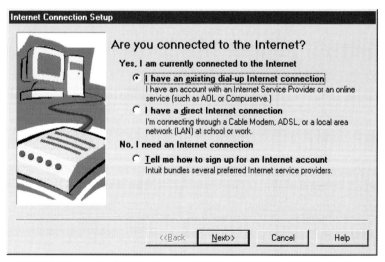

Figure 7.1 Before you can bank online, you have to tell Quicken how to connect to the Internet.

2. Choose one of the connection options:

- **I Have an Existing Dial-Up Internet Connection** Choose this option, click Next, and answer a series of questions about the Internet connection you have. Quicken asks for the name of the service you use and the Web browser with which you connect to the service.

- **I Have a Direct Internet Connection** Choose this option if you are running Quicken on a network.

- **Tell Me How to Sign Up for an Internet Account** Choose this option if you haven't yet signed up with an Internet service provider.

When you are finished telling Quicken about your Internet connection, you see the Internet Connection Options dialog box. Read on.

Telling Quicken When to Close the Connection

The next step is to tell Quicken what to do after you make the Internet connection and finish banking online. To do that, choose Online | Internet Connection | Options if you don't already see the Internet Connection Options dialog box. The most important options in this dialog box are the first two. Choose Disconnect from the Internet if you want to sever your Internet connection as soon as you finish banking online, or choose Stay Connected to the Internet if you prefer to surf the Net after you finish your online banking chores.

GETTING READY TO USE THE ONLINE SERVICES

After you have established a connection to the Internet and told Quicken what to do when you are finished banking online, you can begin using the online services. This part of the chapter explores two of the most useful services, banking online and paying bills online. With these services, you can download information about an account, pay bills, transfer money between accounts, or send e-mail messages to your bank.

The Big Picture:
Online Banking and Online Payment

Before you can bank online or pay bills online, you have to find out if your bank offers the services. If so, you apply for the service by calling the bank and making arrangements to bank online. A few days later, the bank sends you a confirmation notice that includes a PIN (Personal Identification Number) identical to the PINs used at ATM machines. You have to supply a PIN whenever you make an online transaction.

> **DEFINITION**
>
> *PIN: An identification number that safeguards financial transactions. You must submit the correct PIN in order to complete an online transaction with Quicken. PIN stands for Personal Identification Number.*

When you make your first transaction online, you are asked as a security measure to change the PIN that the bank gave you to a PIN you invent yourself. For security purposes, Intuit asks for your PIN whenever you submit an online transaction.

When you bank online, you make a direct connection to the computers at the bank you do business with. When you pay a bill, your computer calls Intuit, and Intuit withdraws the amount of the payment from your account and relays it to the payee either in the form of a paper check or as an electronic funds transfer.

Applying for the Services

Before applying for the services, I suggest calling your bank and speaking to a bank representative. Find out how much the services cost, whether you can transfer money between bank accounts, whether the bank offers a trial period, and whether you will be charged on a per-account or per-customer basis for the services.

When you're ready to apply for the Online Banking and Online Payment services, the next step is to fill out the official application form and download information about your bank into Quicken:

1. Choose Online | Online Financial Services Setup, and click the Apply Now button in the Get Started dialog box.

2. Click the Connect button in the Connect dialog box to go on the Internet.

3. At the Apply for Financial Services Web site, click the name of your bank and then click the Apply Now button.

4. Fill in the online application form. When you are done, data from your bank is downloaded to Quicken so that you can bank online.

Setting Up an Account for Use Online

The next step is to mark the account or accounts you will set up as online accounts. Follow these steps:

1. Choose Online | Online Financial Services Setup.

2. Click the Enable Accounts button in the Get Started dialog box.

3. On the Select Financial Institution screen, open the drop-down menu and choose the financial institution that you bank with, if necessary. Then click Next.

4. On the Online Account Setup screen, find and click on the account that you want to be an online account. Click Next again.

5. On the EasyStep tab, shown in Figure 7.2, click the Yes button beside the services that you want to use. Click Next to forge ahead.

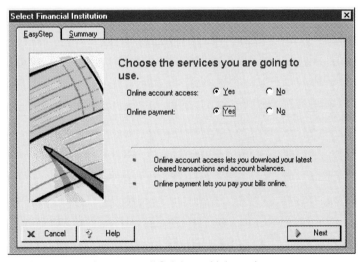

Figure 7.2 Click the Yes button to tell Quicken which services you want to use or have signed up for.

6. Answer the questions and click Next as you go along:

- **Routing Number**   The *routing number* is the first nine numbers in the lower-left corner of checks. On either side of the routing number is a colon. In the case of a savings or other type of account besides checking, get this number from the account information sheet or call your bank.

- **Account Number**   You can get this number from a check, too. It is the last nine or ten digits in the lower-left corner. The routing number comes first, then the check number, then the account number.

- **Account Type**   Click the down arrow, if necessary, and tell Quicken which kind of account this is.

- **Customer ID**   This is the number on your account information sheet—probably your social security number.

7. Glance at the first Summary tab to make sure that the information is correct, and click Next.

8. Glance at the second Summary tab to make sure all is well, and click Done. Quicken asks if you want to set up another account for use online.

9. Either click Yes and Next and start all over, or click No and then click the Next button.

10. Click OK in the Congratulations dialog box.

In the Account List window, a lightning bolt appears next to the account name to show that it is an online account:

| My Checking Account | Bank | ⚡ | Basic checking account | 1141 | 7,832.02 | 👆 |
| My Savings Account | Bank | ⚡ | Stash savings account | 61 | 9,194.03 | |

BANKING AND BILL PAYING ONLINE

At last—you've made the Internet connections, applied for the online banking services, and made an account or two into an online account. Now you are ready to blast into cyberspace with your digital cash. The following pages explain how to go online, download a bank statement, transfer money between accounts, send an e-mail message to a bank, and pay a bill online.

Going Online

Whether you want to bank online, make an electronic payment, send e-mail to the bank, or transfer money between online accounts, the procedure for getting online is the same. Follow these steps to go online and do your banking:

1. Click the Online button or choose Online | Online Center. You see the Online Financial Services Center window.
2. If you are signed up with more than one bank, click the Financial Institution arrow and choose the institution where the account you want to get at is located.
3. Click one of the tabs—Transactions, Payments, Transfers, or E-mail—and give instructions for downloading transactions from the bank, paying a bill, transferring money between accounts, or sending an e-mail message (the following pages explain how).
4. Click the Update/Send button. You see the Instructions to Send dialog box shown in Figure 7.3. The instructions you see are the very same ones you entered on the tabs in the Online Financial Services window.

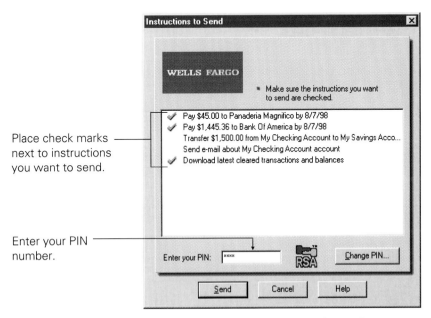

Figure 7.3 Make sure a check mark appears next to each online instruction you want to send.

5. Make sure that a check mark appears beside the instructions you want to send. To keep from sending an instruction, click a check mark to remove it.

6. Enter your PIN in the Instructions to Send dialog box.

7. Click the Send button.

8. In the Connect to dialog box (if it appears), enter your user name and password, and click Connect. After a minute or two, you see the Online Transmission Summary box. It lists the messages and transactions you sent and tells you whether they were transmitted successfully.

9. Click OK to return to the Financial Services Center window.

CAUTION

Depending on how you told Quicken to end the connection (see "Telling Quicken When to Close the Connection" earlier in this chapter), you might still be connected to the Internet. Click Online | Disconnect to disconnect from the Internet.

Getting Accurate, Up-to-Date Account Information

As part of the online banking service, you can find out how much money is in an account and which transactions have cleared the bank. After you get this information, you can compare it to what you entered in the account register and update the register with the downloaded information, if you wish.

To update a bank account, follow the directions earlier in this chapter under "Going Online" and make sure that "Download latest cleared transactions and balances" appears with a check mark beside it in the Instructions to Send dialog box (see Figure 7.3). After the information has been downloaded, Quicken either informs you that no new transactions have been recorded since the last time you went online, or it displays a Transactions tab like the one shown in Figure 7.4.

Peruse the statement to find out the account's balance, to see whether a transaction has cleared the bank, or do whatever it is you went online to do. The balance, dates, and transactions listed here are valid as of four o'clock on the last

Click to compare your
records with the bank's.

		Online Financial Services Center		
Delete Payees Repeating Contact Info			Print Options ▾ How Do I ▾	

Financial Institution:
Wells Fargo

WELLS FARGO

Update/Send...

Transactions | Payments | Transfers | E-mail | Wells Fargo

Cleared transactions and online balances downloaded on 8/1/98.

Compare to Register...

Click any account
to view its
transactions.

Account	Transactions	Online Balance
Wells Checking	185	19,066.83
Savings	0	N/A

Transactions

Date	Num	Payee/Description	Payment	Deposit
7/16/98	2133		7.35	
7/16/98	2134		5.14	
7/20/98	2125		96.56	
7/22/98	ATM	ATM Deposit		6,000.00
7/24/98	ATM	ATM Transfer	6,000.00	
7/24/98	ATM	ATM Deposit		2,000.00
7/24/98	2132		10.00	
7/29/98	ATM	ATM Deposit		3,985.60
7/29/98	ATM	ATM Deposit		1,971.28
7/29/98	2136		92.55	
7/29/98	2137		25.98	
7/29/98	2138		45.00	

Figure 7.4 Downloading a bank statement over the Internet

business-day afternoon when the bank closed. Notice the account list. If you have funneled your money into more than one account at this bank, click another account to see its balance, transactions, and so on.

EXPERT ADVICE

Comparing your records to the bank's in the Online Financial Services window is a convenient way of making sure your records are accurate. When you make the comparison, you get the chance to fix entry errors and enter transactions you forgot to record in registers. Comparing also saves time when you reconcile an account, because transactions that have cleared the bank are checked off automatically in the Reconcile Bank Statement window.

The Compare to Register button is for clearing the transactions you downloaded in the register, fixing discrepancies between your records and the bank's, and entering transactions that you have yet to enter in your register. Follow these steps to "compare" your records to the bank's:

1. Click the Compare to Register button. You see a window like the one in Figure 7.5.

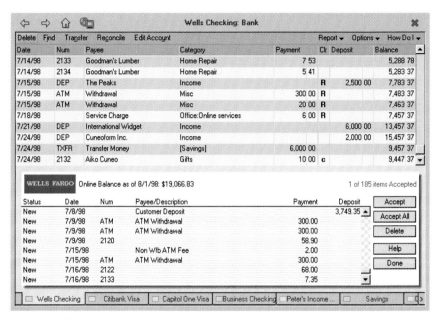

Figure 7.5 Comparing your records to the bank's

The Status column on the left side of the transaction list says "Match" when your records and the bank's jibe. When a transaction either hasn't been entered in the register yet or was entered incorrectly, the Status columns says "New." You can leave the matched transactions alone—they are perfectly okay. The new transactions are what you are concerned with.

2. In the Status column, scroll to the first transaction in the list that says "New" and click to select it.

3. Compare the first new transaction to transactions in the register at the top of the screen and click either the Accept or Delete button, or go into the register to fix a transaction if you entered it incorrectly:

- **Transaction Not Entered Yet in Register** If the transaction is one you haven't entered yet, click the Accept button. A dialog box appears and gives you a chance to categorize the transaction. Click Yes and assign the transaction to a category. Then go into the register at the top of the screen and enter the payee's name and any other pertinent information. When you click the Enter button in the register, the word "Accepted" appears in the Status column at the bottom of the screen.

- **Transaction Already in Register** Because the date you record a transaction in the register and the date that the bank shows the transaction as complete are sometimes different, transactions can be listed as "new" even though they have been entered correctly in the register. When a "new" transaction has been entered correctly, click the Delete button to remove the transaction from the statement you downloaded.

- **Transaction Needs Correcting** Notice in Figure 7.5 that the first transaction in the register at the top of the screen and the last "new" transaction at the bottom of the screen both describe check 2133, but the record in the register and the record from the bank differ. The register shows a payment of $7.53 and the downloaded statement shows a payment of $7.35. In this case, the entry in the register is wrong and needs to be changed (banks rarely err when it comes to dollar amounts). If you click the Accept button to accept a new transaction like the one for check 2133 and then try to record the transaction, you see a dialog box like this one:

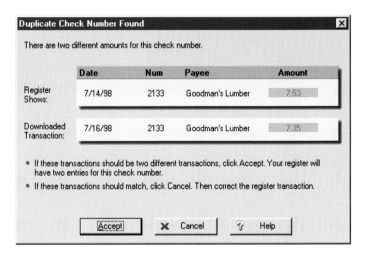

When you see this dialog box, click Cancel, and then fix the entry in the register.

4. Examine each "new" transaction in the list and accept it, delete it, or alter a transaction in the register.

5. When no more new transactions remain and all transactions that had the "New" status have the "Accepted" status instead, click the Accept All button to accept the "Match" transactions, too.

6. Click the Done button.

Chapter 5 explains how reconciling works.

Quicken puts a "C" (for Cleared) in the Clr column to show where transactions have cleared the bank. Next time you click the Recon button to reconcile this account, check marks will appear beside cleared transactions in the Reconcile Bank Statement dialog box. You will be spared the trouble of checking off—and double-checking the accuracy of—the transactions you downloaded.

Transferring Money Between Accounts

To transfer money from one account to another, both accounts must be online accounts and both must be held in the same bank. Follow these steps to transfer the money:

1. Click the Online icon on the iconbar or choose Online | Online Center.
2. Choose a bank from the Financial Institution drop-down list, if necessary.

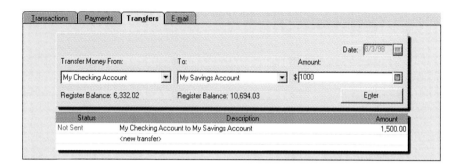

3. Choose the account you are transferring the money from in the Transfer Money From box.
4. Choose the account that will receive the money in the To box.
5. Enter the amount of money to be transferred in the Amount box.
6. Click the Enter button.
7. Click the Update/Send button.
8. See "Going Online" earlier in this chapter to learn how to send the transfer instruction.

CAUTION

Not all banks allow money to be transferred electronically between accounts. Before you attempt to transfer money, make sure your bank permits it.

If you decide against transferring the money, highlight the transfer order on the Status list at the bottom of the Transfers tab and then click the Delete button (it's in the upper-left corner of the Online Financial Services Center window). After a transfer has been sent, the letters "OXfr" (for "online transfer") appear in the Num box of the register where the transfer was recorded. Meanwhile, a "C" (for Cleared) appears in the Clr column. All online transactions are cleared in the register after they are sent:

| 8/3/98 | OXfr | Transfer Money | | 1,500 00 | c | | 6,332 02 |
| | | [My Savings Account] | Electronic Transfer | | | | |

Sending an E-Mail Message to the Bank

As a fringe benefit of banking online, you can send e-mail to a bank. To do that, click the Online icon on the iconbar or choose Online | Online Center and then click the E-mail tab in the Online Financial Services Center window. From there, click the Create button. In the Create dialog box, choose whether the message regards an online account or an online payment, and then click OK. Fill out the Message to dialog box and click OK again.

Back on the E-mail tab, you see the date and the recipient's name. Click on a message on the list and then click Read to read it or click Delete to delete it (the Delete button is in the upper-left corner of the Online Financial Services Center window). To send a message, click the Update/Send button and see the instructions under "Going Online" earlier in this chapter.

Paying the Bills Online

Before you can start paying bills online, you have to make a list of the parties you will pay. The following pages explain how to do that, as well as how to pay a bill online.

Preparing the Online Payee List

The first step to using the Online Payment service is to make a list of the companies and people whose bills you intend to pay online. Follow these steps to make the list:

1. Choose Lists | Online Payees. You see the Online Payee List window shown in Figure 7.6.
2. Click the New button to open the Set Up Online Payee dialog box. In most cases, the parties whom you pay will receive paper checks, so it is important to enter information correctly in this dialog box:

Describe the payee here.

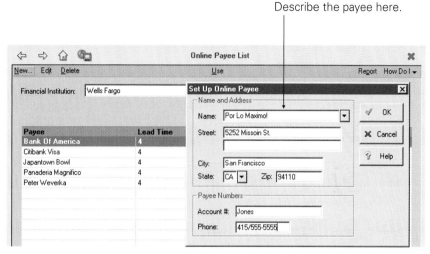

Figure 7.6 Before you can send an online payment, you have to fill in the Set Up Online Payee dialog box.

3. Fill in the dialog box. You can click the down arrow in the name box and choose names from the Memorized Transactions list. If the payee doesn't have an account number, you will be asked to enter the payee's last name in the Account # box.

4. Click OK.

5. In the Confirm Online Payee Information dialog box, make sure the information is indeed accurate and then click the Accept button.

The payee's name appears in the Online Payee List window. The lead time shown in this window is the number of days that the payment is expected to take to reach the payee. After you start sending payments online, Quicken may change lead times in the Online Payee window if it recognizes payees as parties to which it can send electronic payments.

Keep clicking the New button and filling in the Set Up Online Payee dialog box until you put together a list of the parties to whom you will send payments online. You can click the Edit button to change payee information or the Delete button to remove a payee from the Online Payee List window.

Paying Your Bills

After you have listed the parties you intend to pay, you are ready to pay your bills online. Follow these steps:

1. Click the Online icon on the iconbar or choose Online | Online Center to reach the Online Financial Services Center window.

2. Click the Payments tab, shown in Figure 7.7.

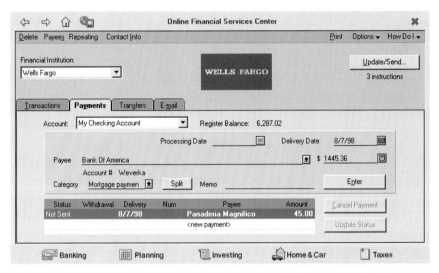

Figure 7.7 Enter payments you want to make online on the Payments tab of the Online Financial Services Center window.

3. Choose the account from which to pay the bill.

4. Choose the name of the party you want to pay from the Payee drop-down list.

5. Fill in this dialog box as you would the Write Checks window or an account register.

6. Click the Enter button.

7. Click the Update/Send button.

8. Follow the directions under "Going Online" earlier in this chapter to send the payment across cyberspace.

After you send payments over the Internet, a message box tells you that they were sent and which check numbers they were assigned. Meanwhile, the Status column on the Payments tab says "Sent" instead of "Not Sent." In the Num box of the register, a lightning bolt appears beside the check number.

SHORTCUT

You can send online payments straight from an account register. To do so, choose Send Online Payment in the Num box menu.

To delete a payment that has been sent, select it on the Status list on the Payments tab and click the Cancel Payment button. You can also click the Update Status button to inquire about the status of a payment—that is, find out whether the payee has received it—the next time you go online.

GETTING SECURITY PRICES ONLINE

You can update the price of securities in your portfolio by way of **Quicken.com**, Quicken's official home on the Internet. Being able to download security prices this quickly is a very, very nice feature of the program. Quicken downloads the current per-share price of all the stocks and mutual funds you own and records those prices in your portfolio. By downloading prices, you save yourself the trouble of entering prices yourself. And to top it off, downloading prices is free. You can even download articles about the securities you own (click the News button in the Security Detail View window to read them).

SHORTCUT

To update your portfolio without starting from the Portfolio View or Security Detail View window, simply click the One-Step Update button. You will find it with the other direction buttons in the upper-left corner of the Quicken screen.

Chapter 14 explains the Portfolio View and Security Detail View windows.

Follow these steps to update your portfolio by way of the Internet:

1. Starting from the Portfolio View or Security Detail View window, click the Update Prices button (or the Update button in Detail view) and choose Get Online Quotes & News from the drop-down menu. You see the Quicken 99 Download Selection dialog box, which has check marks next to Online Quotes and Security News.

2. Click the Update Now button. As shown in Figure 7.8, you see the Quicken 99 Download Status dialog box as share prices are downloaded from the Internet to your computer. After the prices have been downloaded, you see the Quicken 99 Download Summary dialog box, which tells whether new per-share prices were entered in your portfolio and whether more news articles are available.

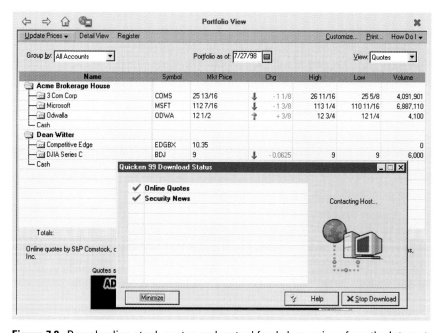

Figure 7.8 Downloading stock quotes and mutual fund share prices from the Internet

3. Click the Done button to close the Download Summary dialog box.

4. If necessary, choose Online | Disconnect and click Yes in the dialog box that appears to disconnect from the Internet (see "Telling

Quicken When to Close the Connection" earlier in this chapter if you want Quicken to disconnect by itself when you are through downloading prices).

To find out when you last updated your portfolio on the Internet, choose Online | Download Summary. You see the Quicken 99 Download Summary dialog box, which lists the dates and times that you last visited the Internet to bring your portfolio up to date:

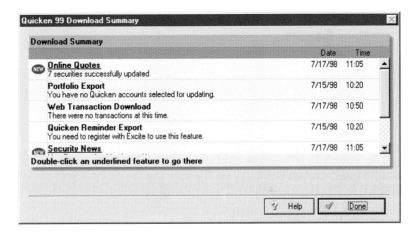

RUNNING A CREDIT CHECK ON YOURSELF

Anyone who intends to apply for a loan ought to run a credit check. Lenders favor people with clean credit records, so finding out whether your credit history has a blemish and erasing that blemish is worthwhile. You can obtain one free credit report with the program, and Quicken also offers a baffling assortment of other options for subscribing to a credit report service called Experian. Yes, you can request a credit report on someone else, but to do so you need their social security number, birth date, mother's maiden name, and address.

To run a credit check, choose Online | Quicken on the Web | Credit Check. Then read about the various ways to run a credit check (click a More Information button to learn all the details), click an Order Now! Button, and either print an order form and fill it out or submit information over the Internet.

RESEARCHING INVESTMENTS AND COMPANIES AT QUICKEN.COM

By way of its Web site, **Quicken.com**, Quicken offers a bunch of different ways to go on the Internet and research companies and get financial news. And you can get to **Quicken.com** from inside the Quicken program in numerous ways.

Starting from the Investing Center (choose Features | Centers | Investing Center to get there), click a hyperlink under "Internet Links" to read financial news, commentary about financial markets, and so on. When you click a link, you go to a page inside **Quicken.com** with the information you asked for. To go to the Quicken.com home page and rummage for financial news there, choose Online | Quicken on the Web | **Quicken.com**. You land at the **Quicken.com** home page shown in Figure 7.9, which offers financial news, advice for investors, up-to-date reports about the financial markets, and the like.

INTERNET

Links

Today's Headlines
Market Commentary
Market Movers
World Equity Watch
Earnings Release Calendar

Figure 7.9 Quicken.com offers numerous ways to research investments.

To research stocks and mutual funds, learn the ticker symbol of the stock or mutual fund you want to research and choose Online | Quicken on the Web | Investment Research. In the Quicken Investment Research window, enter the ticker symbol and click the Go Online button. You can also get reports about certain kinds of stocks and mutual funds from this window.

Quicken As Your Executive Secretary

137

FAST FORWARD

Tell Quicken to Alert You to Financial Events ➤ *pp. 140-141*

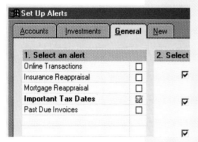

1. Choose Features | Reminders | Alerts. You see the Set Up Alerts window.
2. In box 1, click to choose what you want to be alerted about.
3. In box 2, enter the information that the program needs in order to alert you on the Home Page.
4. Click OK.

Enter a Reminder Note So It Appears on the Home Page ➤ *p. 142*

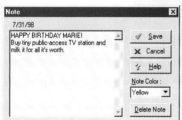

1. Click the Calendar icon on the iconbar or the Jot a note hyperlink on the Home Page.
2. Click the day on which you want to write the note.
3. Click the Note button.
4. Write a note in the Note window.
5. Click the Save button.

Schedule a Future Transaction So You Don't Forget to Make It ➤ *pp. 142-146*

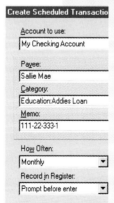

1. Choose Lists | Scheduled Transaction (or press CTRL-J).
2. In the Scheduled Transaction List window, click the New button to see the Create Scheduled Transaction dialog box.
3. At the top of the dialog box, tell Quicken which account to make the payment from and what type of transaction you want to make.
4. In the middle of the dialog box, tell Quicken who the payee is, how to categorize the payment, the amount of the payment, and when the next payment is due.
5. In the bottom of the dialog box, say how often to make payments or deposits, how many to schedule, whether they should be recorded automatically, and how many days in advance you want to be warned of the scheduled transaction.

Record a Scheduled Transaction in a Register ➤ pp. 146-149

1. On the Home Page, right-click a scheduled transaction and
   make a choice from the shortcut menu:
   - **Edit this Scheduled Transaction** Opens the Record
     Scheduled Transaction dialog box so you can change the
     amount or date
     of the transaction.
   - **Skip this Scheduled Transaction** Removes the scheduled
     transaction from the Highlights Center (and Reminders window).
   - **Enter this Scheduled Transaction** Records the transaction
     automatically in the register.

Scheduled Transactions

- Do you know that Scheduled Transactions can be used as a Remin
  transactions that are not constant in amount. Click here to learn mor

Type	Account	Date	Payee/Description
Sched. Tr...	My Check		
	My Checkin	Create a Scheduled Transaction	
	My Checkin	Edit this Scheduled Transaction	
Check to Print	Business Ch	Skip this Scheduled Transaction	
	My Checkir	Enter this Scheduled Transaction	

Look Up an Address You
Have Stored in Quicken ➤ pp. 151-152

1. Click the AddrBk icon on the iconbar or choose Lists |
   Track Important Addresses.
2. Either scroll to and double-click on the person or
   organization whose address you need, or type the first
   few letters of the person or organization in the Find box.
3. Click the Close button when you are done with the Address
   Book.

Qdata - Financial Address Book

File Edit Sort Options Help

New   Edit   Delete   Search   Print   Help

Find *Last Name* :   Group:

Last Name	First Name	Organization
<<New>>		
		Peter Weverka
		Gunne Sax
		Panaderia Magnifico
		Esmerelda Gonzalez
		SF Bay Area Educato
Yoshikawa	Ken	

This chapter takes a giant leap toward the future when, according to science fiction writers, everyone will have two or three robots on hand to do all the chores and all the work. In this chapter, you learn how to make Quicken serve as your robo-secretary.

This chapter describes how to have Quicken alert you to upcoming financial events and how to keep track of important addresses and phone numbers with Quicken. You also learn how to schedule important transactions in advance so you don't forget to make them and how to use the Financial Address Book and Financial Calendar to organize your chaotic life. Sounds like the tasks secretaries do, doesn't it? Don't forget to give Quicken flowers on National Secretary's Day.

BEING ALERTED TO FINANCIAL EVENTS

The Home Page is the first window you see when you start Quicken. "Choose for Yourself What Appears on the Home Page" in Chapter 3 explains how to put items, including alerts and reminders, on the Home Page.

To help you keep on top of your finances, Quicken puts alerts on the Home Page under the heading "Alerts & Reminders." Alerts appear, for example, when you allow an account balance to drop below a certain minimum, you exceed your credit card limit, or you overspend in a certain expense category. Alerts also appear in message boxes in registers and in the Quicken Reminders window.

Alerts & Reminders

7/9/98	The balance for your Citibank Visa is over the credit limit.
7/11/98	The balance for your Capitol One Visa is over the credit limit.
7/21/98	Your account balance in My Checking Account is at or over the maximum. Click here to go to your account register.

To tell Quicken to alert you on the Home Page and Quicken Reminders window when an untoward incident is about to occur, choose Features | Reminders | Alerts. You see the Set Up Alerts dialog box shown in Figure 8.1.

In box 1, choose what you want to be alerted about. Depending on what you choose, instructions at the top of box 2 tell you what type of information is needed in the right side of the dialog box. In box 2, enter the information that Quicken asks for. Click all four tabs—Accounts, Investments, General, and New—to see all the different ways of staying alert.

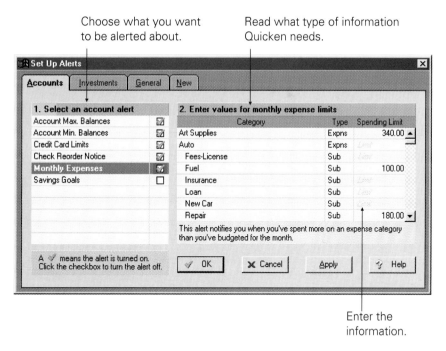

Choose what you want to be alerted about.

Read what type of information Quicken needs.

Enter the information.

Figure 8.1 The Home Page broadcasts alerts if you exceed the limits you impose on yourself when you make entries in this dialog box.

WRITING REMINDER NOTES FOR THE HOME PAGE

See "Choose for Yourself What Appears on the Home Page" in Chapter 3 if you need to know more about the Home Page. See "Choose What You See When you Start Quicken" in Chapter 3 if you want a particular window, not the Home Page, to appear when you start the program.

Under "Alerts & Reminders" on the Home Page and "Alerts and Calendar Notes" in the Quicken Reminders window, you can write notes to yourself. As you surely know, the Home Page is the first screen you see when you start Quicken. It's hard to miss a reminder note in a prominent place like the Home Page. Personally, I like to write notes to remind myself when friends' and relatives' birthdays are near.

To write a note to yourself, start by going to the Financial Calendar window: Either click the Calendar icon on the iconbar or choose Features | Reminders | Financial Calendar. The Financial Calendar shows all recorded and scheduled transactions. On the right is a menu of memorized transactions. I don't cover the Calendar in this book because I think it's too cluttered to be useful, but you are free to make choices on the Options menu and play with the Calendar if you want.

From the Financial Calendar window, follow these steps to write a note that will appear on the Home Page and Quicken Reminders window:

1. Click a day. Notes start appearing on the Home Page seven days prior to the day you select.
2. Click the Note button. You see the Note dialog box.
3. Type your note and click the Save button.

To decide for yourself how many days in advance notes appear on the Home Page and Quicken Reminders window, choose Edit | Options | Reminders and enter a number in the Days in Advance text box.

SCHEDULING TRANSACTIONS SO YOU DON'T FORGET TO MAKE THEM

Most people make transactions of the same kind over and over. Mortgage payments, car payments, the rent, and quarterly tax payments, for example, are made at regular intervals—monthly, bimonthly, or quarterly. Certain kinds of deposits are made on a regular basis, too. Most salaried employees receive the same twice-a-month or biweekly pay whether they take long lunches or work on weekends.

To help you record and remember to make transactions that you make over and over again, you can schedule them. After you schedule a transaction, it appears under "Scheduled Transactions" on the Home Page and in the Quicken Reminders window where you can plainly see it. Scheduled transactions also appear in the Billminder window when you start your computer (see "Letting the Billminder Tell You What Needs Doing" later in this chapter).

Read on to learn how to schedule a transaction, record one in a register, postpone one, and delete one. You also learn how to handle automatic paycheck deposits.

In Chapter 3, see "Choose for Yourself What Appears on the Home Page" and "Choose What You See When You Start Quicken" in the same chapter if you need help with the Home Page.

EXPERT ADVICE

By all means, schedule a transaction if it will help you to pay it on time. Credit card companies and banks, to name only two hard-nosed institutions, charge a penalty when payments arrive late. It takes little time and effort to set up a scheduled payment, and scheduling payments can help save money, especially if you are the forgetful type as I am. It's hard to miss making a payment when you are reminded to do so on the Home Page each time you start the program.

Scheduling a Transaction

Follow these steps to schedule a transaction, such as a mortgage payment, credit card payment, rent payment, transfer to a savings account, or deposit that is made at regular intervals:

1. Choose Lists | Scheduled Transaction (or press CTRL-J). You see the Scheduled Transaction List window.
2. Click the New button. The intimidating Create Scheduled Transaction dialog box shown in Figure 8.2 appears.

Tell how the transaction is made.

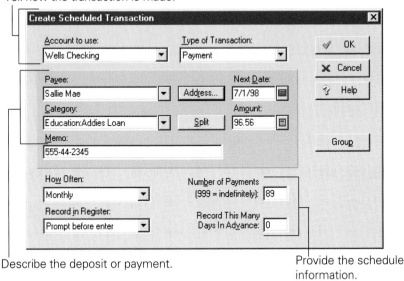

Describe the deposit or payment.

Provide the schedule information.

Figure 8.2 Describe the scheduled transaction in great detail in the Create Scheduled Transaction dialog box.

SHORTCUT

The fastest way to schedule a transaction is to right-click in a register on a transaction that you want to schedule, choose Schedule Transaction from the shortcut menu, and then fill out the Create Scheduled Transaction dialog box.

Actually, this dialog box isn't as intimidating as it seems. Many of these text boxes, buttons, and drop-down lists also appear on registers.

3. On the top of the dialog box, tell Quicken where the transaction goes to or comes from and how it is to be made:

- **Account to use** Choose the account that the transaction is to be paid from or paid to.

- **Type of transaction** The first two choices, Payment and Deposit, are self-explanatory. Choose Print Check if you intend to print the checks by which the payment is made. Choose the last option,

Online Pmt, if you are enrolled in the online banking service and want to make the scheduled transaction electronically.

4. In the middle of the dialog box, tell Quicken about the payee or the party from whom you receive payments. I trust that these boxes look familiar—they are the same ones that appear on account registers. If you chose Print Check in the Type of drop-down list, you can click the Address button and enter an address for the payee. Only the Next Date box might seem mysterious:

To tell Quicken how many days in advance you want to be warned of payments, see "Choose for Yourself What Appears on the Home Page" in Chapter 3.

- **Next Date**   Enter the date when the first of the series of scheduled transactions is to be made. In effect, the next date is the due date. For example, if your monthly credit card payments are due on the seventh of each month, enter 1/7. Simply enter whatever the next due date happens to be. On the Quicken Reminders screen, you will be reminded seven days before each monthly due date to make the payment.

EXPERT ADVICE

It isn't really necessary to enter an amount in the Amount box. If you know exactly what the payment or deposit will be, enter it. For credit card payments and other important transactions whose amounts change from month to month, enter the average amount you pay in the Amount box. Quicken uses amounts in scheduled transactions when formulating budgets and debt-reduction plans (see Chapter 12) and when forecasting future income (see Chapter 13).

5. In the bottom of the dialog box, give Quicken the following information:

- **How Often**   The frequency at which the transaction is to take place. Intervals range from Only Once at the top of the scroll list to Yearly at the bottom.
- **Number of Payments**   In the case of a paycheck, leave the number of payments at 999. You will be paid at least that many times, I hope. The 999 setting simply means that the deposit or payment is

an ongoing one. If you know the number of payments, enter it. To schedule 359 mortgage payments, for example, enter **359**.

- **Record in Register** Choose Automatically enter to record transactions like direct-deposited paychecks automatically in the register. With this option, the transaction goes in the register and you don't review it first on the Home Page. Choose "Prompt before enter" if you want the chance to review the transaction first on the Home Page or the Quicken Reminders window.

- **Record This Many Days in Advance** If you want, enter a number here to record the transaction in the register a few days in advance of its due date. The transaction is entered as a post-dated transaction.

- **Group** Believe it or not, you can schedule groups of scheduled transactions by clicking this button. See Quicken's Help program if you are banking online and this slice of esoterica interests you.

6. Click OK when you are done filling in the Create Scheduled Transaction dialog box.

EXPERT ADVICE

Besides the Home Page, scheduled transactions also appear in the Quicken Reminders window. To see that window, choose Features | Reminders | Reminders. In earlier versions of Quicken, the Reminders window appeared first when you started the program. See "Choose What You See When You Start Quicken" in Chapter 3 if you want it to appear first in this version of the program, too.

Recording a Scheduled Transaction

Now that you've gone to all that trouble to schedule a transaction, you will be glad to know that paying and recording it is far easier than scheduling it. Each scheduled transaction appears seven days in advance of its due date on the Home Page.

As Figure 8.3 shows, the Home Page lists the account that the transaction is to be paid from or paid into, the due date, the payee name, and an amount (the

Change the transaction.

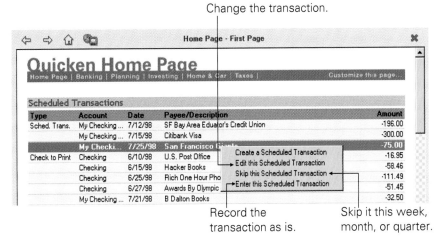

Figure 8.3 Recording a scheduled transaction. Scheduled transactions appear on the Home Page and Quicken Reminders windows.

Quicken Reminders window lists this information as well). How you handle a scheduled transaction depends on whether you want to record it as it appears on the Home Page or alter it in some way before you record it. Right-click the transaction that you want to record and then do one of the following:

- **Record the transaction as-is** To record a transaction exactly as it is shown in the window, choose Enter this Scheduled Transaction (click the Enter in Register button in the Reminders window). The

EXPERT ADVICE

Unfortunately, Quicken isn't smart about entering check numbers when you right-click and choose Enter this Scheduled Transaction to record a scheduled payment that you want to make from a checking account. When you choose the option, a notice tells you that you are recording a duplicate check number. To get around this problem, choose Edit this Scheduled Transaction (or click the Edit button in the Reminders window) instead of choosing Enter this Scheduled Transaction to record a check payment. Then, in the Record Scheduled Transaction dialog box, choose Next Check Num from the Number drop-down list.

transaction is recorded instantaneously in the register, as of the date shown onscreen.

- Change the transaction before you record it   If you want to change the amount of the transaction, the payee name, the date on which the transaction is recorded, or the account in which it will be entered, choose Edit this Scheduled Transaction (click the Edit button in the Reminders window). You see the Record Scheduled Transaction dialog box. Change the transaction as you please and then click the Record button.

By the way, after you change the amount or any other part of the scheduled transaction, your original transaction stays intact. If you want to change a scheduled transaction permanently, see "Changing and Deleting Scheduled Transactions" later in this chapter.

Skipping a Scheduled Transaction

To bypass a scheduled transaction and tell Quicken that you won't make it this week, month, quarter, or whatever, right-click the transaction and choose Skip this Scheduled Transaction from the shortcut menu, as in Figure 8.3 (click the Skip Payment button in the Reminders window). That's all there is to it. Quicken pushes the due date ahead and you aren't reminded to record the transaction until a week, month, quarter, or whatever has passed.

Paying Early and Often

Suppose you are taking a month-long trip to Greece. Before you go, you want to pay off scheduled transactions in the next month so that you don't come home to a mountain of unpaid bills. To make a scheduled transaction early, choose Lists | Scheduled Transaction (or press CTRL-J). You see the Scheduled Transaction List window shown in Figure 8.4. From there, click the transaction you want to pay early, and then click the Pay button. You see the Record Scheduled Transaction dialog box. Change the date in the Date box, choose an option from the Number drop-down list if necessary, and click the Record button.

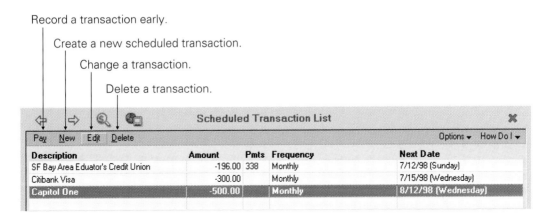

Record a transaction early.

Create a new scheduled transaction.

Change a transaction.

Delete a transaction.

Figure 8.4 From the Scheduled Transaction List window, you can create, change, delete, or record a transaction early.

Changing and Deleting Scheduled Transactions

To change or delete a scheduled transaction, you have to go to the home of scheduled transactions—the Scheduled Transaction List window (see Figure 8.4). In this window, find and click the transaction you want to change or delete, and then click the Edit or Delete button:

- **Edit** You see the Edit Scheduled Transaction dialog box. This behemoth works exactly like the Create Scheduled Transaction dialog box (see Figure 8.2). Change the settings to taste and then click OK.

- **Delete** A dialog box warns that you are about to delete a scheduled transaction. Click OK.

Tracking Income and Deductions from a Paycheck

If you are a salaried employee and your paycheck is deposited automatically by your employer, you can schedule a deposit of your paycheck. Not only that, you can also record how much of your gross income is devoted to taxes, social security, employee-sponsored IRA accounts, health plans, and what-all, so you can keep track of that stuff. If you deposit part of your income in a retirement account, Quicken will ask which account to deposit the money in.

If you are a stickler for keeping good records, get out your most recent paycheck stub and choose Features | Banking | Set Up Paycheck. Then answer the questions and fill in the screens, clicking the Next button as you go along. To schedule the paycheck deposit, be sure to click the Yes button when Quicken asks if you want to be reminded automatically to enter your paycheck deposit.

Personally, I see no reason to complicate your life by tracking your taxes, social security payments, and the like when your employer does it for you. You can, however, record a scheduled deposit for your net pay if your employer deposits your paycheck for you automatically on each payday. Do that by following the standard procedures for scheduling a transaction, in this case a deposit (see "Scheduling a Transaction" earlier in this chapter).

LETTING THE BILLMINDER TELL YOU WHAT NEEDS DOING

"Choose for Yourself What Appears on the Home Page" in Chapter 3 explains how to put items on the Home Page.

As the last section in this chapter explains, scheduled transactions appear where you can't miss them on the Home Page, the first window you see when you start Quicken. That's fine and dandy, and if you want to be deadly certain to pay your bills on time, you can also see scheduled transactions in the Billminder window each time you turn on your computer. The Billminder can also list checks to print, online payments that haven't been sent yet, investment reminders, and notes from the Financial Calendar.

Figure 8.5 shows the Billminder window. Click the Run Quicken button to start Quicken. Or click the Turn Off Billminder check box if you tire of seeing the Billminder window whenever you sit down before your computer.

If the Billminder is for you, choose Features | Reminders | Reminders to open the Quicken Reminders window. Then click the Options button and choose Billminder | Show Billminder when starting Windows.

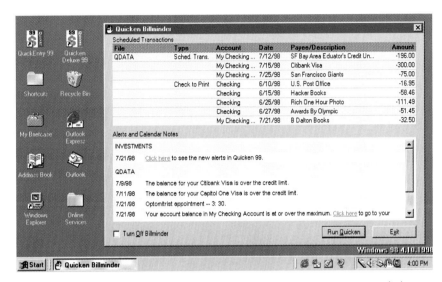

Figure 8.5 The Billminder appears whenever you start your computer to remind you that bills need paying and checks need printing, among other things.

KEEPING TRACK OF ADDRESSES AND PHONE NUMBERS

Occasionally you have to look up a person's or a company's address in order to send a check or bill. For those occasions, Quicken offers the Financial Address Book. It is easy to look up addresses in the Address Book, and entering them is pretty easy, too, as the following pages explain.

Recording an Address in the Financial Address Book

When you write an address on a check, it is recorded automatically in the Address Book. Any addresses that you enter on the Scheduled Transactions List, the Memorized Transaction List, and the Online Payees List are entered automatically as well. However, you can easily enter an address on your own—just use the following steps:

1. Click the AddrBk icon on the iconbar or choose Lists | Track Important Addresses. The Financial Address Book opens, as shown in Figure 8.6.
2. Click the New button.
3. Fill in the lower half of the screen. To move from place to place, either click or press the TAB key.
4. Click the Record button when you are done.

Looking Up an Address

Follow these steps to look up an address in the Address Book:

1. Click the AddrBk icon on the iconbar or choose Lists | Track Important Addresses to open the Financial Address Book.
2. Either scroll to and click on the person or organization whose address you need, or type the first few letters of the person's or organization's name in the Find box. The address appears in the bottom half of the screen.

Type here to look for an address...

...or scroll and double-click the person whose address you need.

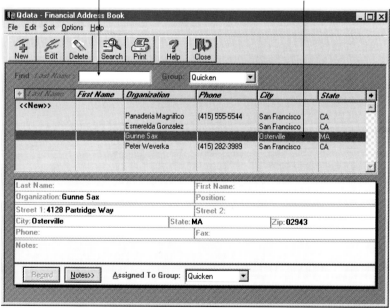

Figure 8.6 Use the Financial Address Book to keep track of the important addresses you require from time to time.

Reports and Graphs for Assessing Your Finances

INCLUDES

- The 29 kinds of Quicken reports and how to generate them

- Creating a report of your own

- Memorizing a customized report so you can use it later

- Creating a graph that depicts your financial situation

- Tailoring a graph

- Changing the appearance of a graph

- Printing reports and graphs

FAST FORWARD

Create an EasyAnswer Report in Seconds ➤ pp. 157-158

1. Choose Reports | EasyAnswer Reports.
2. In the EasyAnswer Reports & Graphs dialog box, click the question that needs answering.
3. In the Details part of the dialog box, provide the information that Quicken needs to construct the report or graph.
4. Click the Show Report or Show Graph button.

Generate One of Quicken's Reports ➤ pp. 158-161

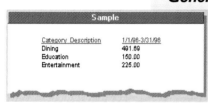

1. Click the Reports button on the iconbar.
2. Find the report you want to generate in the Create Report window. You might have to click tabs and use the scroll bars to find the one you want. Click a report's name (not its icon) to get a sample glimpse of what it looks like when it has been generated.
3. Change the report dates, if necessary.
4. Click the icon beside the report you want to generate.

Generate a QuickZoom
"Report Within a Report" ➤ pp. 159-161

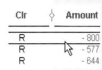

1. Move the mouse pointer over a part of a report that arouses your curiosity.
2. When the pointer changes into a magnifying glass with a Z (for "zoom") inside it, double-click.

Create a Custom-Made Report of Your Own ➤ pp. 161-164

1. Create the report that most resembles the one you want to create.
2. In the report window, click the Customize button.
3. Choose options in the Customize Report dialog box. The Display tab handles the title and layout of the report; the Accounts tab lets you choose which accounts to include; the Include tab lets you choose categories and classes; and the Advanced tab lets you choose which transactions to include and exclude.
4. Click the Create button.

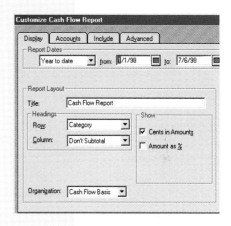

Memorize a Report for Later Use ➤ p. 164

1. Generate your report and click the Memorize button.
2. Enter a title for the report.
3. Choose the Report Dates option that specifies the period of time you're reporting on.
4. Enter a description of your report.
5. Click an icon if you'd like one to appear beside the report name.
6. Click OK.

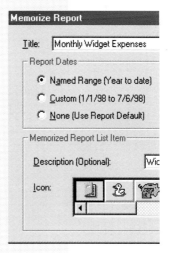

Create One of Quicken's Five Graphs ➤ pp. 164-169

1. Choose Reports | Graphs.
2. Click one of the five graph types—Income and Expenses, Budget Variance, Net Worth, Investment Performance, or Investment Asset Allocation.
3. In the Graph Dates part of the dialog box, tell Quicken which time period to use for generating the graph.
4. Click the Create button.

See What a Pie Slice or Bar on a Graph Represents in Monetary Terms ➤ pp. 166-167

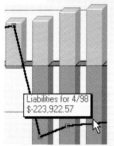

1. Move the mouse over the part of the graph you are interested in. The pointer changes into a magnifying glass and a box appears with the numeral that that part of the graph represents.
2. Double-click to see another graph that gives more detail about the thing you clicked on.

Change the Look of a Graph ➤ pp. 169-170

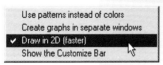

1. With the graph onscreen, click the Options button.
2. Choose Use patterns instead of colors to see a black-and-white graph, or Draw in 2D (faster) to see a two-dimensional graph.

A picture is worth a thousand words, so they say, and one financial graph is worth a fair number of words, too. With Quicken, you can get pie charts, bar charts, and other kinds of charts that show right away where you stand financially. You can also get detailed reports— 29 kinds in all—about everything from investment performance to missing checks.

This chapter explains how to get the lowdown on your finances by generating reports and graphs. It describes how to use one of Quicken's prefab reports and how to fashion reports of your own. It tells how to generate and tinker with graphs. It explains how to print graphs and reports, too. This chapter is an important one. Reports and graphs can be very useful. After I discovered the Tax Summary report, I stopped staying up late on April 14 and spent the evening instead lolling around in my Bermuda shorts.

SHORTCUT

You can make many different reports and graphs appear on the Home Page, the window you see when you start Quicken. See "Choose for Yourself What Appears on the Home Page" in Chapter 3.

EASYANSWER REPORTS AND GRAPHS

The surest way to find out anything is to ask, and that is the premise behind the Reports | EasyAnswer Reports command. Choose this command to generate a simple report or graph that answers a common question about finances. When you choose Reports | EasyAnswer Reports, you see the EasyAnswer Reports & Graphs dialog box shown in Figure 9.1.

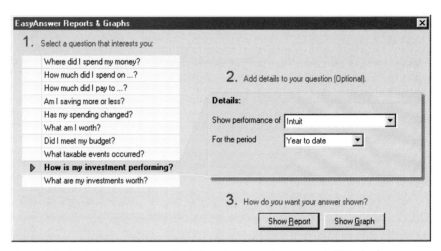

Figure 9.1 Click the question on the left that you want answered, fill in the box or boxes on the right, and then click either Show Report or Show Graph.

If one of these questions is the one you have been aching to have answered, click it. One, two, or three boxes appear in the Details section, depending on the question you clicked. Usually, all you do is choose a time period, but Quicken needs category names and account names to answer some of the questions. When you have made entries in the Detail boxes, click the Show Report or Show Graph button.

READY-MADE
REPORTS FROM QUICKEN

Chances are, you can find a ready-made report that tells you exactly what you need to know about your finances. Quicken offers 29 different reports. And if one of them isn't quite right, you can always tweak it. This part of the chapter describes Quicken's ready-made reports and explains how to generate them. "Fashioning a Report of Your Own," a few pages hence, explains how to get a tailor-made report of your own.

SHORTCUT

A fast way to create a report or graph is to start from inside a register: Select a transaction whose payee or category assignment you want to know more about and then click the Report button. From the Report menu, you can generate a by-date category report of all transactions you assigned to the category; a by-date payee report of all payments you made; a by-date listing of all transactions in the register; or a pie chart of the ten highest expenditures by category.

The Different Kinds of Reports

Later in this chapter, "Memorizing Your New Report So You Can Call on It Again" explains how to create your own reports for the Memorized tab.

To see the different kinds of reports that Quicken offers, click on the Reports menu and slowly slide the mouse pointer past Banking, Planning, Investment, Taxes, and Business. The submenus list all the reports you can generate. Chances are, one of these reports will do the trick.

You can find out more about these reports and even see small samples of what they look like by clicking the Reports button on the iconbar. When the Create Report window shown in Figure 9.2 appears, click one of the tabs, click a report description, and watch the sample box (sometimes you have to scroll to see all the reports that are available on a tab). Between the sample report and the description, you can usually tell what a report is good for. Whatever you do, don't click a report icon unless you want to generate a report. Clicking an icon tells Quicken to generate the report.

Generating Reports and QuickZoom Reports

When you've selected a report style from the Create Report window (see Figure 9.2), specify report dates to tell Quicken which time period to cover in the report. Then either click the report's icon or the report's name and click the Create button. Soon you see your report in all its glory. You probably have to click the scroll bar to move down the "pages" and read the whole thing.

Report description

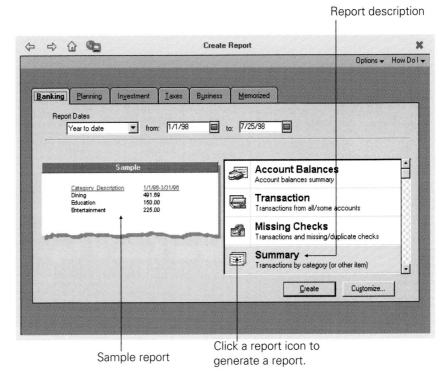

Sample report

Click a report icon to
generate a report.

Figure 9.2 Scroll down the list of reports if necessary, then click on a report name
(not its icon), and glance at the sample to see what the report is.

SHORTCUT

*The last four reports you generated appear at the bottom of the Reports
menu. Click one of the four to generate it again.*

If something on a report arouses your curiosity, move the mouse pointer
over it. With any luck, the mouse pointer changes into a magnifying glass with a
Z (for "zoom") in it. Double-click at that point and you either go to the transaction

in the register or you see what Quicken calls a *QuickZoom report*—a "report within a report" that clarifies the thing you clicked on, whatever it happened to be.

EXPERT ADVICE

You can export a report to a word processing or spreadsheet program. To do so, generate the report and click the Copy button in the Report window. The report is copied to the Windows Clipboard. From there, you can copy it elsewhere.

FASHIONING A REPORT OF YOUR OWN

Mavericks will be glad to know that you don't have to rely on ready-made reports, because you can fashion reports of your own. To create a report tailored especially for your finances, you start by generating a ready-made report, and then you click the Customize button in the Create Report window to mold the report into something entirely new.

Besides creating new reports, you can change the way they look. And when you're finished doing that, you can tell Quicken to "memorize" your new report so you can call on it again without having to go through all that shaping and molding a second time.

"Massaging" a Quicken Report

After you have generated a ready-made report, you can start fooling with it by clicking the Customize button in the report window (for that matter, you can start fooling around from the get-go by clicking the Customize button at the bottom of the Create Report window). When you click the Customize button, you see a Customize Report dialog box similar to the one in Figure 9.3. The four tabs in the dialog box—Display, Accounts, Include, and Advanced—are for tweaking the report in different ways.

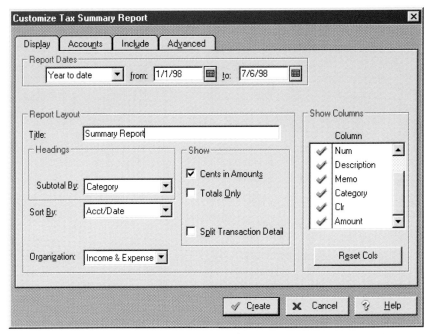

Figure 9.3 The Display tab of the Customize Report dialog box offers options for customizing a summary report.

EXPERT ADVICE

When it comes to fashioning a report of your own, consider starting with one of these reports on the Reports | Banking submenu: Account Balances, Transaction, Summary, or Comparison. These four reports are the basic report types on which all of Quicken's ready-made reports are built.

Depending on the kind of report you are trying to modify, the options in the Customize Report dialog box differ a little bit. Don't be afraid to click the Help button in the dialog box to get descriptions of the options you have to choose from. When you are done filling in the four tabs of the Customize Report dialog box, click the Create button to generate your newfangled report. Here is a brief rundown of what is on the four tabs:

Tab	What It Does
Display	Changes the title and layout of the report
Accounts	Tells Quicken from which accounts to draw data for the report
Include	Tells Quicken which categories, classes, or category groups to report on
Advanced	Weeds out transactions that you want to exclude from the report

EXPERT ADVICE

Unless you change the report date settings, all Quicken reports gather data from transactions made in the year to date. To change the default date settings, choose Edit | Options | Reports and enter a new Default Report Date Range in the Report Options dialog box.

Changing the Look of a Report

"Printing Reports and Graphs" at the end of this chapter explains how to establish the size of the margins for a report, print on different-sized paper, and print in landscape mode.

Besides changing the layout and content of a report, you can change its appearance. By dragging the column markers, you can change the width of columns. And you can also choose a new typeface for the column headings and the body text of a report.

To change the width of a column in a report, move the mouse pointer over a diamond-shaped marker that separates the name of one *header*—that is, one column heading—from the next. If you do this correctly, the mouse pointer changes into a cross with arrowheads on two sides. Click, hold down the mouse button, and drag the cross to widen or narrow the column. This illustration shows the headers and diamond-shaped markers at the top of a report:

Cat/Sub ◇ Date ◇ Acct ◇ Num ◇ Description ◇ Memo ◇Clr◇ Amount

The Print Report dialog box is the starting point for changing the typeface that is used in the headers and body text of a report. To get there, click the Print button in a report window (or press CTRL-P) and then click either the Heading Font or Body Font button. The Heading Font button opens a dialog box for changing the font, font style, and font size of headers in a report. The Body Font button opens a dialog box for choosing a typeface for the main text.

EXPERT ADVICE

As you experiment with the report's appearance in the Print dialog box, be sure to click the Preview button from time to time. Click this button and you see a window that shows precisely what your report will look like on the page after it is run though the printer.

Memorizing Your New Report So You Can Call on It Again

After you go to the trouble of creating a report of you own, you might as well tell Quicken to "memorize" it. That way, you can generate the report again without having to go to all the trouble of modifying one of Quicken's reports. When you memorize a report, you give it a name, and Quicken puts the name on the Memorized tab of the Create Report window so you can call on it again. The Step by Step box over on the next page explains how to memorize a report that you've created.

To remove a report from the Memorized tab of the Create Report window, click its name, click the Delete button, and click OK when Quicken asks if you really want to delete your report.

GRAPHING YOUR FINANCES

The quickest way to see how you stand financially is to generate a graph. Graphs tell it like it is. The slices of the pie and the bars on the graph tell you instantly what your finances look like. It's pretty easy to create a graph with

STEP BY STEP Memorizing a Report

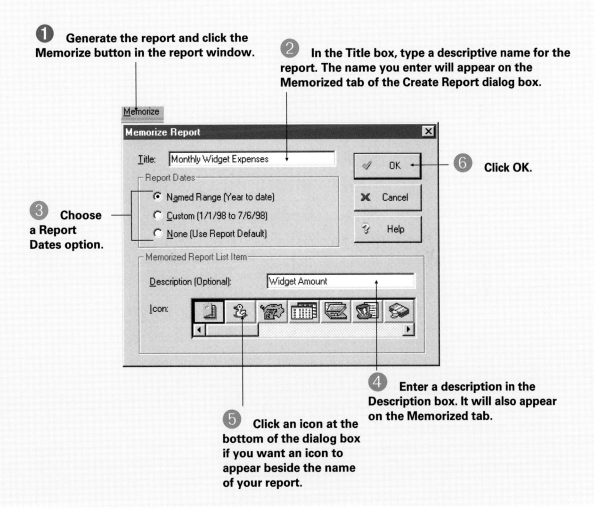

1 Generate the report and click the Memorize button in the report window.

2 In the Title box, type a descriptive name for the report. The name you enter will appear on the Memorized tab of the Create Report dialog box.

3 Choose a Report Dates option.

6 Click OK.

4 Enter a description in the Description box. It will also appear on the Memorized tab.

5 Click an icon at the bottom of the dialog box if you want an icon to appear beside the name of your report.

Quicken. And, like reports, you can tinker with graphs to make them display the financial data you are curious about. This part of the chapter shows you how to create a graph, "zoom in" to look at it more closely, create customized graphs of your own, and change the appearance of graphs.

The Five Types of Graphs

To create one of Quicken's five ready-to-wear graphs, choose Reports | Graphs, and then click one of the five graph commands on the menu. No matter which command you choose, you end up at the Create Graph dialog box shown in Figure 9.4. This dialog box serves up five types of graphs, two of which are shown in Figure 9.5. Click the icon next to the graph you want to create (or click the graph description and then click the Create button):

- **Income & Expenses Graph** A bar graph comparing monthly income and expenses and a pie chart showing each expense as a percentage of total expenses.

- **Budget Variance Graph** Two bar graphs, one that compares your budget income goals to your actual income and another that compares your actual spending by category to your budget's spending goals.

- **Net Worth Graph** A bar graph that shows, month by month, how your assets and liabilities stack up to produce your net worth.

- **Investment Performance Graph** Two bar charts, one that shows the month-by-month value of your portfolio and another that shows your average return for the year. The charts can report by type, goal, security, account, or asset.

- **Investment Asset Allocation** Bar charts that show how investments perform by allocation. When you set up an investment or security, Quicken gives you the opportunity to classify it by asset type.

Getting a Closer Look at Graph Data

Graphs are plotted from the data in registers. As such, each bar, pie slice, line, and box represents a number of some kind. To find out what those numbers are, move the mouse pointer over the part of the graph you are interested in. The pointer changes into a magnifying glass and you see a dollar figure.

If you double-click while the magnifying glass is onscreen, Quicken shows you a "QuickZoom graph" with detailed information about the thing you clicked.

Choose dates for the graph.

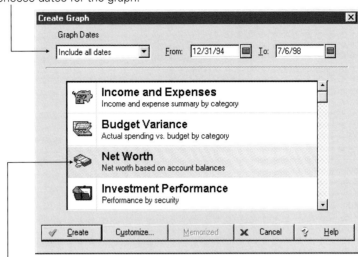

Click a graph icon or click a graph type and then click Create.

Figure 9.4 The Create Graph dialog box is where you tell Quicken what kind of graph to make.

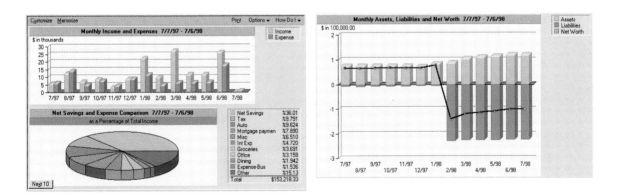

Figure 9.5 An Income and Expenses graph (left) and a Net Worth graph (right)

QuickZoom graphs are a convenient way to look more closely at the data on a graph. When you are finished scrutinizing a QuickZoom graph, click the Close button to get back to the original graph.

Creating Your Own Graph

When Quicken makes a graph, it includes data from all the accounts. All categories and all classes go into the making of a graph. As for the time period covered, Quicken graphs cover the year to date. You can, however, change these settings. You can also exclude certain accounts, certain categories, and certain classes. And you can tell Quicken to plot data from past years or from this quarter or from last month.

Follow these steps to create a customized graph of your very own:

1. Choose Reports | Graphs and select a graph to open the Create Graph dialog box (see Figure 9.4).
2. Click the graph that most resembles the one you want to create.
3. Click the Customize button. You see the Customize Graph dialog box shown in Figure 9.6.

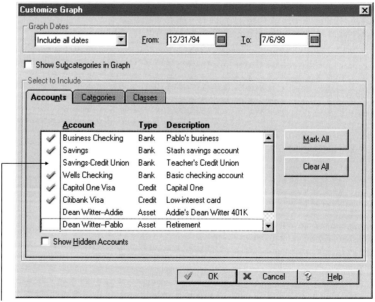

Accounts, categories, and classes without check marks are not plotted in the graph.

Figure 9.6 The Customize Graph dialog box is where you tweak a graph and tell Quicken precisely what data you want it to display.

4. Click the Accounts, Categories, or Classes tab to keep data from accounts, categories, or classes from being plotted in the graph.

5. Click items to exclude them. As you click beside account, category, or class names, the check marks beside items are removed. Only items with check marks beside their names are plotted in the graph.

6. Choose a new date for plotting the graph, if you want to.

7. Click the Create button to create your newfangled graph.

Memorizing a Graph So You Can Use It Later

Graphs, like reports, can be memorized and called to use another day. If you have gone to the trouble to create an elaborate, intricate graph, you owe it to yourself to save it so you can use it again. To do that, click the Memorize button in the graph window. In the Memorize graph dialog box, enter a description for your graph and click OK.

To call on the graph again, choose Reports | Graphs | Memorized Graphs, click the name of the graph in the Memorized Graphs window, click the Use button, and click OK in the Recall Memorized Graph dialog box. By the way, the Edit button in the Memorized Graphs window is for changing the names of memorized graphs, and the Delete button is for removing them from the Memorized Graphs window.

Changing the Look of a Graph

Appearances count for a lot, so Quicken gives you a handful of ways to change how graphs look. The most dramatic way to change the look of a graph is to click the Options button in a graph window. You see a submenu with these options:

```
Hide Customize Bar
Draw in 2D (faster)
Draw in Patterns
Create Graphs in Separate Windows
```

- **Hide (or Show) the Customize Bar**   Displays (or removes) the menus along the top of the graph for changing the dates between which the graph data is plotted.

- **Draw in 2D (faster) (or in 3D)**   Robs one dimension from the graph and renders it in two dimensions instead of three. If you are drawing graphs in two dimensions, choose Draw in 3D to go back to three-dimensional graphs.

- **Draw in Patterns (or in Color)** Shows crosshatch patterns in graphs instead of colors. If your printer is a black-and-white job, choose this option. Choose Draw in Color to use colors instead of patterns.
- **Create Graphs in Separate Windows** Tells Quicken to print graphs like Income & Expenses, which is really two graphs, on separate pages. It is a printing option, truth be told.

Another way to change the appearance of a graph is to do it from the Report Printer Setup dialog box. To get there, choose File | Printer Setup | For Reports/Graphs. Click the Heading Font button to open a dialog box where you can choose a new typeface for headings and titles. Click the Body Font button to get to a dialog box where you can choose a new typeface for the text and labels in you graphs.

EXPERT ADVICE

If you find yourself constantly having to improve the look of your graphs, choose Edit | Options | Graphs and select check boxes in the Graph Options dialog box to change the default appearance of graphs.

PRINTING REPORTS AND GRAPHS

Before you can print a report or graph, you have to visit the Report Printer Setup dialog box and tell Quicken how to lay it out. The following pages explain how to do that and how to actually send a report or graph to the printer. By the way, choices made in the Report Printer Setup dialog box apply to all your reports and graphs, so choose wisely.

Telling Quicken How to Print Reports and Graphs

Follow these steps to tell your printer how to print reports and graphs:

1. Choose File | Printer Setup | For Reports/Graphs. You see the Printer Setup dialog box.

2. If necessary, choose the correct printer from the Printer drop-down list.

3. In the Margins boxes, change the settings if you want wider or narrower margins.

4. Click the Settings button to print on different-sized paper or print in landscape mode instead of portrait mode. The Landscape option prints on paper that is wider on top than it is on the sides (like a landscape painting). It is easier to print a wide report or graph in landscape mode. Click OK to return to the Printer Setup dialog box.

5. Click OK.

Printing a Report or a Graph

Printing a graph is pretty darn simple. All you have to do is glance at your graph to make sure it is just so, and then click the Print button or press CTRL-P. The thing is printed immediately.

When you click the Print button or press CTRL-P in a Report window, however, you see the Print dialog box. From there, you can make last-minute adjustments to the report's appearance. As you fool with the options in this dialog box, be sure to click the Preview button from time to time to see what your changes amount to.

NOTE

Getting the Housekeeping Done

- Backing up a Quicken data file

- Restoring a file from a backup copy

- Deleting and renaming accounts

- Creating archive and year-end files

- Renaming, copying, and deleting a file

- Protecting files and transactions with passwords

- Changing and removing passwords

FAST FORWARD

Back Up a Quicken File ➤ pp. 177-178

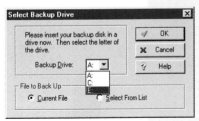

1. Put a floppy disk in the drive to which you will make the backup copy.
2. Choose File | Backup (or press CTRL-B).
3. Click Yes in the dialog box that asks if you have labeled the floppy disks and are ready to back up the file.
4. If necessary, click the down-arrow in the Select Backup Drive drop-down list and choose a new drive letter, and then click OK.
5. Click OK when Quicken tells you the file backed up successfully.

Replace the On-Disk Copy of a Quicken File with Its Backup ➤ pp. 178-179

1. Put the floppy with the backup copy on it in the A drive of your computer.
2. Choose File | Restore Backup File. You see the Select Restore Drive dialog box.
3. If necessary, choose a new letter from the Restore files from Drive drop-down list, and then click OK.
4. In the Restore Quicken File dialog box, click the file that is to replace the data file on your computer, and then click OK.
5. In the dialog box that asks if it is okay to overwrite the file in use, click OK.
6. Click OK in the dialog box that tells you that the file restored successfully.

Create an Archive File for Storing
the Previous Year's Transactions ➤ pp. 186-187

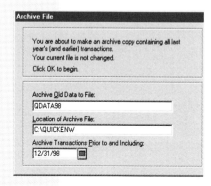

1. Choose File | File Operations | Year-End Copy.
2. Since Archive is already selected, click OK in the Year-End Copy dialog box.
3. In the Archive File dialog box, enter a name for the archive file in the Archive Old Data to File box.
4. Enter a date in the Archive Transactions Prior to and Including box. Transactions recorded previous to the date you enter and transactions recorded on the date you enter will be stored in the archive file.
5. Click OK.
6. Click OK in the dialog box that tells you the file copied successfully.

Create a Password to Keep Others
from Seeing Your Financial Data ➤ pp. 188-191

1. Choose File | Passwords | File.
2. Type the password twice in the Set Up Password dialog box, once in the Password and once in the Confirm Password box.
3. Click OK.

175

This important chapter explains the necessary housekeeping chores you have to do in Quicken. It tells how to back up Quicken data for safe-keeping and how to create a year-end or archive file of the previous year's financial transactions. It also explains how to rename, copy, and delete accounts and Quicken data files. You learn how to copy records from one account to another. Last but not least, this chapter has something for the espionage fan: it explains how to create passwords so others can't look at your precious financial data.

PROTECTING DATA AGAINST A COMPUTER FAILURE

Computers are marvelous machines until they break down. A broken computer is worse than useless. The data stored on its hard disk is trapped inside and will never be of use to anyone. Unless someone had the foresight to back up the data, no one will ever be able to see or use it again.

In computer lingo, *backing up* means to make a second copy of a computer file and keep it in a safe place where nothing can harm it. Usually, files are backed up to floppy disks or zip drives. If the hard disk gets warped, the computer is stolen, the house catches on fire, or another morbid catastrophe strikes, you can get the file back—as long as you made a backup copy. Backing up a Quicken data file and restoring data from a backed up file are the subjects of this part of the chapter.

Backing Up Financial Data

Nothing could be easier than backing up a Quicken data file. Here's how:

1. Put a floppy disk or zip disk in the floppy drive or zip drive and glance at the computer screen to make sure that the Quicken file you want to back up is onscreen.
2. Choose File | Backup (or press CTRL-B).
3. Click Yes in the dialog box that asks if you are ready to back up the data file.
4. In the Select Backup Drive dialog box, choose a new drive letter, if necessary, from the Backup Drive drop-down list and then click OK.
5. Click OK in the message box that tells you the file backed up successfully.

EXPERT ADVICE

Quicken makes it very easy to back up a data file. Do it each time you finish running the program. That way, you always have an up-to-date copy of your financial records that you can use if the original copy gets bent, mutilated, or spindled. To be reminded to back up each time you finish running Quicken, choose Edit | Options | Quicken Program, click the General tab in the General Options dialog box, and enter 1 in the Remind to Backup after Running Quicken text box.

By the way, backing up data is so important, Quicken reminds you to back up if you forget to do it. If you lackadaisically use the program on three different occasions without backing up your data, you see the Automatic Backup dialog box. This dialog box is your cue to get with it and back up your financial records:

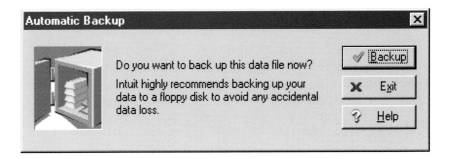

Restoring Data from Backed Up Files

If something wicked this way comes and you lose your Quicken financial data, you can always restore it from the backup copy you made. Or, if you bungle a find-and-replace operation, for example, and make a hash of your data file, all is not lost, because you can get a clean copy of your financial records from the backup copy. Replacing the original copy of a data file with the backup copy is called *restoring*. Follow these steps to restore data from backed up files:

1. Put the floppy or zip disk with the backup copy on it in a drive on your computer.
2. Choose File | Restore Backup File. You see the Select Restore Drive dialog box.
3. If necessary, choose a new letter from the Restore files from Drive drop-down list, and then click OK.
4. In the Restore Quicken File dialog box shown in Figure 10.1, click the file that is to replace the data file on your computer, and then click OK.
5. In the dialog box that asks if it is okay to overwrite the file in use, click OK.
6. Click OK in the dialog box that tells you that the file restored successfully.

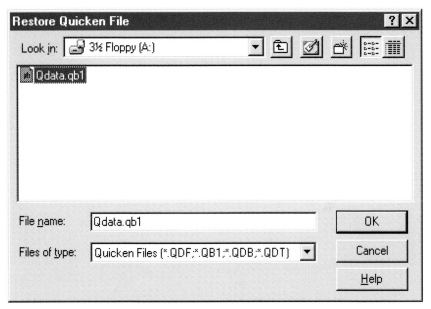

Figure 10.1 When you restore a Quicken file, you erase the copy on the hard disk and replace it with the backup copy. Click the backup file in this dialog box and then click OK.

Now all you have to do is enter the financial transactions that you entered between the time you last backed up the file and the time you "restored" it. I hope there aren't many transactions to enter.

EXPERT ADVICE

Quicken keeps backup copies of files in a folder on the hard drive called C:\Quickenw\Backup. If you forgot to back up your data file and you need to restore it, you might try getting backup copies from that folder. However, files in the Backup folder are made sporadically, so I wouldn't count on them to be up-to-date and accurate.

MOVING RECORDS FROM ONE FILE OR ACCOUNT TO ANOTHER

You recorded transactions in the wrong account? Making that mistake is easy because Quicken offers many different kinds of accounts. Perhaps you recorded transactions in a 401(k) account when you should have recorded them in an investment account. Perhaps you want to move transactions from one Quicken file to another.

Moving transactions is a three-step business. You start by copying them to a floppy disk, where they are saved in a QIF (Quicken Interchange Format) file. Then you import the transactions you copied from the QIF file into the account where they belong. Then you delete the original transactions that you copied. Before you copy transactions, take note of the dates of the transactions you want to move. You will be asked for inclusive dates when you copy the transactions to the QIF file. And make a backup copy of the file, too, in case you regret copying and deleting the transactions.

Put a floppy disk in the disk drive and follow these steps to move transactions from one account to another:

1. Choose File | Export. You see the QIF Export dialog box:

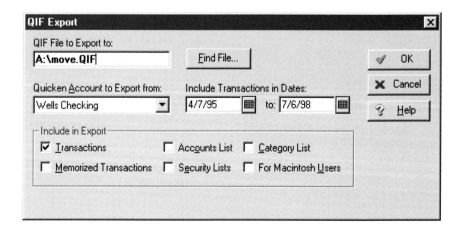

2. Click the Find File button to open the Export to QIF File dialog box.

3. Click the Save in down arrow, choose 3 Floppy (A:), enter a name for the file in the File name box, and click OK.

4. In the QIF Export dialog box, choose the account from which you will remove transactions and the dates of the transactions you want to move, and click OK. The transactions are copied to a QIF file on the floppy disk.

5. Choose File | Import | QIF File. You see the QIF Import dialog box, which already lists the QIF file with the transactions you want to move:

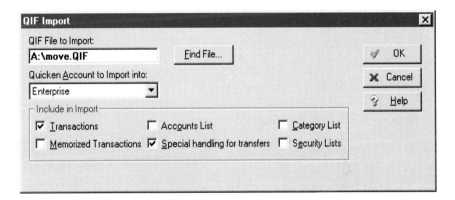

6. From the Quicken Account to Import into drop-down list, choose the account where the transactions rightfully belong, and then click the OK button.

7. Click OK in the message box that tells you how many transactions were imported.

8. Go back to the original transactions that you copied and delete them. If you copied all the transactions in an account, you can do this by deleting the account. The next section explains how.

RENAMING, UPDATING, AND DELETING ACCOUNTS

When you close a bank account, when you want to change its name in the Quicken register, or when a bank's phone number or other pertinent information needs updating, go to the Account List window. To get there, either click the Accts icon on the iconbar or choose Lists | Account. You see the Account List window shown in Figure 10.2. From here, click the name of the account that needs touching up, and follow these steps to rename, update, or delete it:

- **To Rename** Click the Edit button and enter a new name in the Edit Bank Account dialog box.
- **To Update** Click the Info button and record new information in the Additional Account Information dialog box.
- **To Delete** Click the Delete button. You see the dialog box shown in Figure 10.2. Type **yes** in the text box and click OK.

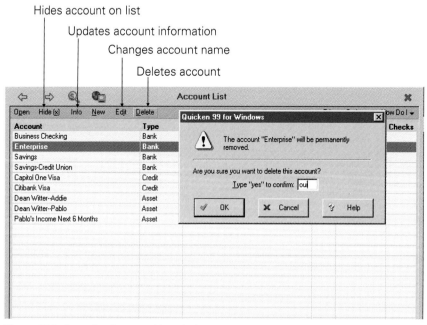

Figure 10.2 From the Account List window, you can rename, update, and delete accounts.

CAUTION

As Chapter 3 explains, hiding an account in the Account List is better than deleting an account. When you delete an account that you have closed, you lose all its financial records. Its records do not figure into reports and charts. You can't examine your financial history as carefully. If you disregard my advice and delete an account instead of hiding it, be sure to back up your Quicken data file in case you regret losing the account records you deleted.

RENAMING, COPYING, AND DELETING DATA FILES

In Chapter 1, "Creating a New File for a Business or a Second Party" explains how to launch a new Quicken data file.

On the File menu are commands for renaming, copying, and deleting the data files in which transactions are stored. Most people never have to touch these commands, since most people only use one data file, but I have included instructions for executing the commands in case you're not one of "most people."

Renaming a Quicken File

To rename a Quicken file, all you have to do is choose File | File Operations | Rename. You see the Rename Quicken File dialog box. Enter a new name for the file in the New Name for Quicken File box and click the file you want to rename. When you have christened the file with a new name, click the OK button.

Copying a Quicken File

Follow these steps to make a copy of all or part of a Quicken file:

1. Open the file and choose File | File Operations | Copy. You see the Copy File dialog box:

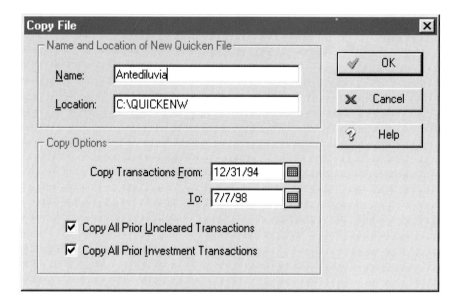

2. Enter a descriptive name in the Name box.

3. Quicken suggests putting the copy alongside the other files in the Quickenw folder, but you can put it elsewhere by entering a path name in the Location box.

4. Choose Copy Options to tell Quicken which transactions to copy:

   - **Copy Transaction From/To**   To begin with, Quicken wants to copy all the transactions, but you can change these dates. Do so if you want to copy a part of the file.

   - **Copy All Prior Uncleared Transactions**   Click this check box if you are copying part of the file and you want to copy uncleared transactions that fall before the date range you entered in the Copy Transactions From and To boxes. Unless you copy the uncleared transactions, you can't reconcile your accounts in the copied file.

   - **Copy All Prior Investment Transactions**   Make sure this check box is clicked if you want the copied file to show a complete history of your investment transactions.

5. Click OK.

6. In the File Copied Successfully dialog box, click OK to keep working in the original file, or click the New copy option button and click OK to open the copy you just made.

Deleting a File

Before you delete a Quicken file, make a backup copy. Someday you might need the file you deleted. Moreover, unlike other files, Quicken data files don't land in the Windows Recycle Bin after they are deleted.

After you've made the backup copy, choose File | File Operations | Delete. You see the Delete Quicken File dialog box. Click the to-be-deleted file and then click the OK button. An ominous message box appears and warns you that the file will be permanently deleted. The message box gives you a last chance to keep the file. Type **yes** in the confirm box and click OK, or click Cancel if you get cold feet and decide not to go through with it.

CLOSING OUT THE YEAR

In traditional accounting methods, the books are "closed" at the end of the year and a new set of books is "opened." To accommodate traditionalists, Quicken offers a command for starting a new file at the end of the year. You can also create an *archive file,* a second file where all the transactions prior to a certain date are kept.

When you create an archive copy of a file, the original file you have been working with all along stays intact and you end up with two files, one with data prior to a certain date and one with all your Quicken data. When you create a *year-end file,* on the other hand, the original file does not stay intact—instead, it is broken in two, and all transactions from the previous year are removed from it and stored in the year-end file. Meanwhile, the original file is "shrunk" be-cause—except for investment records—only transactions from the present year remain in the original file. Quicken keeps investment records from past years in the original file so you can track investment histories.

CAUTION

Don't create a year-end or archive file on January 1. Wait until you have filed your income taxes, made the necessary end-of-the-year reports, and reconciled all transactions from the past year.

Putting Data from the Past in an Archive File

Follow these steps to create an archive file:

1. Choose File | File Operations | Year-End Copy. You see the Year-End Copy dialog box.
2. The Archive option button is already selected, so click the OK button. You see the Archive File dialog box shown in Figure 10.3.

Enter the name for the file.

The file holds all transactions made up to and including this date.

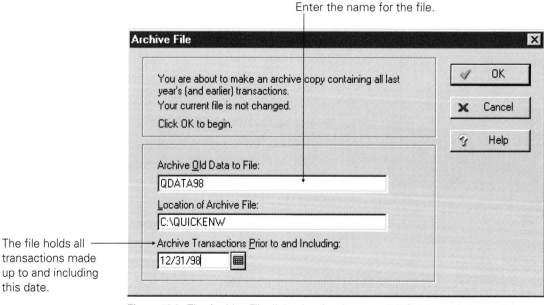

Figure 10.3 The Archive File dialog box is where you tell Quicken what to call the archive file and which transactions to put in it.

3. In the Archive Old Data to File box, Quicken suggests calling the archive file by its present name followed by the last two digits of the previous year's name, but you can choose a name of your own by typing it in the box.

4. In the Archive Transactions Prior to and Including box, Quicken has entered the last day of the previous year. The archive file will hold all financial transactions made prior to and including this date, unless you enter a new date or click the baby calendar and choose a new date.

5. Click OK. Quicken copies transactions for the archive file.

6. In the File Copied Successfully message box, either click OK to return to your Quicken data file, or click the Archive file option button and click OK to visit the archive file.

To view an archive (or any Quicken file, for that matter), choose the File | Open command, select the archive file in the Open Quicken File dialog box, and click OK.

Creating a Year-End File for Your Financial Records

Be sure to back up the Quicken data file before you create a year-end file. That way, if you regret shrinking the original file, you can restore it from the backup copy. Follow these steps to create a year-end file for your financial records and remove past years' records from the Quicken data file:

1. Choose File | File Operations | Year-End Copy.

2. In the Year-End Copy dialog box, click the Start New Year option button and click OK. You see the Start New Year dialog box.

3. In the Copy All Transactions to File box, enter a name for the year-end file.

4. In the second box, the one with the long name, enter the cut-off date (probably January 1). All transactions (except investment transactions) before the cut-off date will be removed from the file you work with and be placed in the year-end file.

5. Quicken keeps the year-end file in the Quickenw folder along with all the other data files, but if you want to put the file elsewhere, enter a new path name in the Move Current File to box.

6. Click OK. You see the File Copied Successfully dialog box.

7. The File for New Year option is already selected, so click OK to see the original file *sans* the transactions you just removed from it.

To see transactions in a year-end file, do what you would do to open any Quicken file: choose the File | Open command, select the file in the Open Quicken File dialog box, and click OK. You can look at the file, but don't alter it in any way.

CAUTION

Don't change data in the year-end file. The ending balances of the accounts in the year-end file are the beginning balances of the accounts in the original file. If you alter an ending balance, the beginning balance in the original file won't be adjusted accordingly.

PROTECTING YOUR FINANCIAL RECORDS WITH PASSWORDS

To keep others from snooping, you can assign passwords to Quicken files. After a password has been assigned to a file, no one can open it without the password. Besides protecting a file, you can also keep transactions that were recorded prior to a certain day from being changed. For example, you might protect the previous year's transactions with a password.

EXPERT ADVICE

An ideal password is hard to decipher but also easy to remember. Here's a trick for choosing a password: Decide what your favorite foreign city is and spell it backwards. If I needed a password for my Quicken file, it would be "yclekreB."

A password can be any combination of characters. Quicken doesn't distinguish between upper- and lowercase letters in passwords. As long as "Peter" is the correct password, it doesn't matter if you enter **peter**, **Peter**, or **PETER** in Quicken's password dialog boxes.

It almost goes without saying, but you must never, never, never forget a password. A Quicken file whose password has been forgotten is as good as useless, because no one can get into it. Write down passwords in a secret place where no one would expect to find them.

Assigning a Password to a File

Follow these steps to clamp a password on a file and keep others from opening it:

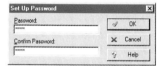

1. Choose File | Passwords | File.
2. In the Set Up Password dialog box, type your password twice, first in the Password and then in the Confirm Password box. Instead of letters, you see asterisks in case anyone is looking over your shoulder (a cunning spy, however, could watch your fingers on the keyboard and get the password that way!).
3. Click OK.

Next time you or a cat burglar starts Quicken and tries to open the data file, the Quicken Password dialog box bars the door:

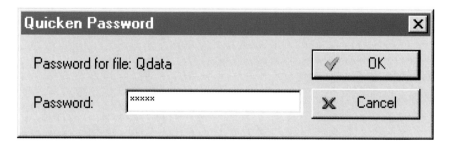

Enter the password and click OK. Devious souls who try to get into your data file without knowing the password are told that they have the incorrect password and are sent packing.

Assigning a Password to Register Transactions

Assigning a password to transactions in a register is similar to assigning a password to a file. The only difference is, you tell Quicken to protect transactions that were recorded before a certain day.

To assign a password to register transactions, open the register whose transactions you are so keen on preserving and choose File | Passwords | Transaction. In the Password to Modify Existing Transactions dialog box, enter the password twice, once in the Password box and once in the Confirm Password box. In the Required For Dates Through box, enter the date on or before which a password will be required in order to alter a transaction. For example, if you enter 12/31/98, users need the password to change transactions entered on or before that date.

If you or anyone else goes into the register, changes a transaction that occurred on or before the date, and clicks the Enter button, the Quicken Password dialog box appears. As long as you enter the password correctly in this dialog box, you hear the beep when you click OK and the transaction change is recorded. Enter the password incorrectly and Quicken stamps on your toe.

Changing and Doing Away with Passwords

Follow these steps to change or get rid of a password to either a file or transactions in a register:

1. Choose File | Passwords and click either File or Transaction on the submenu.

If you choose Transaction, you see the Change Transaction Password dialog box shown in Figure 10.4. The dialog box for changing or dropping file passwords looks the same except it doesn't have a Required For Dates Through box.

2. Either remove or change the password:

- **Remove** Enter the password in the Old Password box and click the OK button.

- **Change** Enter the present password in the Old Password box and the new password in both the New Password and Confirm Password boxes, marvel at all those asterisks, and then click OK.

In the case of transaction passwords, you can also change the date through which a password is required for altering transactions. Do that by entering a new date in the Required For Dates Through box.

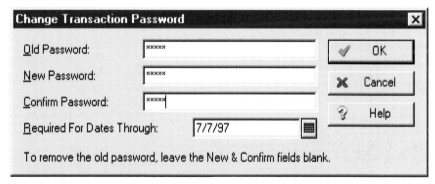

Figure 10.4 To change or remove a password, type the password in the Old Password box. To remove the password, click OK immediately. Otherwise, enter the new password in the New and Confirm boxes, and then click OK.

Keeping Track of Loans, Liabilities, and Assets

INCLUDES

- What liabilities and assets are

- Telling Quicken how to track an amortized loan

- Recording an extra loan payment

- Keeping track of adjustable-rate loans

- Tracking liabilities and debts

- Tracking the value of assets

- Cataloging the items that you own

FAST FORWARD

Record a Loan Payment ➤ pp. 203-204

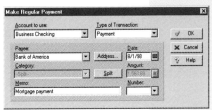

1. Click the Loans button on the iconbar or choose Features | Bills | Loans (or press CTRL-H) to get to the View Loans window.
2. Click the Choose Loan button and choose the loan to make a payment on, if necessary.
3. Click the Make a Payment button to see the Loan Payment dialog box.
4. Click the Regular button to see the Make Regular Payment dialog box.
5. Enter the date the payment will be made.
6. From the Account to use drop-down menu, choose the account that the payment will be made against.
7. Click OK.

Record an Extra Payment Along with the Payment You Usually Make ➤ pp. 204-206

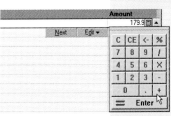

1. Click the Loans button on the iconbar or choose Features | Bills | Loans and record the payment as you normally would.
2. Go to the register where the transaction was recorded, click the payment amount, and click the calculator icon to open the mini-calculator.
3. In the calculator, click the plus sign, enter the amount you want to pay above and beyond what you usually pay, and click the Enter button.
4. Click the Split button.
5. In the Split Transaction window, click the principal portion of the payment, and then click the calculator icon to open the calculator.
6. Click the plus sign in the calculator, enter the amount you entered in step 3, and click the Enter button.
7. Click the Next button and then click OK to close the Split Transaction window.
8. Click the Enter button in the account register.

Track Your Debt in a Liability Account ➤ *p. 207*

Liability accounts work like the other Quicken accounts, except that payments made toward reducing the debt are recorded in the Decrease column, and increases in debt are recorded in the Increase column.

Increase	Clr	Decrease	Balance
223,750 00			223,750 00
		161 95	223,588 05
		662 97	222,925 08
500 00			223,425 08

Track Your Value Possessions in an Asset Account ➤ *p. 208*

Assets include IRAs, real estate, and even personal items like jewelry. Set up an asset account and categorize asset transactions as you would if you were working in another kind of Quicken account register. Record increases in the asset's value in the Increase column and decreases in the Decrease column of the register.

Decrease	Clr	Increase	Balance
		9,203 00	9,203 00
		6,698 48	15,901 48
493 17			15,408 31
		602 43	16,010 74

Catalog Items That You Own with the Quicken Home Inventory Program ➤ *pp. 208-211*

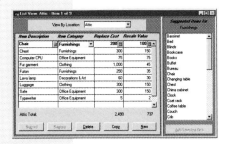

1. Click the Inventry button on the iconbar or choose Features | Planning | Quicken Home Inventory.
2. Choose a room from the View By Location drop-down menu.
3. Under Item Description, enter the name of an object of value, and then choose a category from the Item Category drop-down menu.
4. Enter the replacement cost and resale value of the item.
5. Click the Record button.

This chapter delves into a subject that most people know more about than they care to know: paying off loans. It tells how to track how much of a loan payment goes toward paying the interest and how much goes toward reducing the principal.

This chapter also explains how to keep track of liabilities and assets with Quicken, including the value of the items in your household. A *liability* is simply a debt that you owe. Liabilities count against net worth. When Quicken lists net worth in the Account List window, for example, it subtracts liabilities from the money in savings and checking accounts. Credit card debt is an example of a liability. So is tax owed to the IRS. So is a mortgage, a car loan, and a student loan.

An *asset* is something of value that you own—stock, a house, jewelry, an IRA, a baseball card autographed by the great Willie Mays. Money that is owed you is an asset. The money in checking and savings accounts is considered an asset as well. Assets add to net worth. Create asset accounts in Quicken to get a better picture of what you are worth—not as a human being of course, but as a financial entity.

THE BIG PICTURE: LOANS AND LIABILITIES

Although all loans are liabilities, since they count against net worth, Quicken makes a distinction between amortized loans and no-interest debt when it comes to setting up a liability account. If you are tracking an amortized loan, choose the Features | Bills | Loans command, but if you are tracking no-interest debt or if you don't care to keep track of how much of your debt payment goes toward interest and how much goes toward reducing the principal, set up a liability account. Either way, you end up with a liability account register for tracking how much you owe and how much you have paid on the debt.

TRACKING AN AMORTIZED LOAN OR MORTGAGE

"Calculating the Price of a Loan or Mortgage" in Chapter 13 tells how to determine how much you can borrow and what the payments on a loan will be.

Setting up a liability account for tracking an amortized loan or mortgage takes a while and can get pretty complicated, so before reading how to do it you ought to consider whether doing it is even necessary. It probably isn't necessary. As long as the lender tells you how much you owe after each payment and how much you are paying in interest, you really don't need to track the loan. You can simply get the numbers from the lender.

In the case of mortgages, business loans, and investment loans, the lender should send you a 1098 tax form at the end of the year that explains how much of your payments went toward interest. That is the amount you need to know, because the amount you paid to service interest on the loan is tax deductible. As long as the lender tells you how much you can deduct from your income taxes in interest payments, you don't need to track the amortized loan yourself. Instead, create a liability account and, as the principal decreases, record it in the liability account's register.

Setting Up the Loan Account

The first step in tracking an amortized loan is to set up the loan liability account. When you are done setting up the account, Quicken will have created a schedule for paying off the loan. The program will also have created a memorized transaction for the loan payment. Follow these steps to set up a liability account for an amortized loan:

1. Click the Loans button on the iconbar or choose Features | Bills | Loans (or press CTRL-H) to open the View Loans dialog box. When

Loans

you are done setting up the account, the View Loans window will look like the one in Figure 11.1.

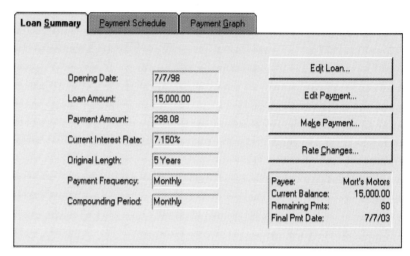

Figure 11.1 When you finish setting up the loan account, the View Loans window looks like this.

2. Click the New button to get to the Loan Setup dialog box.

   This dialog box probably looks familiar because it is similar to all account setup dialog boxes.

3. Click the Next button to get to the EasyStep tab, and then start filling out the screens and clicking Next as you complete each one.

   The following list describes the questions you have to answer to set up the account:

   - **What type of loan is this?** Make sure the Borrow Money option button is selected.

   - **Choose a Quicken account** Enter a descriptive name for the account you will use to track this loan.

   - **Have any payments been made?** Click Yes or No.

   - **Enter the initial loan information.** Enter the date the loan commenced and the original balance of the loan. In other words, enter the amount of the loan.

CAUTION

If you've made payments on the loan already, be sure to enter the original balance and not how much you currently owe. Quicken needs to have the original balance in order to create a payment schedule for the loan.

- **Does this loan include a balloon payment?** Click Yes or No.
- **Enter the original length of the loan.** Enter a number and the length of the loan in years, months, or weeks. For a 30-year mortgage, you would type **30** and choose Years from the menu, for example.
- **Enter the payment period.** Tell Quicken how often you will make payments. Either click the down arrow and choose a time period or click the Other Period option button and enter the number of payment periods per year in the Payments per Year box.
- **Enter the compounding period.** Interest is compounded daily, monthly, or semiannually. Check the paperwork that came with your loan and choose an option.
- **Do you know the current balance of this loan?** (This question appears only if you already made payments on the loan.) Click Yes or No. If you click Yes, enter the date of your last statement from the lender and how much that statement says you owe.
- **Enter the date of the first (or next) payment.** Tell Quicken when the first payment is due or was made.
- **Do you know the amount of the first (or next) payment?** Click Yes or No.
- **Enter the amount of principal and interest in the next payment.** This confusing request simply means to enter the amount of the next payment.
- **Enter the interest rate for this loan.** Enter the interest rate that you are being charged for taking out this loan. If the loan you are

setting up is an adjustable-rate loan, enter the current rate of interest.

- **Summary tabs** Take a look at the information you entered to make sure everything was entered correctly.

4. Click the Done button when you've answered all the questions.

   You see the Set Up Loan Payment dialog box shown in Figure 11.2. In this dialog box, you get one last chance to change the specifics of your loan. You also tell Quicken how to make payments and who is to be paid. Everything under Transaction in this dialog box gets "memorized."

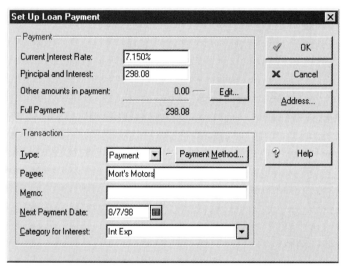

Figure 11.2 Quicken "memorizes" the information in the Transaction part of the Set Up Loan Payment dialog box

5. Choose Payment or Print Check in the Type box to say how you intend to pay the loan installments.

6. If you want to schedule loan payments or online repeating payments, click the Payment Method button and fill out the Select Payment Method dialog box.

EXPERT ADVICE

Lenders charge hefty penalties for late loan payments. If scheduling loan payments will help you make loan payments on time, by all means, schedule them. Chapter 8 explains how.

7. In the Payee box, enter the lender's name, and, while you're at it, enter a few words that describe the loan in the Memo box.

8. Click the down arrow in the Category for Interest box and choose an expense category for recording the interest portion of the loan payments you will make, probably Int Exp (Interest Expense) or Mort Int (Mortgage Interest).

9. Click OK.

A dialog box asks whether an asset is associated with this loan. Only click Yes and create an asset account if you are tracking a mortgage. As you pay off the mortgage, more of the house will become yours, not the bank's, and the house will count as an asset and not a debt. With each payment, the part that goes toward paying down the principal will be transferred to your asset account.

10. Click Yes or No. If you click Yes, answer the questions in the Asset Account Setup dialog boxes to create your asset account.

Later in this chapter, "Keeping Track of Assets" explains asset accounts.

Back in the View Loans window (see Figure 11.1), you can see everything you need to know about your loan in all its naked glory. The lower-right corner of the dialog box sums up what is owed, how many payments remain, and when the last payment is to be made.

As shown in Figure 11.3, click the Payment Schedule tab to get a look at when payments are due and what portion of each payment goes toward interest and what portion goes toward reducing the principal of the loan.

Click the Payment Graph tab, also shown in Figure 11.3, to see how the balance of the loan will decrease as you make future payments. That green line that slopes upward, by the way, shows what your total interest payments are on

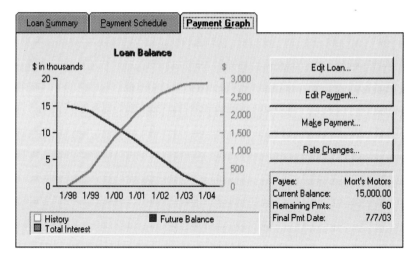

Figure 11.3 The Payment Schedule tab (top) shows when payments are due and how the principal is reduced over time; the Payment Graph tab (bottom) shows how the amount you owe decreases over time.

the loan. If you had saved and bought the thing without having to take out a loan, you would have been able to devote all the money on the right side of the graph to your pleasure or your principles instead of to a lender. As Figure 11.3 shows, it costs nearly $3,000 in interest payments to service a $15,000 loan made at 7.15 percent interest. Over five years, the total payments will be about $18,000.

Recording a Loan or Mortgage Payment

Follow these steps to record a payment on a loan or mortgage for which you set up an account in Quicken:

1. Click the Loans button or choose Features | Bills | Loans (or press CTRL-H) to go to the View Loans window.
2. In the View Loans window, click the Choose Loan button at the top of the window and choose the loan for which you want to make a payment.
3. Click the Make a Payment button.
4. In the Loan Payment dialog box, click the Regular button. You see the Make Regular Payment dialog box:

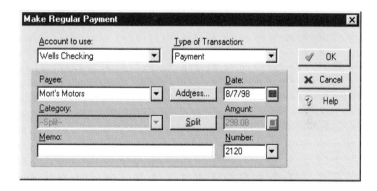

5. Enter a date in the Make Regular Payment dialog box.
6. From the Account to use drop-down menu, choose the account that the payment will be made against.
7. In the Number box, tell Quicken how the payment will be made.
8. The rest of the boxes should be filled in correctly, since this is information you gave Quicken when you set up the loan account, but go ahead and make new choices if you wish.
9. Click OK.

When a payment is made, the amount that goes toward paying the principal of the loan is recorded as a money transfer to the loan liability account you set up (or the asset account if you made a mortgage payment). The amount that goes toward the interest is recorded as an interest expense. To see how this works, click the Split button in the Make Regular Payment dialog box and peek at the Split Transaction window:

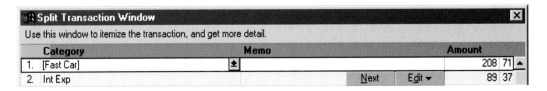

When a loan payment is recorded in the liability account register, the total amount you owe is reduced by the portion of your payment that went toward reducing the principal:

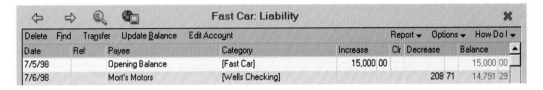

By the way, you can record a loan payment directly from a register and save a little time that way. The Step by Step box explains how to do it.

Changing the Particulars of a Loan

When you need to change the particulars of a loan—the lender's name, the compounding period, or whatnot— click the Loans button or choose Features | Bills | Loans to get to the View Loans window (see Figure 11.1). Then choose the loan that needs changing from the Choose Loan drop-down menu and click the Edit Loan button. That takes you to the Edit Loan dialog box, where you can make changes to your heart's content. When you're finished doing that, click Done.

Paying More Than What Is Expected of You

It goes without saying, but the faster you pay off an amortized loan, the less you have to pay altogether, because much of the cost of an amortized loan goes toward paying interest.

STEP BY STEP Making a Loan Payment Directly from a Register

① Open the checking account from which you will make the payment.

③ In the Confirm Principal and Interest dialog box, adjust the principal and interest, if necessary.

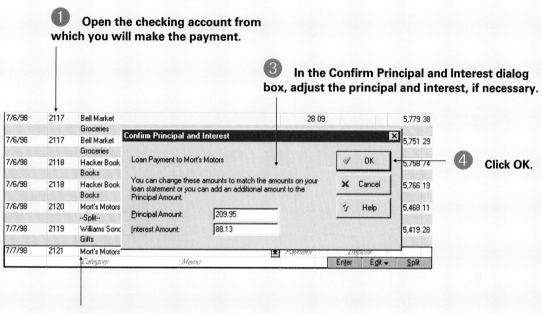

④ Click OK.

② Enter the lender's name in the Payee box and press TAB.

How you record a payment you've made that's above what the lender expects of you depends on whether you combine the extra money with your current payment due or submit it as a separate payment. For example, if your mortgage payment is $900 a month and you want to pay an extra $300, you can either write a check for $1,200, or two checks—one for $900 and one for $300.

- **Single check** The Fast Forward section at the start of this chapter gives all the details, but here are the thumbnail instructions: Click the Loans button or choose Features | Bills | Loans and record the payment as you normally would, and then go to the register where the transaction was recorded and select the transaction. From there, add the extra amount you paid to the normal payment, click the Split button, and add the extra amount to the principal portion of the payment in the Split Transaction window. Then go back to the register and enter the transaction.

● **Two checks** To record the second check for the extra amount you want to pay, choose Features | Bills | Loans to get to the View Loans window (see Figure 11.1). From there, choose the loan from the Choose Loan drop-down menu, if necessary, and click the Make Payment button. In the Loan Payment dialog box, click the Extra button. You see the Make Extra Payment dialog box. Fill in this box as you would the Make Regular Payment dialog box. Notice that the Category box in the register doesn't say "Split" as it usually does. That is because the entire amount of the extra payment counts toward reducing the principal of the loan:

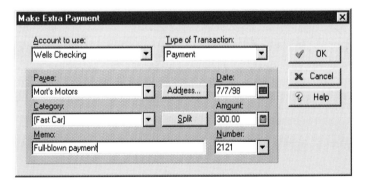

Handling Adjustable-Rate Loans

If you took out a variable-interest loan and the interest rate changed, you need to tell Quicken what the new interest rate is and have the program adjust your payments accordingly. To do that, go to the View Loans window and click the Rate Changes button. You see the Loan Rate Changes dialog box. Click the Edit button. The Edit Interest Rate Change dialog box appears.

This dialog box is for changing the interest rate and for having Quicken calculate what the new payment will be. The numbers you enter here mean nothing to the amounts already recorded in your registers—those numbers will not change. You do not need to enter anything in the Regular Payment box, because Quicken calculates what your new regular payment will be based on the new interest rate you enter. However, if you do enter a regular payment amount, Quicken changes the length of the loan to accommodate the new payment schedule.

TRACKING A LIABILITY

A liability account tracks money you owe. A credit card account, for example, is a liability account, because it tracks the negative balance of what you owe the credit card issuer. Open a liability account in Quicken to track loans for which you pay no interest (or loans you do pay interest on but for which you don't care to track the interest and principal), income taxes, or anything else that counts against your net worth.

"Setting Up an Account" in Chapter 1 explains how to set up an account. Follow the directions there and choose Liability to set up a liability account.

Figure 11.4 shows a liability account register. One glance at this figure tells you that a liability account is exactly like the other accounts in Quicken. It has places for entering dates, categories, and amounts. The only difference is that Increase and Decrease columns appear where Payment and Deposit columns might usually be. When something adds to your debt, enter it in the Increase column. When you pay off part of your debt, record the payment in the Decrease column. The Balance column (always negative, always red) lists your total debt.

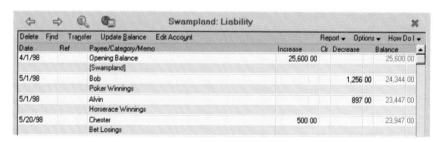

Figure 11.4 A liability account for tracking money owed for swampland. By tracking liabilities, you know your net worth and can plan your spending better.

KEEPING TRACK OF YOUR ASSETS

Set up an asset account in Quicken to track things of value that contribute to your net worth: jewelry, a collection of nineteenth-century Shaker furniture, a Ming vase, an apartment building. In Figure 11.5, an author has set up an asset account to keep track of future royalty payments. The author is owed this money and, by tracking it in an asset account, the author can figure it into spending and budgeting plans.

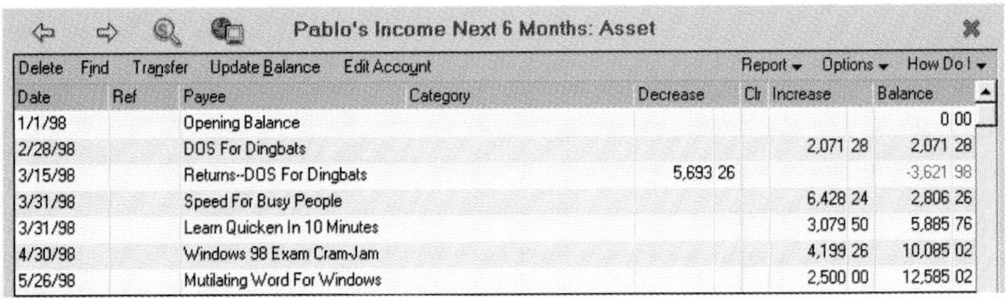

Date	Ref	Payee	Category	Decrease	Clr	Increase	Balance
1/1/98		Opening Balance					0 00
2/28/98		DOS For Dingbats				2,071 28	2,071 28
3/15/98		Returns--DOS For Dingbats		5,693 26			-3,621 98
3/31/98		Speed For Busy People				6,428 24	2,806 26
3/31/98		Learn Quicken In 10 Minutes				3,079 50	5,885 76
4/30/98		Windows 98 Exam Cram-Jam				4,199 26	10,085 02
5/26/98		Mutilating Word For Windows				2,500 00	12,585 02

Pablo's Income Next 6 Months: Asset — Delete Find Transfer Update Balance Edit Account — Report ▾ Options ▾ How Do I ▾

Figure 11.5 An asset account register. Set up asset accounts to track things of value that contribute to your net worth.

When the asset increases in value, enter the amount it has increased by in the Increase column. When it decreases in value, enter a number in the Decrease column. Rather than categorize an item when you record its purchase in the checking register, you might record the expense as a transfer to an asset account. To see how this works, suppose you have an asset account to track the value of a house, and you pay $2,000 for a new deck for the house. Rather than categorize the expense, you could record it as a transfer to the asset account. In theory, anyway, the house is worth $2,000 more with its new deck.

CATALOGING THE ITEMS IN YOUR HOUSEHOLD

Owners of Quicken Deluxe can catalog the items in their houses with Quicken Home Inventory, a program for taking stock of what you own. Use the

Inventory program to establish the cumulative value of the things that you own or simply to make a detailed list of where all your stuff is. When you are done tabulating the value of your belongings, you can record the amount in an asset account called Home Inventory that Quicken sets up for you.

To start the Quicken Home Inventory program, click the Inventry button on the iconbar or choose Features | Planning | Quicken Home Inventory. The program opens and you see the List View window shown at the top of Figure 11.6. Room by room, describe the things you own in this window. To describe an item in detail, click the small button in the Item Description column and enter the particulars in the Detail View window shown on the bottom of Figure 11.6.

After you have recorded the name, location, and value of all that you own, you can take advantage of the buttons in the Quicken Home Inventory screen to do the following:

- **Locations**   Lists, room by room, the value of the stuff you own.
- **Categories**   Lists the value of the stuff you own by category instead of by room.
- **Policies**   Opens a dialog box for describing your insurance policies and making sure that they cover the value of your belongings.
- **Claims**   Opens a dialog box for describing and putting a value on insurance claims.
- **Find**   Lets you search for items when you can't remember which room you lost them in.
- **Move Item**   Opens the Move Item dialog box so you can move items you have cataloged to different rooms.
- **Update**   Updates the Home Inventory asset account, a Quicken account that is created for you automatically when you use the Home Inventory program.
- **Goto Qkn**   Takes you back to Quicken. Click the Quicken Home Inventory button on the taskbar to return to the Inventory screen.
- **Help**   The ubiquitous Help button, which you can click if you need help inventorying your stuff.

Choose a category.

Click to go to
Detail View.

Choose a room in
your house.

Enter an item. ——

When you're ——
satisfied, click to
enter the item in
the list.

Click to return to
List View.

Enter the details.

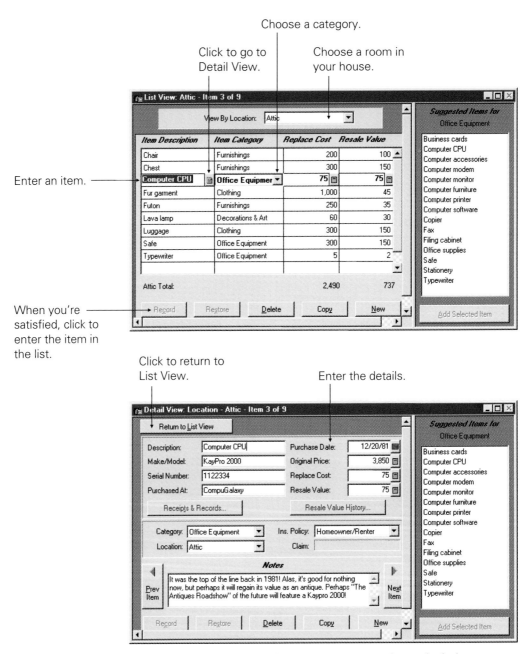

Figure 11.6 Use the Quicken Home Inventory program to take stock of what you
own, what it's worth, and where all the darn things are located.

When you exit the Home Inventory program, you are invited to back up the data you entered. Do it and store the backup file in a very safe place! You can use it for insurance claims purposes if you become the victim of a theft, a natural disaster, or an attack by killer bees.

EXPERT ADVICE

Another way to inventory the things you own is to film them with a video camera. Go from room to room and film all the things that you have accumulated, and while you do so, describe them in intimate detail as though you were touting their merits to the audience of a TV game show.

Planning Ahead with Quicken

INCLUDES

- Planning ahead at the Quicken.com site

- Calculating how much to save for retirement

- Seeing what your present savings will generate in retirement income

- Planning for a child's college education

- Devising a plan to get out of debt

- Formulating a budget

- Getting Quicken's help to save toward a goal

FAST FORWARD

Plan for the Future at Quicken.com ➤ p. 216

1. Choose Features | Centers | Planning Center.
2. Under "Internet Links" in the Planning Center window, click a hyperlink.
3. Enter your password in the Connect to dialog box and click Connect.
4. Click a hyperlink in the **Quicken.com** site.

Find Out How Much You Need to Save Annually for Retirement ➤ pp. 216-220

1. Choose Features | Planning | Financial Calculators | Retirement.
2. In the Retirement Calculator dialog box, click the Annual Contribution option button under Calculate For.
3. Fill in the boxes under Retirement Information. These boxes ask for your current savings and how much income by percentage you expect them to generate, how old you are now and when you expect to retire, how long you expect to live on your retirement savings, and what you want your income in the retirement years to be.
4. In the Tax Information part of the dialog box, say whether your investments for retirement are tax-sheltered (tax-deferred) or not.
5. In the Inflation area, tell Quicken what you expect the inflation rate to be in the future, whether you want the calculations Quicken makes to appear in today's dollars, and whether you want to increase your contributions to account for inflation.
6. Click the Calculate button.
7. Look next to Annual Contribution in the dialog box to see how much you need to set aside each year.

Find Out How Much to
Save for a Child's College Education ➤ *pp. 220-222*

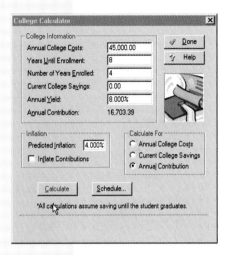

1. Choose Features | Planning | Financial Calculators | College.
2. In the College Planner dialog box, click one of the Calculate For buttons: Annual College Costs to figure out how expensive a college education you can afford, Current College Savings to see how much you need to have saved to reach a savings goal, or Annual Contribution to see how much you need to contribute each year.
3. Under College Information, tell Quicken what you expect college to cost, information about your child's enrollment, what you've saved, and how much you can save annually.
4. Under Inflation, specify what you expect the inflation rate will be and whether you want to make larger contributions as the years go by.
5. Click the Calculate button.

Generate a Budget Report or Budget Graph ➤ *pp. 225-230*

1. Choose Reports | EasyAnswer Reports and click the "Did I meet my budget?" question in the EasyAnswer Reports & Graphs dialog box.
2. In the Details part of the dialog box, choose a time period from the list.
3. Click the Show Report or Show Graph button.

4/1/98 Actual	- Budget	6/30/98 Difference
0.00	417.00	- 417.00
8,827.38	5,985.00	2,842.38
- 128.09	- 240.00	111.91
- 290.39	- 798.00	507.61
- 750.70	- 156.00	- 594.70
- 2,610.00	- 3,504.00	894.00
0.00	- 132.00	132.00
- 758.00	0.00	- 758.00
4,290.20	1,572.00	2,718.20

Display the Progress Bar to See If
You Are Meeting Your Budget or Savings Goal ➤ *pp. 230-231*

1. Right-click below the Quick Tabs and click Show Progress Bar.
2. If you want, click the Cust (Customize) button on the Progress bar, click Choose Category in the Customize Progress Bar dialog box, and choose a new category to display a different budget category onscreen.
3. Click the Close button to remove the Progress bar.

This chapter takes on something that is either dreadful or wonderful, depending on your point of view: It takes on the future.

If you are a pessimist, this chapter shows how to avoid financial ruin in old age. It shows how to give your children the overpriced college education that everyone thinks is necessary these days. It shows how to create a budget that is impossible to live within, formulate a plan to claw your way out of debt, and save toward an unrealistic goal.

If you are an optimist, this chapter shows how to plan for a glorious old age and how to give your children the college education that the little darlings so richly deserve. It shows how to create a budget so that you live within your means, get out of debt, and save toward a wonderful Mediterranean vacation.

QUICKEN.COM SITES THAT CAN HELP YOU PLAN AHEAD

INTERNET
Links

Financial Health Checkup
Saving & Budgeting
Retirement Planning
Your Credit Report
Life Events Planner

At **Quicken.com** are several Web pages that offer tools and articles to help you plan ahead. To visit one of these Web pages, go to the Planning Center (click the Planning link on the Home Page or choose Features | Centers | Planning Center), look under "Internet Links," and click a hyperlink. When you arrive at the **Quicken.com** home page, click a link to learn how to plan for retirement, save money, or reduce debt. You can also reach **Quicken.com** by choosing Online | Quicken on the Web | Quicken.com.

PLANNING FOR YOUR RETIREMENT

Everyone has heard dire warnings about the imminent demise of the social security system. That being the case, setting aside money now for retirement is wise indeed. Moreover, with IRA and Keogh plans, the federal government has made saving for retirement very enticing, since money placed in IRAs and Keoghs is not subject to taxes.

With the Retirement Calculator, Quicken offers three ways to plan ahead for retirement: you can target how much income you need for retirement, calculate how much you need to save annually to reach the retirement income you want, or see how much income your present savings will produce in old age. Follow these steps to peer into the future and plan for retirement:

1. Choose Features | Planning | Financial Calculators | Retirement. You see the Retirement Planner dialog box shown in Figure 12.1.

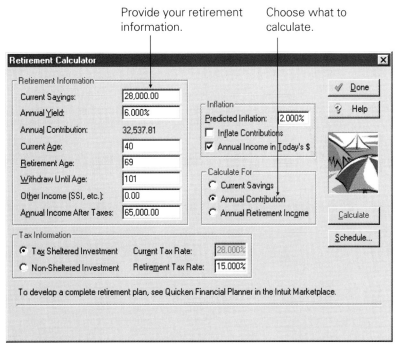

Provide your retirement information.

Choose what to calculate.

Figure 12.1 The Retirement Calculator dialog box, where Quicken figures out how much you need to save, how much income you need to contribute annually, and how much income you will have in retirement

2. Under Calculate For, tell Quicken how you want to plan for retirement:

- **Current Savings** Click this button to find out how much you need to have saved already to meet or help meet your retirement income goal.

- **Annual Contribution** Click here to find out how much you need to contribute each year to meet your retirement income goal.

- **Annual Retirement Income** Click here to find out what your current savings plus annual contributions will produce in annual income after you retire.

3. Answer the Retirement Information questions. Depending on which option button you clicked in step 2, you don't need to fill in some of these boxes—Quicken will fill them in for you.

- **Current Savings** How much you have saved so far.

- **Annual Yield** How much income, by percentage, you expect your investments to produce. As a yardstick, the stock market's average return in the past 70 years has been 10 percent, long-term corporate bonds have yielded 5 percent over the same time, and U.S. Treasury Bills have yielded 3.5 percent.

- **Annual Contribution** How much you can set aside each year for retirement.

- **Current Age** How old you are. And no lying!

- **Retirement Age** What age you would like or expect to retire.

- **Withdraw Until Age** To what age you expect to live. For you, I foresee a ripe old age.

- **Other Income (SSI, etc.)** Your annual social security or pension income. You can find out what your social security benefits will be by submitting form SS-4 to the Social Security Administration.

- **Annual Income After Taxes** How much you want your annual income to be in your retirement years. After you retire, you will withdraw this amount each year from your retirement savings. Be modest. As an old woman or man, your income probably doesn't need to be what it is now. The duplex might be paid off. The kids might be living on communes in Oregon. The dog might be dead.

"Forecasting Your Future Income and Expenses" in Chapter 13 explains how to estimate what your income in the coming years will be.

4. Answer the Tax Information questions:

   - **Tax-Sheltered Investment** Click this option button if you are saving for retirement with IRAs, 401(k) plans, or other tax-deferred savings options.

   - **Non-Sheltered Investment** Click this option button if the investments you are squirreling away for retirement can be taxed before you reach retirement. Enter the marginal tax rate you expect to pay on these investments in the Retirement Tax Rate box.

5. Test your prognostication skills in the Inflation area of the dialog box:

   - **Predicted Inflation** What you expect the inflation rate to be on average between now and the time you retire. If it's any help, inflation in the past six decades has averaged 3.3 percent annually.

   - **Inflate Contributions** If you intend to make larger and larger contributions over the years to account for inflation, click this check box. If you choose this option, Quicken will make a schedule in which your annual contributions get larger as the years go by.

   - **Annual Income in Today's $** Click this box if you want to see what the money you are saving will be worth when you retire. If you want to see the figures in today's dollars, which are worth considerably more than tomorrow's dollars, remove the check mark. With the check mark removed, the figures are higher.

6. Click the Calculate button.

7. Under Retirement Information, glance at the Current Savings box to find out how much money you need to have already saved to meet your retirement income goal, glance at the Annual Contribution box to find out how much you need to set aside each year to reach your goal, or glance at the Annual Income After Taxes box to find out how much your savings and contributions will produce in retirement income.

8. Play around with the figures some more and then click the Done button.

EXPERT ADVICE

To get advice for planning your estate, choose Features | Planning | What-if Scenarios, click the Estate Plan hyperlink, and start reading.

SAVING FOR A CHILD'S COLLEGE EDUCATION

The American middle class is extremely nervous about sending its children to good (that means expensive) colleges and universities, and to make the middle class even more nervous, Quicken offers the College Planner. Using the College Planner, you can find out how swanky a college you can afford, how much you can pay for college with your present savings, or how much you need to save annually. Follow these steps to use the College Planner:

1. Choose Features | Planning | Financial Calculators | College. You see the College Planner shown in Figure 12.2.

2. Under Calculate For, choose how you want to conduct your investigation:

   • **Annual College Costs**   Click to figure out how much in college expenses you will be able to pay annually with the money you've already saved plus the amount you intend to set aside each year till your child goes to college. In other words, click here to find out how swanky a university you can afford to send your daughter or son to.

   • **Current College Savings**   Click to figure out how much you need to have saved already in order to send your child to college, not counting the amounts you intend to set aside annually till your child goes.

   • **Annual Contribution**   Click to figure out how much you need to contribute each year in order to cover the annual costs of sending your child to college.

Enter the college information.

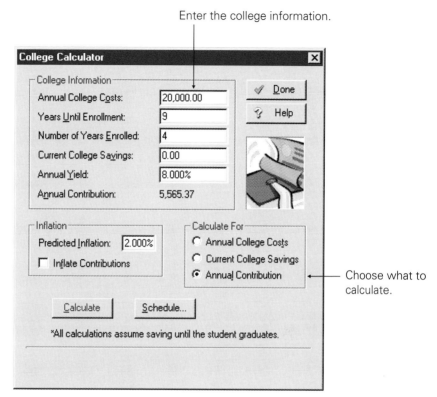

Figure 12.2 The College Calculator, where you find out whether you can afford to buy your child a nasal Ivy League accent

3. Fill in the boxes under College Information.

   Except for Annual College Costs, in which you list the yearly cost (expenses plus tuition) of sending the child to college, most of this stuff is self-explanatory. To find out college costs, you can always call a university's administrative offices (call 617-495-1551 to find out how much it costs to send an undergraduate to Harvard University for a year).

4. Under Inflation, put what you think the inflation rate will be in the Predicted Inflation box, and click the Inflate Contributions check box if you intend to make your contributions larger over the years to account for inflation.

5. Click the Calculate button.

You find out how much you are able to pay, how much you need to have saved, or how much you need to contribute annually. If you wish, click the Schedule button to see how much you need to set aside each month. Sigh, and then click Done when you've finished marveling at how much college costs.

EXPERT ADVICE

Quicken's College Planner offers advice for saving for college and many excellent links to sites on the Web where you can find information about college scholarships, financial aid, student services, and colleges themselves. Choose Features | Planning | What-if Scenarios and click the College link in the Interactive Planner window.

DEVISING A PLAN TO GET OUT OF DEBT

"Running a Credit Check on Yourself" in Chapter 7 explains how to obtain a credit report that shows your credit history.

Debts, especially credit card debts, are the single most daunting obstacles that come between people and their financial well-being. If you owe exorbitant sums on a credit card or credit cards, you need to find a way to pay off or pay down that debt. Credit card companies charge outrageous interest rates. Money that you could be saving for your pleasure, your retirement, or other worthwhile causes is instead going to a credit card company. It's time for you to do something about that.

To see your way out of debt, users of Quicken Deluxe can take advantage of the Debt Reduction Planner. Using the Planner, you find out precisely how much debt you have, how much you can devote each month toward reducing the debt, and where you can reduce your monthly expenses. When you are done, you see a Debt Reduction window like the one in Figure 12.3. The window shows how much you need to pay monthly to climb out of debt and when you will be out of debt. You also can print an "Action Plan to Get Out of Debt" with specifics about how much you need to pay each month, where you can cut expenses, and where you can go for help to solve your debt problems.

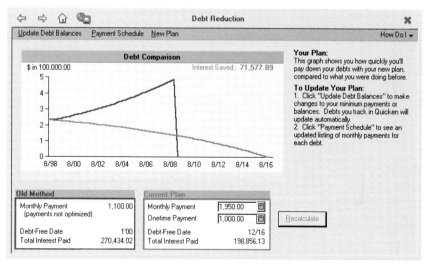

Figure 12.3 Use the Debt Reduction Planner to help see your way out of debt.

Click the Debt Reduction link in the Planning Center window or choose Features | Planning | Debt Reduction Planner to start devising your plan. The Debt Reduction dialog box appears. If necessary, click the New Plan button, and then, clicking the Next button as you go along, enter information in the following five tabs:

- **Debts** Lists how much debt you have, to whom you are indebted, and the interest rate on each debt. These figures come from your account registers (click the Update Debts button to make sure all figures are accurate).

  Select a debt and then click the Remove button to keep a debt from being considered in the plan; click Add to add a debt that isn't listed on the Debts tab.

  Before you can leave this tab, you must tell Quicken the interest rate charged for each debt, roughly how much your current monthly payment is, and what the minimum monthly payment you are required to make is. Select a debt and click the Edit button to give Quicken this information.

- **Order** Lists your debts in the order that you should pay them off, given their amounts and interest rates. The Suggested Pmt column lists how much you need to pay each month to pay off each debt. Click the Change Payment Order? check box before clicking the Next button if you want to change the order in which you will pay off your debts.

- **Savings** Lists the amount of your current savings and investments, and asks how much of this money you can devote to paying off debt. This is where you tell Quicken whether you can spare money from savings and investments for paying off debt. Glance at the Results box, enter the amount of a one-time payment you can make, and click the Recalculate button. Notice how the debt free date and total interest amount for paying off debts change. Experiment by entering different one-time amounts and clicking the Recalculate button.

- **Budget** Lists your top four spending categories and how much you spend monthly in each category. On this tab, you figure out where you can spend less in order to devote the savings to reducing debt. If necessary, choose new categories from the drop-down lists, and then enter how much you can cut back in the Amount to cut back text boxes. Then click the Recalculate button.

- **Plan** Shows your "Action Plan to Get Out of Debt." Click the Print this Action Plan button to read the plan carefully.

When you are done, the Debt Reduction window appears (see Figure 12.3). Periodically revisit this window and click the Update Debt Balances button to see whether you are sticking with your plan. You can always click the New Plan button if your plan proves too ambitious and you need to devise a new one. To return to the Debt Reduction window, choose Features | Planning | Debt Reduction Planner or click the Debt Reduction link in the Planning Center window.

BUDGETING WITH QUICKEN

When bills arrive in the mail with ominous red warnings on them or when you want to start saving for a house or a vacation to the Greek isles, it is time to put yourself on a budget. Budgeting with Quicken is a two-step business. First, you prepare the budget by telling Quicken what you expect your income to be and how much you would like to spend in each category or category group. After a few months pass and Quicken accumulates enough data to see whether you have met your budget, you create a budget report or budget graph. The report or graph compares what you thought you would earn and spend with what you really earned and spent, so you can see right away whether you stuck to your budget and where you need to tighten your belt.

EXPERT ADVICE

Before you draw up a budget, choose Reports | EasyAnswer Reports and generate a "Where did I spend my money?" report. Create an Income and Expense graph, too. They will help you formulate your budget.

Deciding How to Draw Up the Budget

Quicken gives you lots of choices when it comes to drawing up a budget. You can budget by month, by quarter, or by year, and you can crunch the budget numbers by category group or by category. Follow these steps to draw up a budget:

See "Make Your Own Categories and Subcategories" in Chapter 3 if you don't understand categories. Categories are essential for budgeting.

1. Choose Features | Planning | Budgets or click the Budgeting link in the Planning Center window. A Budget window like the one at the top of Figure 12.4 appears. In the figure, the budget numbers have been entered.

   The Budget window might look confusing at first, but stare at it for a while and you notice that the window lists income categories first and expense categories second. Besides entering how much you would like

By-month columns

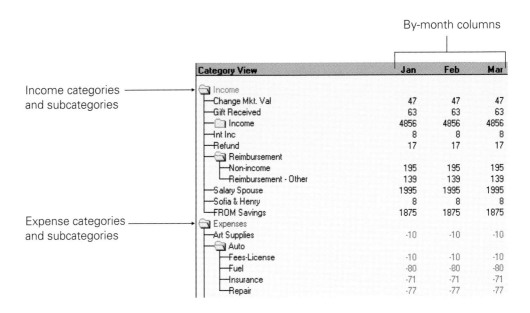

Income categories and subcategories

Expense categories and subcategories

By-quarter columns

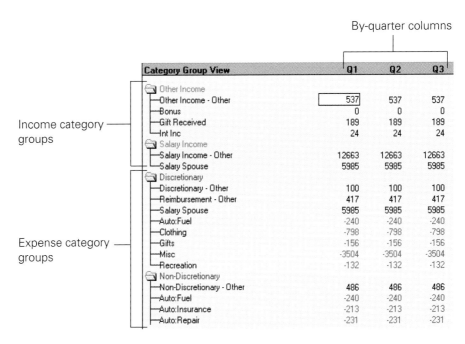

Income category groups

Expense category groups

Figure 12.4 Entering the numbers in Category view by month (top); entering the numbers by Category Group view by quarter (bottom)

To learn how to create and manage category groups, see "Setting Up and Managing Category Groups" in Chapter 4.

Display <u>C</u>urrent Month
Display C<u>u</u>rrent Quarter
Display Current <u>Y</u>ear
Display <u>M</u>onths
✔ Display <u>Q</u>uarters

✔ Show Category <u>G</u>roups

<u>S</u>ave Budget
<u>R</u>estore Budget

Other <u>B</u>udgets
Category <u>G</u>roups

to spend in expense categories, you estimate what your income will be in income categories. Click the down arrow on the scroll bar along the right side of the window to see the expense categories.

Figure 12.4 demonstrates two ways to formulate a budget in the Budget window, by category group or by category and subcategory. The Budget window at the top of Figure 12.4 shows a category and subcategory budget; at the bottom is a category group budget. In the category group budget, income category groups come first and are followed by expense category groups.

Notice that the Budget window at the bottom of Figure 12.4 is set up for budgeting on a quarterly instead of a monthly basis. This budget would be easy to prepare because you would only enter four quarterly amounts instead of twelve monthly amounts, and you would only enter a few category group amounts instead of dozens of category and subcategory amounts. However, it wouldn't provide as much insight as the monthly, category-and-subcategory budget shown at the top of Figure 12.4.

2. If you want to enter the numbers by category group, click the Options menu and choose Show Category Groups from the drop-down list.

3. If you want to budget by quarters, click the Options menu and choose Display Quarters.

You have drawn up the budget. Now it's time to enter the numbers.

Entering the Budget Numbers

Entering the numbers is the hard part. This is where you give serious consideration to how much money you take in and how much you spend. My advice is not to be ambitious. Set realistic goals for yourself (and for your family, too, if you are preparing a budget for them). The idea is to curb your spending, not set yourself up for failure.

The fastest way to enter the numbers is to get them directly from the Quicken registers. Not only are the numbers entered for you automatically, but you can start with real data about your income and spending habits. After the numbers are entered, you can tinker with them in the Budget window. The other way to enter numbers is to do it yourself. Both techniques are described herewith.

Entering the Budget Numbers Automatically

Follow these steps to "autocreate" a budget and enter the numbers automatically from your account registers:

1. Click the Edit button in the Budget window and choose Autocreate from the drop-down menu. You see the Automatically Create Budget box.

2. In the From and To boxes, enter the date range for Quicken to draw data from.

3. In the Round Values to Nearest box, choose $1, $10, or $100 to tell Quicken how to round out the numbers it puts in the budget.

4. Click the Use Monthly Detail option button if you want Quicken to use real amounts from the time period you chose, or else click Use Average for Period if you want Quicken to average out your spending or income and enter the same figure across all columns in the Budget window.

5. Click the Categories button to tell Quicken which categories to include in the budget. In the Select Categories to Include dialog box, check marks appear beside the categories that will be included in the budget. Click the Clear All button to remove the check marks and then go down the list and click on each category that you want to include in the budget to put a check mark beside it. When you are done, click OK.

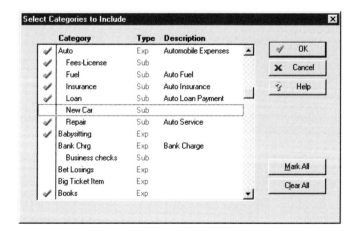

6. Back in the Automatically Create Budget dialog box, click OK.

Now examine the numbers in the budget and change them if you like.

Entering the Budget Numbers from Scratch

To enter the numbers from scratch, click in the Budget window or press TAB or SHIFT-TAB to move from column to column. As you enter the numbers, click a closed folder to see the categories or subcategories inside it. Click an open folder to tuck the categories or subcategories back into their parent category group or category. Don't forget to click the Options button and choose Save Budget button from time to time as you work on the budget. This way you won't lose your work and, if you botch things up, you can choose Restore budget from the Options menu and get the last saved copy of your budget back.

Meanwhile, the Edit button in the Budget window offers some handy options for entering numbers quickly:

2-Week	Click this button to budget for biweekly paychecks. In the Set Up Two-Week budget dialog box, enter the amount you receive and the date that you will receive your next two-week paycheck.
Copy All	Copies the budget to the Windows Clipboard.
Clear Row	Removes the budget amounts in the row the cursor is in so you can enter all zeros or start from scratch.
Clear All	Removes all amounts from the Budget window so you can start all over.
Autocreate	Enters data automatically from your account registers (see the preceding section of this chapter).
Fill Row Right	Copies the amount at the location of the cursor across the entire row to the right of the cursor.
Fill Columns	Copies the amounts in the column that the cursor is in to all the columns to the right of the one the cursor is in. For example, to copy the amounts from the top to the bottom of the third column to all the columns to its right, click anywhere in the third column and choose this option.

Seeing Whether You've Met Your Budget

Chapter 9 explains how you can customize graphs and reports so they report only on specific categories or category groups.

Now comes the moment of truth. You created a budget and you have been doing your best to live with it for several months. It is time to find out how much self-discipline you have. To create a budget report and budget graph, follow these steps:

1. Open the budget you want to see a report on in the Budget window.
2. Click the Report button.
3. Choose one of the following options:

   Budget Report
   Monthly Budget Report
   Budget Variance Graph

   • **Budget Report** A comprehensive report showing your actual income and spending and your budgeted income and spending in the year so far. Where red numbers appear in the Difference column of the report, you failed to meet your budget in a category or category group.

   • **Monthly Budget Report** A month-by-month report comparing your spending to budgeted spending and income. Look for red numbers in the Difference column—they show where you went over budget.

   • **Budget Variance Graph** The bars at the top of the graph tell how your actual income and budgeted income compare. The bars at the bottom tell how actual spending and budgeted spending compare. In the top chart, you know you received less income than you calculated if you see red bars dipping below the zero line. On the bottom chart, Over Budget bars tell where you went over budget and by what amount.

You can put several different budget graphs and reports on the Home Page window. See "Choose for Yourself What Appears on the Home Page" in Chapter 3.

You can also generate budget reports and graphs by choosing Reports | EasyAnswer Reports, clicking the seventh question on the list, "Did I meet my budget?" and clicking the Show Report or Show Graph button. To see whether you are meeting your budget in a certain category, you can display it on the Progress bar, as the next part of this chapter explains.

Using the Progress Bar to See If You Have Met a Budget Goal

Besides generating reports, another way to see whether you are meeting a budget goal is to list the budget goal on the Progress bar. By right-clicking below the Quick Tabs and choosing Show Progress Bar from the shortcut menu, you can make the Progress bar appear at the bottom of the Quicken window. The Progress bar shown here lists two budget goals, Books Budget and Gifts Budget. This month the user has not exceeded the $72 that he allotted for books and the $52 that he allotted for gifts in his budget:

Follow these steps to choose which budget categories to display on the Progress bar:

1. If necessary, right-click the blank spot below the Quick Tabs and choose Show Progress Bar on the shortcut menu to see the Progress bar.
2. Click the Cust (Customize) button. You will find it on the right side of the Progress bar.
3. Under Left Gauge Type or Right Gauge Type in the Customize Progress Bar dialog box, open the drop-down menu and choose Budget Goal Progress.
4. Click the Choose Category button.
5. Click a new category for the Progress bar and click OK.
6. Click OK to close the Customize Progress Bar dialog box.

When you want to remove the Progress bar from the screen, click its Close button.

SAVING TOWARD A FINANCIAL GOAL

To help squirrel away money for trips, presents, and other enticing objectives, Quicken offers a feature called a "savings goal account." A savings goal account is a sort of ghost bank account. You transfer money into it, but not really. When you transfer money from a checking account to a savings goal account, the checking account balance shows a decrease and the savings goal account shows an increase, even though no real money has passed between the real checking account and the ghostly savings account.

The idea is to keep you from getting your hands on the money you want to save. It is hidden in the savings goal account. In the checking account, you think you have less money than you really do, so you learn to live with less money.

Starting a Savings Goal Account

To start a savings goal account, choose Features | Planning | Savings Goals or click the Savings Goals hyperlink in the Planning Center window. You see the Savings Goals window. Click the New button to get to the Create New Savings Goal dialog box.

In the Goal Name box, enter a descriptive name for the goal. Enter the amount you want to save with the help of the savings goal account in the Goal Amount box. In the Finish Date box, Quicken has entered the day a year hence. Change that date to the date by which you want to have saved the money and click OK.

In Chapter 11, "Keeping Track of Your Assets" explains asset accounts.

Back in the Savings Goals window, you see the name of your goal and the other information you entered. Notice the "Projected Monthly Contribution" at the bottom of the window that Quicken says you need to set aside each month to reach your goal. Quicken creates a new asset account for tracking contributions toward the goal.

Setting the Money Aside

To set the money aside, you make a "contribution" to the savings goal account. To do that, open the Savings Goals window, select a savings goal (if you've established more than one), and click the Contribute button. You see the Contribute to Goal dialog box with the projected monthly contribution. In the From account list, choose the account from which to withdraw the ghost money. The dialog box shows how much money is in the account. If necessary, enter a number in the Amount box and then click OK:

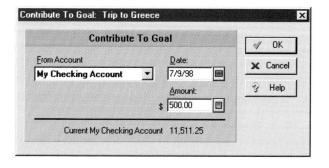

The Progress bar in the Savings Goals window shows how close or far you are from attaining your goal. Meanwhile, the account from which you withdrew the money shows a decrease. Where normally you would see an account name in brackets to show that money had been transferred from one account to another, you see the name of your savings goal asset account in brackets:

| 7/9/98 | Contribution towards goal | 500 00 | 11,011 25 |
| | [Trip to Greece] | | |

Managing and Closing
Savings Goal Accounts

| Trip to Greece Goal |
| 4,250.00 |

Periodically choose Features | Planning | Savings Goals and see how close you are to reaching your goal. To chart the progress of a savings goal on the Progress bar, right-click below the Quick Tabs and choose Show Progress Bar. Then click the Cust button, choose Savings Goal Progress from a Gauge Type drop-down menu in the Customize Progress Bar dialog box, and click OK.

When you reach your savings goal or you want to abandon it, click the Accts button and select the name of the savings goal account in the Account List window (click the Options button and choose Display Other Accounts if you have trouble finding it). Then click the Delete button, type **yes** in the "Are you sure?" dialog box, and click OK. Money transfers from accounts to your old savings goal account are instantly deleted from all registers.

13

Quicken as a Financial Analysis Tool

INCLUDES

- Getting advice on the Internet for buying houses and comparing loans

- Calculating the payments on a loan or mortgage

- Deciding whether to refinance your house

- Forecasting your future income and expenses

- Determining the future value of an investment

- Calculating how to reach an investment goal

- Generating investment reports and graphs

FAST FORWARD

Go on the Internet and
Get Advice for Buying a House ➤ pp. 238-239

More Sites

Applying for a
Mortgage
Credit Resources
Owning Your Home
Planning to Buy a
Home
Shopping for a
Home or Mortgage

- Choose Online | Quicken on the Web | Mortgage Center to visit a site that offers tools for comparing mortgages and finding out how expensive a house you can buy.
- Choose Online | Quicken on the Web | Quicken Live and click the Home & Mortgage hyperlink under "Best of the Web" to see a list of sites made for home buyers.

Find Out How Big a Loan or
Mortgage Payment You Can Handle ➤ pp. 239-241

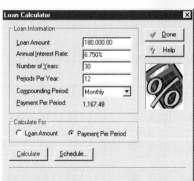

1. Choose Features | Planning | Financial Calculators | Loan.
2. Under Calculate For in the Loan Calculator dialog box, click the Payment Per Period option to find out how large your payments will be on a loan, or click the Loan Amount button to find out how large a loan you can realistically take out.
3. In the Loan Amount box, enter the amount of the loan you would like to take out.
4. In the Annual Interest Rate box, enter the interest rate you will be charged for the loan.
5. Enter the length of the loan in the Number of Years box.
6. Enter the number of payments you will make each year in the Periods Per Year box. If payments are due each month, for example, enter **12**.
7. Click the arrow in the Compounding Period box and choose Semi-Annually, if necessary.
8. In the Payment Per Period box, enter the amount you can realistically pay each month.
9. Click the Calculate button and look beside Loan Amount or Payment Per Period to find out either how big a loan you can take out or what your monthly payments will be.

Forecast What Your Future
Account Balances Will Be ➤ *pp. 243-245*

1. Choose Features | Planning | Forecasting.
2. A graph shows you, on the basis of Quicken's forecast, what your account balances in the next several months will be.
3. Click the Prev or Next button below the time period menu to "page through" your future or past account balances.

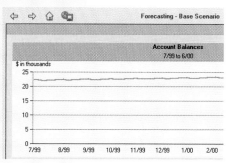

Calculate the Rate by Which an Investment Grows
and How to Reach an Investment Outcome ➤ *pp. 245-248*

1. Choose Features | Planning | Financial Calculators | Savings. You see the Investment Savings Calculator dialog box.
2. Under Calculate For, click Opening Savings Balance to find out how much money you need to start with to reach an investment goal, click Regular Contribution to see how much you need to contribute periodically to reach the goal, or click Ending Savings Balance to find out what your present investment will be worth over time.

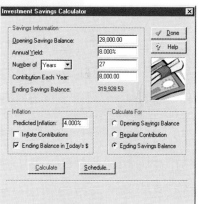

3. In the Opening Savings Balance box, enter how much the investment is worth today.
4. In the Annual Yield box, enter the percentage amount you think the investment will grow each year.
5. If necessary, click the down arrow in the Number of menu and choose a time period other than years, and enter a number in the box to the right as well.
6. Enter the amount of money you will contribute periodically to the investment in the Contribution Each Year box.
7. In the Ending Savings Balance box, enter the amount you would like the investment to be worth when the time period is over.
8. Click the Calculate button.

This chapter explains how Quicken can help you make wise financial decisions. Instead of having to estimate how an investment will grow over time or how much taking out a mortgage will cost, you can get the precise numbers—no ifs, ands, or buts.

This chapter explains how to shop for loans and mortgages on the Internet and how to calculate what the monthly payments on a loan or mortgage will be. In other words, you can find out in this chapter how much you can afford to borrow. For people who already make mortgage payments, this chapter shows how Quicken can help you decide whether refinancing is worthwhile. This chapter also tells how to peek into the years ahead and see what your net worth will be in the future, how to calculate the future value of an investment, and how to use Quicken's investment reports to figure out whether your present-day investments are making you richer or poorer.

GETTING HOME-BUYING ADVICE FROM QUICKEN

INTERNET
Links

Current mortgage & loan rates
Advice on buying a home
Should you refinance?
Find lenders online
Are you over or under insured?

Through Quicken, you can climb aboard the Internet and investigate the hundred and one things you need to know as you shop for a house or decide whether to refinance a mortgage. Either click the Home & Car hyperlink on the Home Page or choose Features | Centers | Home & Car Center to go to the Home & Car Center window. Under "Internet Links," click a hyperlink to visit the Quicken Mortgage Center site shown in Figure 13.1. This site offers worksheets for comparing loans and finding out how expensive a house you can buy. It also lists interest rates from leading lenders and gives advice about home buying and refinancing. You can also reach the Mortgage Center by choosing Online | Quicken on the Web | Mortgage Center.

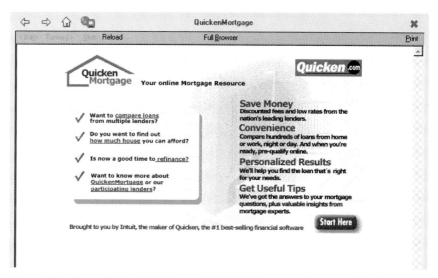

Figure 13.1 Chose Online | Quicken on the Web | Mortgage Center to visit what Quicken calls "your online mortgage resource."

Another way to get home-buying advice on the Internet is to choose Online | Quicken on the Web | Quicken Live. That takes you to **Quicken.com**, where, under "Best of the Web," you can click the Home & Mortgage link to see a list of the ten sites that Quicken deems the most useful to home buyers. Click the name of a site to visit it.

CALCULATING THE PRICE OF A LOAN OR MORTGAGE

When you are contemplating a mortgage, car loan, student loan, or other kind of loan, the two most important questions to ask are "What will the monthly payments be?" and "How much can I afford to borrow?" Quicken's Loan Calculator can answer these questions very, very quickly. To use the Loan Calculator:

1. Choose Features | Planning | Financial Calculators | Loan. You see the Loan Calculator shown in Figure 13.2.

The amount you
can afford to borrow

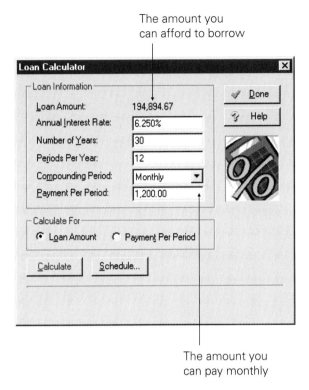

The amount you
can pay monthly

Figure 13.2 Use the Loan Calculator to find out how much you can afford to borrow and what the monthly payments on a loan will be. These calculations show that a renter who pays $1200 in rent each month can afford a $195,000 house.

2. Under Calculate For, click an option button:

- **Loan Amount** Click this button to find out how much you can borrow, given the monthly payment that you know you can afford.

- **Payment Per Period** Click this button to find out what your monthly payments will be, given the amount of money that you want to borrow.

3. In the Loan Amount box, enter the amount of the loan. (If you clicked the Loan Amount button, it says CALCULATED here, so enter

nothing. Quicken will enter a number here when it determines how much you can afford to borrow.)

4. Enter the interest rate you will be charged for the loan in the Annual Interest Rate box.

5. Enter the length of the loan in years in the Number of Years box.

6. In the Periods Per Year box, enter the number of payments you will make each year. For example, if payments are due each month, enter **12**.

7. In the unlikely event that the lender compounds interest on a semi-annual rather than a monthly basis, click the arrow in the Compounding Period box and choose Semi-Annually.

8. Enter the amount of money you can realistically pay each month on the loan in the Payment Per Period box. (If you clicked the Payment Per Period option to find out how much monthly payments will be, it says CALCULATED here. Quicken will enter a number when it computes how much you have to pay each month on the loan.)

9. Click the Calculate button.

10. Glance at the Loan Amount box to find out how much you can borrow or the Payment Per Period box to find out how much your monthly payments will be.

By clicking the Schedule button in the Loan Calculator, you can see the Approximate Future Payment Schedule dialog box. It shows how much of each payment is devoted to paying interest on the loan and how much is devoted to actually reducing the principal.

DEFINITION

Principal: The actual amount of money borrowed on a loan. The principal is different from the interest, which is the price—expressed as a percentage of the loan amount—that you pay for borrowing the money.

TO REFINANCE OR NOT TO REFINANCE

When interest rates start to fall, homeowners get itchy. They ask themselves whether now is a good time to refinance and lower their monthly mortgage payments. When it comes to refinancing, the question is whether the money saved by making lower monthly payments covers the cost of getting the new mortgage. With Quicken's Refinance Calculator, you can find out whether you save each month by refinancing and how many months of lower monthly payments it takes to recoup the cost of getting the new mortgage.

Follow these steps to use the Refinance Calculator:

1. Choose Features | Planning | Financial Calculators | Refinance. You see the Refinance Calculator dialog box shown in Figure 13.3.

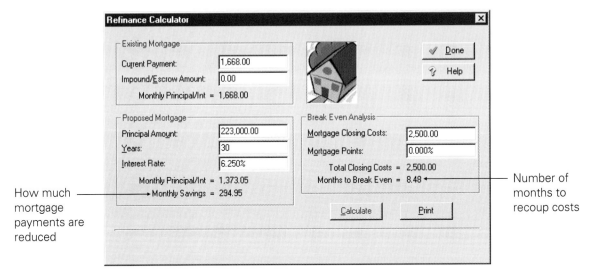

How much mortgage payments are reduced

Number of months to recoup costs

Figure 13.3 Under Proposed Mortgage, the Monthly Savings figure shows how much you save monthly by refinancing; under Break Even Analysis, the Months to Break Even figure shows how long it takes to recoup refinancing costs.

2. Under Existing Mortgage, enter how much your current monthly payment is in the Current payment box. If part of the monthly payment is impounded or is tucked away in escrow accounts for

insurance or property taxes, enter that amount in the Impound/ Escrow Amount box.

3. Under Proposed Mortgage, tell Quicken how much the new mortgage is, how many years it takes to pay it off, and its interest rate. Be sure to use the interest rate that the lender gives you, not the annual percentage rate, which is the *total* cost of borrowing, including loan fees and discount points.

4. Under Break Even Analysis, enter the closing costs in the Mortgage closing costs box. Closing costs include processing fees and appraisal fees.

5. In the Mortgage Points box, enter the loan fee and discount points. *Points* are expressed as a percentage of the loan. If 4 is the number of points the lender wants to charge you, enter 4.

6. Click the Calculate button.

7. Under Proposed Mortgage, look at the monthly savings figure. It shows how much you save monthly by refinancing.

8. Look under Break Even Analysis at the Months to Break Even figure. It shows how many months of lower mortgage payments it takes to recoup the cost of refinancing.

CAUTION

The Refinance Calculator doesn't take into account total interest payments on new mortgages. When you refinance, the amount of each monthly payment goes down, but the total number of payments, reset to 360, goes up, so you pay more in interest.

FORECASTING YOUR FUTURE INCOME AND EXPENSES

Quicken offers a means of forecasting what your future account balances will be, although I'm not sure how useful this device is. In the first place, no one can say what the future will bring, and in the second place, all Quicken does to make a forecast is total the amount in all the accounts, average out how much the total increases or decreases are each month, take into account scheduled transactions in the future, and extrapolate like a madman.

Figure 13.4 shows the Forecasting window. To see one of your own, click the Forecasting hyperlink in the Planning Center window or choose Features | Planning | Forecasting. If you haven't been using Quicken very long, you see the Automatically Create Forecast dialog box, where Quicken asks for a time period from which to get the data for the forecast. Enter a time period and click OK to get to the Forecasting window.

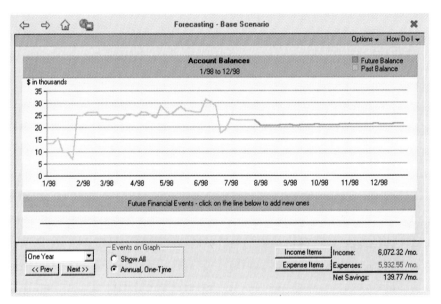

Figure 13.4 In the Forecasting window, the crooked line represents past account totals and the relatively straight line represents what Quicken thinks future totals will be.

The crooked line represents the sum of accounts in the past, and the blue line represents what they will be in the future. Funny how one line is crooked and one line isn't. Personally, I think it's kind of interesting to click the Prev button in the lower-left corner of the dialog box to get a graph of past account totals, which is what I did for Figure 13.4. Notice, in the lower-right corner of the

Forecasting window, that Quicken lists your average monthly income, average monthly expenses, and average monthly savings.

CALCULATING THE FUTURE VALUE OF AN INVESTMENT

If, starting in 1998, you set aside $3,000 in a mutual fund account each year for the next 30 years, the fund grows by 6.25 percent annually, and the inflation rate is a steady 2 percent, how much will your shares in the fund be worth 30 years from now in 1998 dollars?

A. $307,250.61

B. $169,624.12

C. A bundle

D. None of the above

Questions like these, which have stumped Econ 101 students for years, can be answered in about ten seconds with Quicken (the correct answer is B). By using the Investment Savings Calculator, you can find out how an investment will grow over time, how much annual contributions will be worth altogether over time, or how much you need to contribute and save to reach an investment goal. Here's how to use the Investment Savings Calculator:

1. Choose Features | Planning | Financial Calculators | Savings. You see the Investment Savings Calculator dialog box shown in Figure 13.5.

2. Under Calculate For, click an option button:

   - **Opening Savings Balance** Click to find out how much you need to invest to begin with to reach an investment goal. For example, to find out how much you need to invest now in a mutual fund for the investment to reach $100,000 in 15 years, click this button.

   - **Regular Contribution** Click to find out how much you need to invest each year to reach an investment goal. For example, click this button to find out how much you need to contribute each year for 15 years to a SEP-IRA for it to grow to $100,000.

Enter your investment information.

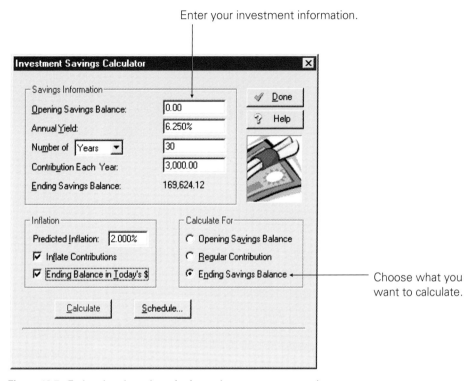

Figure 13.5 Estimating the value of a future investment or security

- **Ending Savings Balance**   Click to find out how much an investment will be worth over time. For example, if you start with $10,000 in a 401(k) plan and contribute $2,000 to it for the next 15 years, click this button to find out what the 401(k) plan will be worth 15 years from now.

3. In the Opening Savings Balance box, enter the amount you have already invested. (If you clicked the Opening Savings button, it says CALCULATED here. Quicken will enter a number here when it determines how much you need to invest to reach your investment goal.)

4. Enter the percentage amount you think the investment will grow each year in the Annual Yield box. On average since 1926, stocks have yielded 10 percent annually, long-term corporate bonds have yielded 5

percent, and U.S. Treasury Bills have yielded 3.5 percent. If you are calculating the return on a mutual fund investment, you can find out what last year's return was. For a savings account, you can get the annual yield from the bank. For real estate, throw darts at a dartboard and don't move to California.

5. Click the Number of arrow and choose a time period if the length of the investment is not to be calculated in years, and enter the number of years, weeks, months, or quarters you will hang on to the investment in the text box.

6. In the Contribution Each Year box, enter the amount of money you intend to add to the investment each year, if you intend to do that. (If you clicked the Regular Contribution option button to find out how much you need to contribute annually to reach an investment goal, it says CALCULATED here. Quicken will tell you how much you need to contribute.)

7. Enter how much you want the investment to be worth over time in the Ending Savings Balance box. (If you clicked the Ending Savings Balance option button to find out how much your investment will be worth, it says CALCULATED here. Quicken will shortly tell you how much it will be worth.)

8. Enter what you think the inflation rate will be during the life of the investment in the Predicted Inflation box. If it helps, the average inflation rate in the United States since 1945 has been 3.3 percent.

9. Click the Inflate Contributions? check box if you made an entry in the Contribution Each Year box and you intend to make larger contributions each year to account for inflation.

10. Click the Ending Balance in Today's $? check box to remove the check mark if you want to see the results of your contribution in the inflated dollars of tomorrow, not in today's dollars. If you uncheck this box, the value of your future investment will seem quite large, but you will have to temper your initial pleasure at seeing how much your money grows by remembering that a dollar won't be worth as much tomorrow as it is today.

11. Click the Calculate button.

12. Glance at the Opening Savings Balance box to see how much you need to invest now to reach your investment goals, the Contribution Each Year box to find out how much you need to contribute annually to reach your goal, or the Ending Savings Balance to see what your investment will be worth in the future.

REPORTS AND GRAPHS FOR ANALYZING INVESTMENTS

Chapter 9 explains how to create reports, tweak them, customize them, and memorize them so you can use them again. It also shows how to create graphs.

If you've already dabbled in investments, you can get Quicken to tell you how well your investments are performing. Do that by creating an investment report or by generating an Investment Performance graph.

To create an investment report, click the Reports button, click the Investment tab in the Create Report dialog box, and then click the icon beside one of these reports:

- **Portfolio Value** Lists the market value of the securities you own, how many shares of each you own, and how much they have increased or decreased in value.

- **Investment Performance** Shows the return, by percentage and amount, of the securities in your portfolio.

- **Investment Income** Totals investment transactions by income category and expense category.

See "Estimating Capital Gains" in Chapter 15 to learn how to estimate the capital gains taxes you must pay when you sell a security.

- **Capital Gains** Lists the capital gain or loss of securities you have sold.

- **Investment Transactions** Lists all transactions from your investment account registers.

You can also gauge the performance of your investments by seeing an Investment Performance graph or Investment Asset Allocation graph. Chapter 9 explains how to create graphs.

CHAPTER

14

Quicken for Investors

INCLUDES

- A look at the Investing Center

- Setting up investment accounts

- Recording the purchase and sales of shares in a security

- Recording income from dividends, interest, and capital gains

- Handling stock splits and other esoteric transactions

- Tracking the market value of securities

- Examining investments in Portfolio view

- Working in Security Detail view

249

FAST FORWARD

Record the Purchase of Shares ➤ pp. 263-264

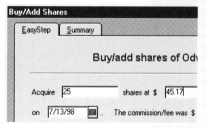

1. Click the Easy Actions button and choose Buy/Add Shares.
2. Click the down arrow in the Which Security? drop-down menu and choose the security whose shares you have purchased. Then click Next.
3. In the next dialog box, tell Quicken where you got the money to purchase the security, either from the cash account you keep with your broker or from an account you track with Quicken; then click Next.
4. In the next dialog box, say how many shares you bought, their per-share price, and the commission you paid, and then click Next.
5. Review the Summary tab to make sure you entered the data right, and click Done.

Record the Sale of Shares ➤ pp. 264-266

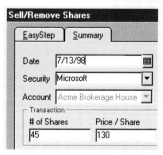

1. Click the Easy Actions button and choose Sell/Remove Shares.
2. Choose the security whose shares you sold and click Next.
3. Click one of the Yes buttons to tell Quicken that you are depositing the money, in either the cash account you keep with your broker or in another account; then click Next.
4. Enter the number of shares you sold, the per-share price, and the commission fee. Then click Next.
5. Review the Summary tab to make sure what you entered is correct, and then click Done.

See the Market Price, Share Price, and Return on Your Investments ➤ pp. 271-272

1. Click the Port icon on the iconbar to switch to Portfolio view.
2. On the Group by drop-down menu, choose which investments you want to examine.
3. On the View menu, choose how you want to examine your investments—by performance, valuation, price updates, stock quote.

Symbol	Mkt Price	
COMS	29	e
MSFT	129 7/8	e
ODWA	12 1/2	e
EDGBX	10.63	e
BDJ	9.625	e

See a Graph that Shows the Price History or Market Value History of an Investment ➤ pp. 272-273

1. Click the Port icon on the iconbar to switch to Portfolio view.
2. Click the Detail View button.
3. Choose a security from the drop-down list in the upper-left corner of the Security Detail View window.
4. From the Market Value/Price History menu, choose an option to graph the security by its price history or the market value of the shares you own.
5. From the time drop-down menu, choose a time option for plotting the data on the graph.
6. Click the News button to see hyperlinks that you can click to go on the Internet and read articles about the security.

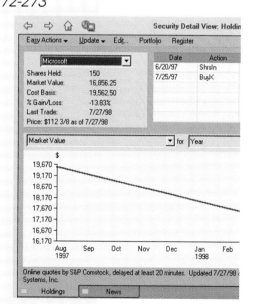

This chapter explains how to use Quicken to track the value of investments, including mutual funds, stocks, bonds, and other securities. Investment accounts are similar to checking and savings accounts. Transactions are recorded by date, and Quicken tracks the value of the securities in a register.

Chapter 7 explains how to research investments online.

What makes investment accounts different, however, is that Quicken tracks the price per share, the number of shares you have (as you buy and sell them), and the shares' market value, not just the account balance. Also, instead of the seven choices in the Num column that you know so well for describing checking and savings account transactions, there are no less than 30 different ways to describe a transaction in an investment account. Better read on...

STUDYING YOUR INVESTMENTS IN THE INVESTING CENTER

Later in this chapter, "Managing Investments in Portfolio View" and "Security Detail View for Focusing on Investments" explain what Portfolio and Security Detail view are.

To see at a glance how well your investments are doing, go to the Investing Center by clicking the Investing hyperlink on the Home Page or choosing Features | Centers | Investing Center. As Figure 14.1 shows, the Investing Center lists securities that you placed on the Watch List (I'll show you how to put securities on this list a little later) and the value of your investment accounts. By clicking a link under "Related Activities," you can see your investments in Portfolio or Security Detail view, go to an investment register, or generate an investment report. Click a hyperlink under "Internet Links" to visit **Quicken.com**, where you can read articles of interest to investors.

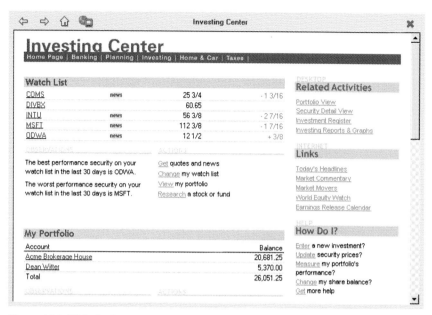

Figure 14.1 Visit the Investing Center when you want to gaze thoughtfully at your investments.

DO YOU NEED TO TRACK INVESTMENTS?

For tax purposes and to understand how well investments are performing, everybody should track investments, except if they are tax-deferred. When it comes to investments like IRAs, SEPs, 401(k) accounts, or tax-deferred mutual funds, have the managers do the work for you. You can create an investment account especially for 401(k) plans, for example, but why bother? If the managers are worth anything, they send statements saying what your profits or losses are. Rather than go to the trouble of recording those profits or losses in an investment account (and the trouble can be significant), set up an asset account and record profits and losses as increases or decreases. You are a busy person. Take my advice about investment accounts and you won't be quite as busy.

In Chapter 3, "Make Your Own Categories and Subcategories" describes how to create a category or subcategory.

When, at the ripe age of 65 or 70, you start withdrawing from the asset account with which you track retirement investments, do not record the withdrawals as transfers to a savings or checking account. Instead, record each withdrawal as a decrease in the asset account *and* as a deposit in a savings or checking account. Create a new category or subcategory for the retirement income you deposit (for example, Retirement Income or Income: Retirement). True, you have to record two transactions each time you withdraw from your retirement savings, which makes for more work, but the asset account will show exactly how much your retirement investments are worth, and the Retirement Income or Income: Retirement category or subcategory will show how much income you got from your retirement investments.

THE BIG PICTURE: TRACKING INVESTMENTS WITH QUICKEN

To track investments with Quicken, you start by setting up an investment account. If you want, you can track all your investments in a single account, but if you are tracking the securities you trade with a brokerage house, create one account for each brokerage house you do business with. That way, you simplify your record keeping, because you can enter data in the investment account straight from the broker's statement and even reconcile your account from the statements the broker sends you.

DEFINITION

Securities: Bonds, stock certificates, and other financial instruments that can be traded and whose value fluctuates.

After you set up the account, you tell Quicken the names of the securities—the stocks, bonds, mutual funds, CDs, and so on—that go in the account. As you do that, you tell the program how many shares you own and what their value is. You can even record past sales and purchases of stock for analysis purposes, as long as you have the paperwork on hand and can record the transactions accurately.

Once the account has been set up and the securities entered, you record purchases, sales, share reinvestments, capital gains, dividends, stock splits, and what all from the register. Or you can examine your investments in the Portfolio View window, which lists all the securities you own and offers ways of studying investments. Figure 14.2 shows the Portfolio View window.

SETTING UP AN INVESTMENT ACCOUNT

Since you've come this far, I'll bet my eyeteeth you know how to set up an account in Quicken. Setting up an investment account is like setting up a savings or checking account, only you have to answer questions about tax deferments and linked checking accounts. Follow these steps to set up an investment account:

1. Click the Accts icon on the iconbar to get to the Account List window, and then click the New button.

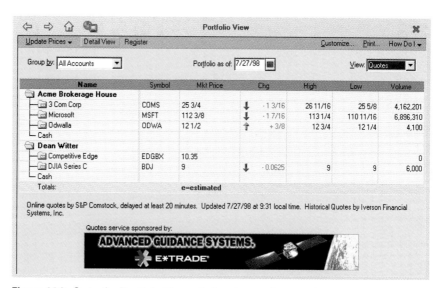

Figure 14.2 Go to the Portfolio View window to examine your investments.

2. In the Account Setup dialog box, click the Investment option button and click Next.

3. When you see the EasyStep tab, bypass it by clicking the Summary tab. You go straight to the screen shown in Figure 14.3. Why not? You've created many accounts by now and you don't need all that hand-holding.

4. Under Account Information, name the account and describe it. If you are setting up an account to track the securities you buy and sell through a brokerage house, you could enter the house's name here.

5. If you are tracking a single mutual fund with this account, click the Account Contains a Single Mutual Fund check box.

6. Fill in the CMA Information part of the dialog box only if this investment account allows you to write checks or use a debit card

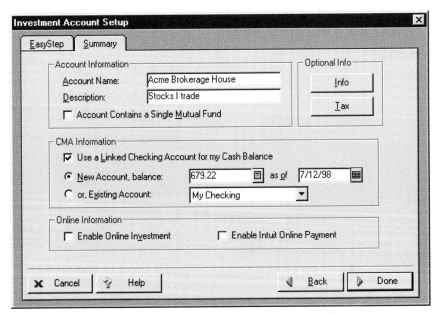

Figure 14.3 The Summary tab of the Investment Account Setup dialog box, where you tell Quicken the name and particulars of the investment account you are creating

With most brokerage accounts, you keep cash in the account as well as securities. The cash is used for buying securities, or else it represents profits from the sale of a security. See "Transferring Cash In and Out of Investment Accounts" later in this chapter to learn how to deposit cash into or withdraw cash from an investment account.

against the account. If that is the case, click the Use a Linked Checking Account check box and then do one of the following:

- **You don't track the account with Quicken** Click the New Account option button and enter the balance of the account and a date.

- **You already track the account with Quicken** Click the Existing Account option button and choose the account from the drop-down list if you have already set up an account to track the checks you write or debit card charges.

7. Click the Tax button if financial activity in the investment account needs to be reported on your income tax form. From the Tax Schedule Information dialog box, click the Tax-Deferred Account check box and then, if you want data in the account to be computed on tax forms, choose the tax form line item where transfers in and out of the account should be reported. Click OK when you're done.

8. Back on the Summary tab, click the Done button. The Security Setup dialog box appears so you can tell Quicken the names of the securities in the account you just created.

9. Click Cancel and then click Yes when Quicken asks if you really want to cancel. Instead of all this hand-holding, there is a faster way to enter the names of securities. Keep reading.

TELLING QUICKEN ABOUT YOUR SECURITIES

No matter what the security you are tracking, you start by telling Quicken everything you know about it—its name, ticker symbol, when you bought it, how much you paid for it, and so on. After that, recording the purchase of more shares, selling shares, recording dividends, and doing all else you can do to a security are all pretty easy to record in Quicken. Read on to find out how to tell Quicken about the securities you own—your mutual funds, stocks, and bonds, as well as IRAs, Keoghs, CDs, treasury bills, annuities, precious metals, collectibles, REITs, unit trusts, and baseball cards.

*See "Buying More Shares of
a Security You Already Track
with Quicken" later in this
chapter if you are already
tracking a security with
Quicken and you want to
record the purchase of
more shares.*

Follow these steps to tell Quicken about securities you already own or just purchased for the first time:

1. Open the investment account register and put the cursor in the first empty row. Make sure you open the investment account, not its associated cash account.

2. Click the Easy Actions button in the upper-left corner and choose Buy/Add Shares from the drop-down menu. You see the Buy/Add Shares dialog box.

3. Type the name of the stock, bond, security, or whatever it is you are trying to track in the Which Security? box. Then click Next. You see the Set Up Security dialog box shown in Figure 14.4.

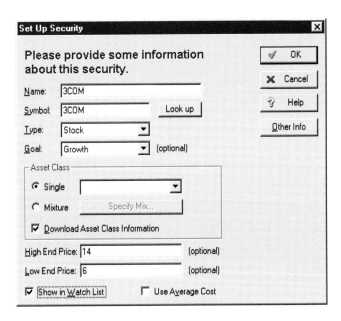

Figure 14.4 In the Set Up Security dialog box, enter the security's name, its ticker symbol, its type, an investment goal (if you want), asset classification, and high and low price.

4. Enter a ticker symbol in the Symbol box if you intend to download information about this security from the Internet. The *ticker symbol* is

How to download stock quotes from the Internet is described in Chapter 7.

At the start of this chapter, "Studying Your Investments in the Investing Center" explains how the Investing Center works.

the abbreviated name of the company. You see them in the cryptic pages of the *Wall Street Journal* and other newspapers. (If you have Quicken Deluxe, you can click the Look up button and find out what the ticker symbol is on the Internet.)

5. From the Type drop-down menu, choose Stock, Bond, CD, or Mutual Fund.

6. Make a choice from the Goal drop-down list if you want to be able to group securities by goal—High Risk, Low Risk, and so on—on reports and graphs and in the Portfolio View window.

7. Make choices in the Asset Class part of the dialog box if you want to group assets in the Investing Center, on reports and graphs, and in the Portfolio View window (see Figure 14.2). If you are tracking a mutual fund, you can click the Specify Mix button and list what percentage of the fund's assets is invested in bonds, stocks, and so on (get this data from the literature that the mutual fund sent to you). Be sure to click the Download Asset Class Information check box if you intend to get share prices from the Internet. Clicking this check box tells Quicken to download news about this kind of security to the Portfolio window.

8. Enter numbers in the High End Price and Low End Price boxes if you want Quicken to alert you on the Home Page and Quicken Reminders window when the security rises above or falls below the prices you enter.

9. Click the Show in Watch List check box if you want this security to appear in the Watch List (see Figure 14.1), a list of important securities that appears in the Investing Center and, if you so choose, on the Home Page.

10. Click the Use Average Cost check box if you are tracking a mutual fund and you want to track it by using the average cost of shares, not the cost of each lot you buy.

11. If this is a bond you are setting up and it has a maturity date, click the Other Info button and fill in the Additional Security Information dialog box. There are also places here for scribbling down a broker's name, phone number, and so on.

12. Click OK in the Set Up Security dialog box. The next dialog box asks from which account you got the money to pay for the securities.

13. Whether you click one of the Yes buttons or the No button depends on whether you just purchased the security or you have had it for some time and are simply recording it in Quicken:

- **Just Purchased the Security**   Click the first Yes button if the security was purchased with cash you keep in your brokerage account; click the second Yes button if you purchased the security with money from an account you track with Quicken, and then choose the account from the drop-down list.

- **Have Had for a While**   Click the No button.

   After you click the Next button, you see the EasyStep tab of the Buy/Add Shares dialog box shown in Figure 14.5. I hope you have the paperwork in front of you, because you are going to need it.

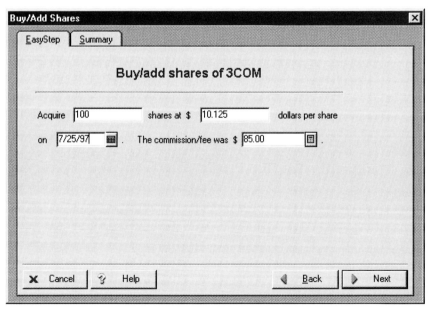

Figure 14.5   Here you list how many shares of the security you own and how much they are worth.

14. Enter the number of shares you own in the Acquire box.

    If the security you are setting up is a bond, enter the number of bonds you bought times ten in the Acquire box, and enter the dollar value of the bond divided by ten in the $ box. In other words, if you are buying a $1,000 bond, enter **10** in the Acquire box and **100** in the $ box. Do this because bonds are quoted at a percentage of their face, or par, value.

    For a CD, put **1** in the shares box and the total value of the bond or CD in the $ box.

15. Enter the dollar value of each share in the $ box. You can enter share prices in eighths—Quicken will convert them to decimals. If you just purchased this security and paid a commission to purchase it, enter an amount in the commission/fee box.

16. Enter the date you purchased the shares or first acquired them.

CAUTION

In the date box, enter the date you purchased the shares, not today's date. Quicken uses the dates you enter to calculate capital gains taxes.

17. Click the Next button. You see the Summary tab.

18. Make sure the information on the Summary tab is correct, and then click Done.

You see your entry in the investment register. In the Action column, it says ShrsIn if you recorded a purchase from the past, or BuyX if you just purchased the stock and recorded it for the first time:

6/20/97	ShrsIn	Microsoft	129 7/8	100	12,987 50	0 00
					12,987 50	
7/25/97	BuyX	3 Com Corp	10 1/8	100	1,097 50	0 00
		[Acme Brokerage	1,097.50	85 00		

CHANGING THE PARTICULARS OF A SECURITY OR AN INVESTMENT REGISTER TRANSACTION

Suppose you go to all the trouble to enter a purchase of shares in a security, but then you discover that you entered the transaction incorrectly or you described the security incorrectly to Quicken. Follow these steps to fix the problem:

- **Security Described Incorrectly**   Click the Port icon on the iconbar to switch to Portfolio view (see Figure 14.2), which lists your securities (if you don't see them by name, choose Security on the Group by menu). Click the name of the security that needs changing, click the Detail View button, and then click the Edit button. You see the Edit Security dialog box, which looks and works exactly like the Set Up Security dialog box (see Figure 14.4). Fix your error there.

- **Investment Transaction Entered Incorrectly**   Open the investment register where you entered the transaction, select it, click the Edit button, and choose Edit Transaction from the drop-down menu. Then, in the dialog box that appears, change the share price, number of shares, or whatever needs fixing, and click the Done button.

SHORTCUT

The fastest way to edit an investment transaction is to go to the Security Detail View window, choose the security from the drop-down list in the upper-left corner of the window, and then double-click the transaction in the mini-register. You see a dialog box for editing the transaction. See "Security Detail View for Focusing on Investments" later in this chapter to learn about Security Detail view.

RECORDING YOUR INVESTMENT ACTIVITY

The Easy Actions menu is also found in the Security Detail View window, so if you prefer to work there, you can perform all the actions described in this section in Security Detail view as well. See "Security Detail View for Focusing on Investments" later in this chapter.

After you have recorded the initial purchase of shares, you can start describing the hundred and one ways to buy and sell securities. The following pages explain how to record a purchase of shares, a sale of shares, a dividend, a reinvestment, and a stock split, among other transactions. You will also find instructions here for recording such esoteric transactions as a margin interest expense and a corporate securities spin-off.

Buying More Shares of a Security You Already Track with Quicken

Buying more shares of a security that you are already tracking with Quicken is very similar to entering shares in the investment account the first time around, which the last handful of pages explained how to do. The difference is that you tell Quicken where the money to buy the shares came from. Follow these steps to record a purchase of more shares:

1. Go to the last line of the investment register, click the Easy Actions button, and choose Buy/Add Shares.
2. Click the down arrow in the Which Security? drop-down menu and choose the security whose shares you have purchased (if you're in Security Detail view, choose which account). Then click Next.
3. In the EasyStep tab of the Buy/Add Shares dialog box, click one of the Yes option buttons to tell Quicken whether the money for the purchase came from the cash account you keep with your broker or from a normal checking account. Choose a new account, if necessary. Then click Next.
4. In the Buy/Add Shares dialog box (see Figure 14.5), enter the number of shares you purchased, how much each share cost, and the commission, if any. Make sure to enter the date of the sale, not today's date. Click Next when you are done.

5. Review the Summary tab to make sure you entered the data right, and click Done.

The purchase is recorded in the register, with the BuyX indicator showing in the Action column.

Selling Shares

If you just read the last few pages, my apologies for being repetitive. The dialog boxes that you get when you choose options from the Easy Actions menu in investment registers start to look alike after a while, but I guess that's good, because, at least where computers are concerned, familiarity doesn't breed contempt; it breeds confidence.

Follow these steps to record a sale of shares:

1. Click the Easy Actions button and choose Sell/Remove Shares.

2. On the EasyStep tab of the Sell/Remove Shares dialog box, click the arrow in the Which Security? box and choose the security whose shares you sold (if you're in Security Detail view, choose an account). Then click Next.

3. In the next dialog box, tell Quicken where you deposited the money from the shares, either in the cash account you keep with your broker or in an account you track with Quicken; then click Next.
   You see a dialog box that looks very similar to the Buy/Add Shares dialog box (see Figure 14.5), only it has a Sell box where the other had an Acquire box.

4. Fill in the dialog box and click Next. You see the Summary tab of the Sell/Remove Shares dialog box shown in Figure 14.6.

5. Click Done if you are selling all your securities or if you purchased the securities all at once. If you bought the securities in lots, however, you need to click the Specify Lots button and read on.

DEFINITION

Lot: A group of securities purchased at the same time at the same price. Also a nephew of Abraham whose wife was turned into a saltshaker.

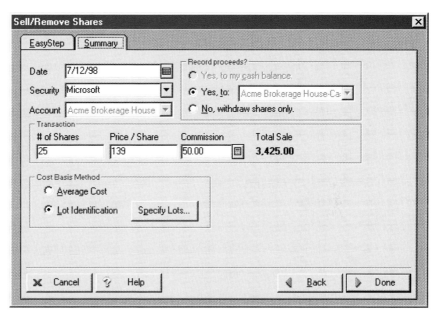

Figure 14.6 From the Summary tab, you can choose which of your stocks to sell by clicking the Specify Lots button.

If you purchased the shares in lots, you need to click the Specify Lots button and tinker with the Specify Lots dialog box shown in Figure 14.7. Select the lot you will be selling the shares from and then enter the number of shares you are selling from the lot in the Selected column. You can also click one of these buttons to get Quicken's help in deciding which shares to sell:

"Estimating Capital Gains" in Chapter 15 tells how to get Quicken's help to determine how much in capital gains taxes you will have to pay when you sell a security at a profit.

- **Maximum Gain** Tells Quicken to sell the shares by which you gain the highest profit.
- **Minimum Gain** Tells Quicken to sell the shares by which you make the least profit to save on capital gains taxes.
- **First Shares In** Sells the earliest shares you bought.
- **Last Shares In** Sells the most recent shares you bought.

Click the Reset button to start all over if you have to, but in any case click OK, click Next, and click Done to record the sale.

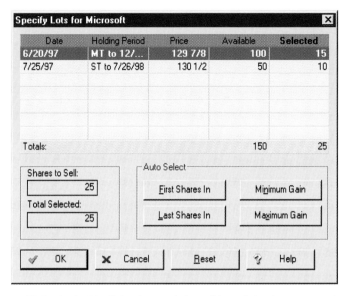

Figure 14.7 Click a lot in this dialog box and then either click a button or make entries to tell Quicken which lots or which parts of lots you sold.

Recording Dividend, Interest, Capital Gain, and Other Income

See "Updating the Market Value of Securities" later in this chapter to learn how to update the per-share price of a security.

You became an investor with the hope that your investments would turn a profit, and when they do, you have to record the income you made in the investment register. The following Step by Step instructions tell how to record income you received by check. The transaction is recorded as a transfer from the investment register to another account. If the income from your investment was reinvested in the security that produced it, see "Reinvesting Shares," the next part of this chapter.

Reinvesting Shares

Sometimes income from a mutual fund or stock is reinvested in the security. To record profits that have been reinvested, follow these steps:

1. Go to the last row in the register.

STEP BY STEP Recording Income from an Investment

① Go to the last row in the register, click the Easy Actions button, and choose Record an Income Event.

② Enter the date of the income disbursement, not today's date.

③ Click the arrow and choose the lucky investment that produced the income.

④ Enter the amount your investment earned in one of the boxes (your statement should tell you how to correctly categorize the income).

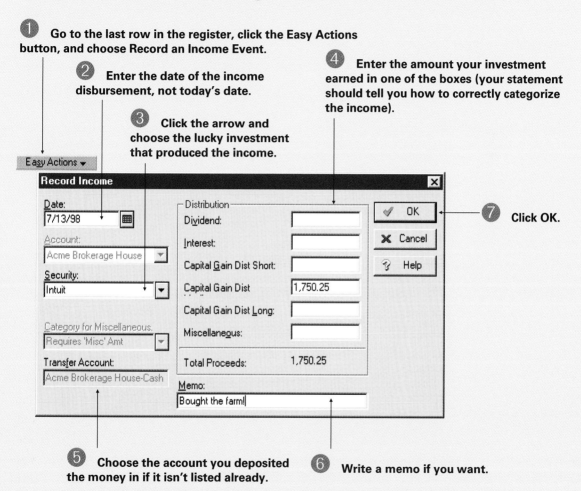

⑦ Click OK.

⑤ Choose the account you deposited the money in if it isn't listed already.

⑥ Write a memo if you want.

2. Click the Easy Actions button and choose Reinvest Income. You see a dialog box by the same name, as shown in Figure 14.8.

3. Fill out this dialog box as you would the Record Income dialog box (see the previous Step by Step box), only enter the number of shares the reinvestment purchased as well in the Number Shares box. Quicken lists the price per share below the Help button in the dialog

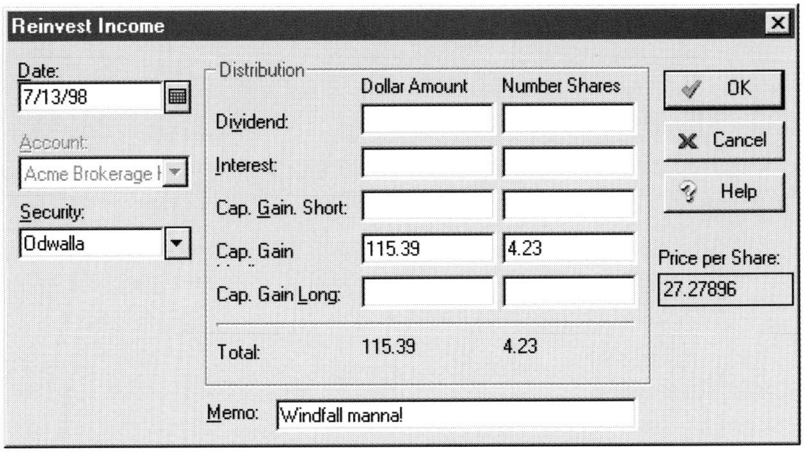

Figure 14.8 When profits from a security are reinvested, fill in this dialog box and enter how many new shares were purchased with the reinvestment.

box. The price per share shown here should match the price per share on the statement you were sent that notified you of the reinvestment.

4. Under Distribution, make one of the following choices (your statement should tell you which one to select):

- **Dividend**   A quarterly (or one-time) stock or mutual fund dividend.

- **Interest**   Interest income from the security.

- **Capital Gain Dist. Short**   A mutual fund capital gains distribution.

- **Capital Gain Dist. Long**   A mutual fund long-term capital gains distribution.

- **Miscellaneous**   A "none of the above" means of acquiring income from an investment.

5. Click OK.

Transferring Cash In and Out of Investment Accounts

If the investment account you set up with Quicken includes an associated cash account, you have to record when you put money in or take money out of the associated cash account. To record a payment, or transfer, into the associated cash account, enter the check to your broker as you would enter any check, but don't categorize the transaction. Instead, go to the bottom of the Category menu and choose the Transfer to/from option and the name of your associated cash account.

| 5/13/98 | 101 | My Broker | | 5,000 00 | | 20,000 00 |
| | | [Acme Brokerage House-Cash] | | | | |

If your broker sends you a check, record it as a transfer from your associated cash account to your checking account or to whichever account you deposited the check in.

Recording Annual Fees, Exit Fees, and Other Miscellaneous Fees

Sometimes you get charged an out-of-the-blue fee from a fund manager or broker. When that happens and a checking account or associated cash account is linked to the investment account you are using to track the security, simply record the fee in the checking account. But if an account is not linked to the investment account, you have to choose another means of recording the fee.

To do that, click the Easy Actions button in the register and choose Miscellaneous Expense to get to the dialog box by that name. Enter the date and, in the Security box, choose a security if the expense is associated with a single security. Then fill in the amount, categorize the expense, choose the account that the money to pay the expense came from, and click OK.

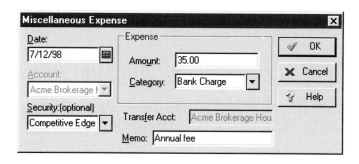

When Stocks or Mutual Fund Shares Are Split

Occasionally, stocks and mutual fund shares are split to lower the price of individual stocks or shares and make them seem more attractive to investors. In a 2-to-1 split, for example, investors are given twice as much stock, but the value of individual stocks is half what it was before, so the owner of 100 shares worth $1,000 now owns 200 shares worth the same amount—$1,000.

To record a mutual fund share split or stock split, click the Easy Actions button and choose Stock Split. In the Stock Split dialog box, enter the date, choose the security whose stock has been split, enter how many shares of the split stock you own and how many shares of the old, unsplit stock you owned. If you want, you can update the price of the stock by making an entry in the Price after Split field. Click OK when you are done.

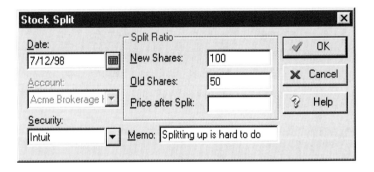

Unusual Stock Transactions

If you click the Easy Actions button in an investment register or in the Security Detail View window (described later in this chapter) and then click the Advanced option at the bottom of the menu, you see a submenu with a number of esoteric options for handling esoteric stock transactions. Here is a rundown of those options and why you would choose them:

- **Margin Interest Expense** Choose this option when you borrow money from a broker to pay for a security. In the Amount box, enter the amount in interest on the loan that you have to pay.

- **Transfer Shares Between Accounts** Choose this option to transfer a security from one investment account to another.

- **Corporate Name Change**   Choose this option to change a security's name without changing the financial records you have diligently kept.

- **Corporate Securities Spin-Off**   When a corporation spins off, drops off, or lops off part of itself and you own shares in the corporation, choose this command to record how many new shares the corporation is issuing for each old share.

- **Corporate Acquisition (stock for stock)**   When one corporation merges with another and the two swap stocks, choose this command to record how many shares are being issued for each share of the parent company and the share price that the parent company has to pay for each share of the company it has swallowed.

- **Stock Dividend (non-cash dividend)**   Choose this command when dividends are paid in stock, not cash.

- **Reminder Transaction**   Choose this command and write a reminder note to yourself. The note will appear under "Alerts & Reminders" on the Home Page and in the Quicken Reminders window. For example, you could remind yourself to buy or sell a stock as of a certain day.

UPDATING THE MARKET VALUE OF SECURITIES

Unquestionably, the best way to update the market value of your securities is to download prices from the Internet ("Getting Security Prices Online" in Chapter 7 explains how). Security prices in your investment accounts are updated automatically when you do it from the Internet. However, if a security doesn't have a ticker symbol and you can't download its price from the Internet, you can always do it yourself the old-fashioned way—by hand.

To update a security price by hand, click the Port icon on the iconbar to switch to Portfolio view. Then click the name of the security whose price you want to update, click the Update Prices button, and choose Edit Price History. You see the Price History for dialog box shown in Figure 14.9. Click the New button to see the New Price for dialog box (also shown in Figure 14.9), enter the price of the security as of a certain day (you can enter the volume of sales and other information as well), and click OK.

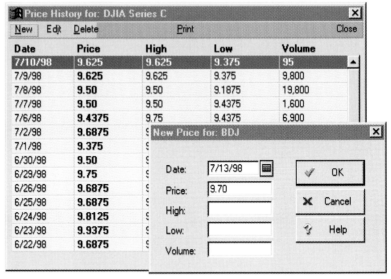

Figure 14.9 To keep your portfolio up to date, enter the current price of securities in the New Price for dialog box.

MANAGING INVESTMENTS IN PORTFOLIO VIEW

After you set up an investment account, Quicken sticks a new icon on the iconbar called Port. Click this icon, press CTRL-U, or choose Features | Investing | Portfolio View to get to the Portfolio View window shown in Figure 14.10. In the Name column are the names of investment accounts. Click a folder to open it and see the securities in an account. The bottom of the window shows the total market value of your investments, their cost basis, and how much you have gained or lost by your investments. The *cost basis* is the total cost of purchasing a security, including commissions, fees, and mutual fund loads.

Click to update price histories.

Click to examine a security.

Go to the account register.

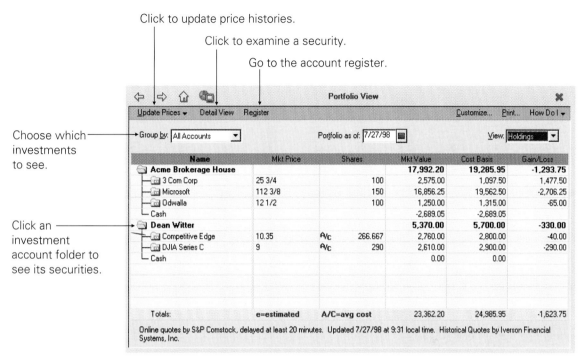

Choose which investments to see.

Click an investment account folder to see its securities.

Figure 14.10 In the Portfolio View window, you can get a good look at how your investments are performing.

EXPERT ADVICE

Besides the standard columns in the Portfolio View window—Price, Shares, Mkt Value, and so on—you can tell Quicken to display other types of information about securities. To do so, click the Customize button. In the dialog box that appears, hold down the CTRL key and click the names of columns in the Available Columns list. Then click the Add button and, finally, click OK.

To choose which accounts and securities appear in the window, experiment with the options on the Group by drop-down menu. Meanwhile, choose these options on the View menu to get a better look at your investments:

- **Holdings** All securities, their price, value, and how much you have earned or lost by them, as shown in Figure 14.10.
- **Performance** How much you've invested, your return on each investment, and the percentage by which each investment has grown or shrunk in relation to the original investment.
- **Valuation** How much you've invested, your return on each investment, and the current market value of each investment.
- **Price Update** The current price, last price, and change in market value.
- **Quotes** Up-to-date stock quotes, including price changes and volume information.

SECURITY DETAIL VIEW FOR FOCUSING ON INVESTMENTS

Detail View

To find out more about an individual security, Quicken offers Security Detail view, as shown in Figure 14.11. To see this view, double-click a security in the Portfolio View window or select it and click the Detail View button.

Everything you can do from a register can also be done from this window by clicking the Easy Actions button and choosing an option from the menu. Click the News button to see a screen with hyperlinks you can click to go on the Internet and read about the security in question. Details about the security, a graph, and the most recent transactions in the register are all there for your viewing pleasure.

For buying shares, selling shares, and so on

For updating share values

Returns to the Portfolio View window

Goes to the investment register

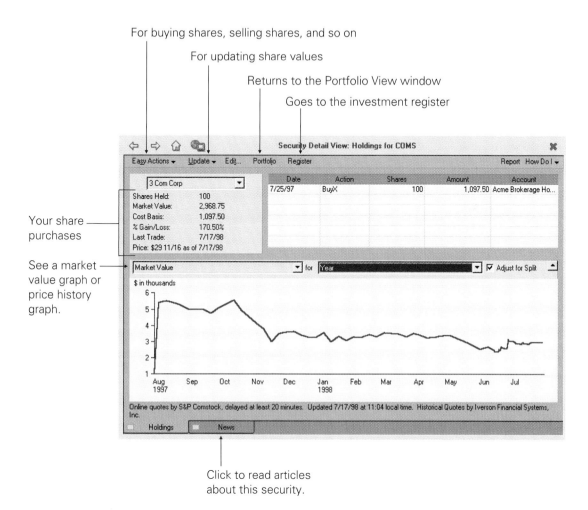

Your share purchases

See a market value graph or price history graph.

Click to read articles about this security.

Figure 14.11 From the Security Detail View window, you can make investment transactions, update market prices, and even graph the history of an investment.

EXPERT ADVICE

Remember, you can do everything from the Security Detail View window that you can do in a register (click the Easy Actions button if you don't believe me). If you're an investor, camp out in the Security Detail View window. It shows the least amount of clutter and lets you focus on the securities you own.

RECONCILING AND UPDATING INVESTMENT ACCOUNTS AND SHARE PRICES

Reconciling an investment account is done the same way as reconciling a savings or checking account. When the statement comes from the brokerage house, open the associated cash account and click the Recon button. You see a dialog box for entering the starting cash balance, the ending cash balance, and the statement date. Click OK in that dialog box and you go to the familiar Reconcile Account window, where you can reconcile the broker's records with your own.

However, a simpler, easier way to reconcile an investment account is to open the account in question and choose either Features | Investing | Update Cash Balance to update the cash value of a brokerage account or Features | Investing | Update Share Balance to record the correct number of shares you own.

Chapter 5 explains the particulars of reconciling an account.

Getting Tax Help from Quicken and TurboTax

INCLUDES

- Finding your way around the Tax Center

- Tagging expense categories so they appear on tax reports

- Identifying tax-deductible expenses

- Estimating what your income taxes will be

- Calculating capital gains taxes

- Getting TurboTax's help to do your income taxes

FAST FORWARD

Tag Categories So That
They Appear on Tax Reports ➤ *pp. 281-283*

1. Choose Lists | Category/Transfer.
2. Click a category or subcategory name on the Category & Transfer List.
3. Click the Edit button.
4. Click the Tax-related check box and click OK.

Assign a Category to a Line on Tax Forms ➤ *pp. 283-284*

Category	Assigned Line Item
Bonus	W-2 : Salary or wages, s
Change Mkt. Val	
Div Income	Sched B : Dividend inco
For Kids	
Gift Received	
Horserace Winnings	
Income	
: IDG	Sched C : Gross receipts
: Nelson Group	Sched C : Gross receipts

1. Choose Features | Taxes | Set Up for Taxes.
2. In the Tax Link Assistant dialog box, click the name of the category or subcategory that you want to assign to a line on a tax form.
3. In the Tax Form Line Items box, click the line item that you want to assign to your category or subcategory.
4. Click the Assign Line Item to Category button and click OK.

Estimate How Much Tax You Will Owe ➤ *pp. 286-289*

Taxable Income	140,004	
Income Tax	34,677	
Other Tax,Credits...	2,500	
Total tax	37,177	
Marginal, Avg. Rate	21.5%	22.2%
Tax Due		
Withholding, W-4...	10,651	
Est. Tax Pmts...	6,000	
Remaining Tax Due	20,526	

1. Choose Features | Taxes | Tax Planner to see the Tax Planner screen.
2. Click the down arrow in the Status box and choose a filing status option.
3. Click the down arrow in the Year box and choose the year for which you want a tax estimate.
4. Fill in the fields in the Tax Planner dialog box. To do that, either enter the numbers yourself or click the buttons to get to dialog boxes that help you calculate the numbers. You can also import the data from Quicken registers by clicking the Quicken Data button.
5. Look at the Remaining Tax Due field in the lower-right corner. It says what your estimated tax bill is.

Estimate the Capital Gains Taxes
You Have to Pay on the Sale of a Security ➤ pp. 289-290

1. Choose Features | Taxes | Estimate Capital Gains.

2. Click a security in the bottom half of the Capital Gains Estimator window.

3. Click the Add button.

4. In the Add to Scenario dialog box, enter how many shares you plan to sell and their per-share price.

5. Note your profit, capital gains tax, and net profit in the top half of the window.

Shares	Sale Price	Gain/Loss	Approx. Tax
100	31	2,002.50	560.70
100	134	412.50	115.50
100	16	285.00	79.80
		2,700.00	756.00

Benjamin Franklin wrote, "In this world, nothing is certain but death and taxes." This chapter explains how to do your best by one of those certainties. As for the other, all you can do about it is eat right, get enough sleep and exercise, and hope for the best.

In this chapter, you learn your way around the Tax Center, how to tag categories that pertain to taxes so they appear on tax reports, and how to find tax-deductible expenses you didn't know about. You also find instructions here for estimating next year's tax bill, calculating the capital gains tax on the sale of a security, and getting the help of TurboTax to do your income taxes.

A TRIP TO THE TAX CENTER

As tax time draws near, click the Taxes hyperlink on the Home Page or choose Features | Taxes | Tax Center to take a trip to the Tax Center window and contemplate your tax situation. As Figure 15.1 shows, the Tax Center offers hyperlinks to Quicken's Tax Planner, Deduction Finder, and Capital Gains Estimator, all of which are explained in this chapter. You can also click hyperlinks to go on the Internet and learn how to improve your tax situation. And you will also find these goodies in the Tax Center:

- **Projected Tax** Roughly how much you owe in taxes. Quicken gets these figures from the Tax Planner (see "Estimating How Much You Will Owe in Taxes" later in this chapter).
- **Tax Calendar** When taxes are due. Quicken gets these dates from the General Tab of the Set Up Alerts dialog box (see "Being Alerted to Financial Events" in Chapter 8).
- **Year-to-Date Income** Your income so far this year in categories that you have tagged for inclusion on tax reports (see "Tagging Categories for Tax Purposes" in this chapter).

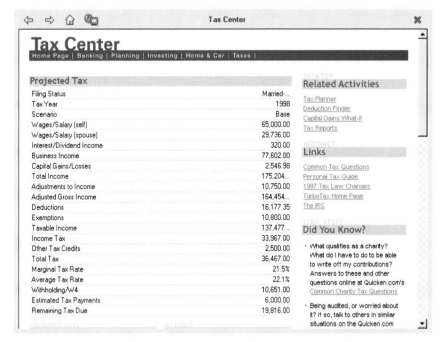

Figure 15.1 In the Tax Center, you can glimpse the future and see what your taxes will be.

- **Year-to-Date Deductions** Expenses so far this year in expense categories that you have tagged for inclusion on tax reports (see "Tagging Categories for Tax Purposes" and "Using the Deduction Finder to Identify Tax-Deductible Expenses" in this chapter).

TAGGING CATEGORIES FOR TAX PURPOSES

Chapter 9 explains how to generate reports, including the Tax Summary report, which lists and totals income and tax-deductible expenses.

One of the most important things you will ever do in Quicken is to tag categories that pertain to income taxes. By doing that, you can tell Quicken to include categories and subcategories in Tax Summary reports like the one shown in Figure 15.2. Accountants charge a small fortune to review registers and find tax-deductible expenses, and, if you do your own taxes, searching for and tabulating tax-deductible expenses can take hours. On the other hand, it takes Quicken

Tax Summary Report
1/1/98 Through 7/13/98

Description	◇ Amount
Office:	
Copying	- 86
Equipment	- 1,378
Furniture	- 60
Online services	- 270
Supplies	- 31
TOTAL Office	- 1,824

Figure 15.2 Part of a Tax Summary Report. This report lays out the numbers for all categories that pertain to income tax reporting.

about four seconds to generate a Tax Summary report that finds and tabulates tax-deductible expenses.

Besides tagging categories so that they appear on Tax Summary reports, you can assign each category to a line on a specific income tax form (Form 1040, Schedule A, Schedule C, and so on). With that done, you can export the information to a tax-preparation program like TurboTax or use Quicken's Tax Planner to get accurate estimates of how much tax you will owe next April.

Tagging Categories for Tax Summary Reports

See "Using the Deduction Finder to Identify Tax-Deductible Expenses" later in this chapter to help find expense categories for Tax Summary reports.

Tagging a category or subcategory so that it appears on tax summary reports is pretty easy. All you have to do is click the Tax-related check box in the Set Up Category dialog box when you create a new category. Or, if you created the category already, you can visit the Edit Category dialog box and click the Tax-related check box there. To open the Edit Category dialog box, choose Lists | Category/Transfer or press CTRL-C to see the Category & Transfer List, click on a category or subcategory, and then click the Edit button. You see the Edit Category dialog box shown in Figure 15.3. Click the Tax-related check box and then click OK.

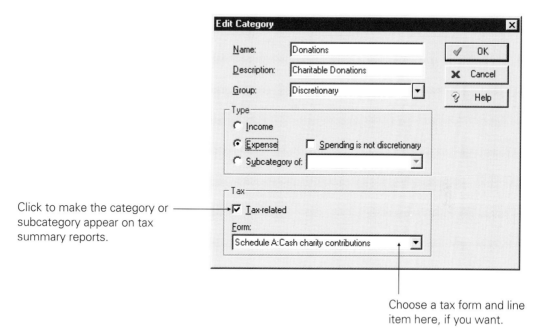

Click to make the category or subcategory appear on tax summary reports.

Choose a tax form and line item here, if you want.

Figure 15.3 Data from tax-related categories appears on Tax Summary reports; assign categories to tax form line items if you use TurboTax or another tax-preparation software.

Assigning Categories to Lines on Income Tax Forms

Assign categories to line items on tax forms if you want to get a head start in using the Tax Planner or if you intend to use a tax-preparation package, such as TurboTax, to calculate your income tax. By assigning categories to line items on tax forms, you can export your data directly into a tax-preparation package and save time calculating your income taxes. However, you have to know the tax forms well to assign line items to tax forms. For example, you have to know that dividend income is reported on Schedule B, and who knows that off the top of their head? If you know the tax forms well or you are willing to study last year's tax returns to find out which line goes on which form, then try assigning categories to lines on tax forms.

To do that, either open the Edit Category dialog box and choose a form and line from the Form drop-down list (see the previous section in this chapter and Figure 15.3), or choose Features | Taxes | Set Up for Taxes to open the Tax Link Assistant dialog box. The three columns in the middle show categories, line items to which they've been assigned (if any), and tax form line items:

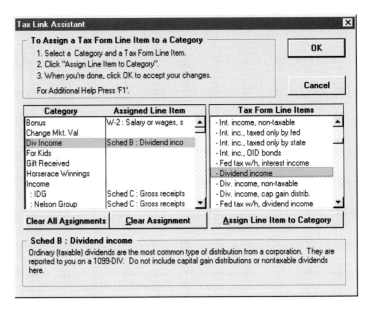

If you've been using ready-made Quicken categories, some categories already have line item assignments. To link a category to part of a tax form, click a category or subcategory, click its corresponding line item in the Tax Form Line Items box, and then click the Assign Line Item to Category button. When you're done assigning the categories that pertain to taxes to line items in tax forms, click OK.

USING THE DEDUCTION FINDER TO IDENTIFY TAX-DEDUCTIBLE EXPENSES

If you are self-employed, or you use Quicken to track business expenses, or you itemize deductions on income tax reports, you owe it to yourself to find every tax-deductible expense you can claim on income tax forms. To help you do that,

Quicken offers a gizmo called the Deduction Finder. The Deduction Finder helps you locate tax-deductible expenses and gives you the opportunity to create a new expense category for tracking each expense you find.

To use the Deduction Finder, either click the Deduction Finder hyperlink in the Tax Center window or choose Features | Taxes | Tax Deduction Finder. You see the Deduction Finder window shown in Figure 15.4. Choose a deduction type from menu 1, a question from menu 2, and then answer the Yes or No questions in part 3, the question list. If you answer a question Yes, you can click the Create a Category button to create a new expense category for tracking the tax-deductible expense.

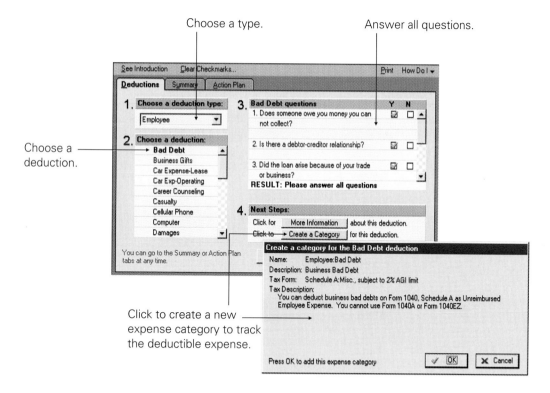

Figure 15.4 Use the Deduction Finder to find expenses that you can deduct from your income taxes.

These questions are the very same ones that tax accountants ask when they determine how to lower your taxes. When you finish answering questions, click the Summary tab to see the deductions you are eligible for and the Action Plan tab to get advice about taking advantage of tax deductions.

ESTIMATING HOW MUCH YOU WILL OWE IN TAXES

Yet another way to plan for tax time is to use Quicken's Tax Planner. It never hurts to know how much tax you will owe, especially if you are the kind who doesn't like surprises. And the Tax Planner is a great way to see how purchasing a house or changing jobs will affect your taxes. Using the Tax Planner, you can fool with the numbers and create one, two, or three different tax scenarios.

Entering the Data

To reach the Tax Planner screen, which is shown in Figure 15.5, either choose Features | Taxes | Tax Planner or click the Tax Planner hyperlink in the Tax Center window (see Figure 15.1). When you finish entering the data in the Tax Planner, Quicken estimates what your total tax, marginal tax, and average tax rates are, and how much tax you owe.

The first thing to do is tell the Tax Planner what your filing status is (Single or Married-Joint, for example) by clicking the Status drop-down menu and making a choice. The Tax Planner on your computer has the correct federal tax rates for 1998, as well as what the fortune-tellers at Intuit think the tax rates for 1999 will be. Choose a year from the Year drop-down menu.

EXPERT ADVICE

A Tax Summary report can be very helpful when it comes to entering data in the Tax Planner. To generate one, click the Reports icon, click the Taxes tab, click Tax Summary, and click the Create button.

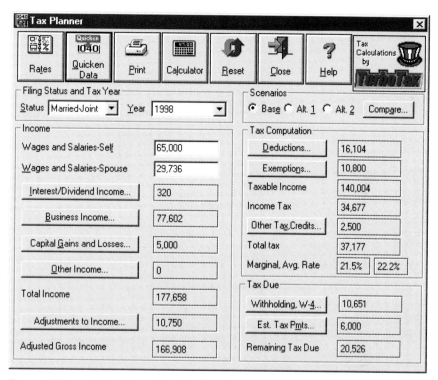

Figure 15.5 Look in the Remaining Tax Due field in the lower-right corner of the Tax Planner window to see what Quicken thinks your tax bill will be.

Next, tell Quicken what your income and expenses are going to be so it can estimate how much you will owe in taxes. Get the paperwork together. You need to know what your income is, what your mortgage interest payments are if you are making mortgage payments, and everything else that you need to fill out tax forms. Of course, you can wing it if you want and make estimates, or you can use last year's tax forms.

Enter what you expect your total wages and salary to be in the first Income field, Wages and Salaries–Self. Then work your way down the Income column on the left side of the screen. Quicken offers buttons to help you fill in some of the fields. For example, if you have or expect to have income from interest and dividends, click the Interest/Dividend Income button, fill in the dialog box, and click OK. After you finish the Income column, work your way down the Tax Computation column, too. As you go along, Quicken calculates your tax bill in the Remaining Tax Due field.

SHORTCUT

Quicken can bring data from categories into the Tax Planner as long as you assigned categories to lines on income tax forms ("Tagging Categories for Tax Purposes" earlier in this chapter explains how to do this). Click the Quicken Data button in the Tax Planner screen. You see the Preview Quicken Tax Data dialog box with its five mighty columns of data. This data comes from the transactions you entered so far this year in Quicken registers. Glance at it and click the OK button. Back on the Tax Planner screen, most of the boxes are filled in. Go down the columns and make sure the data is accurate. If it isn't, enter the tax data yourself.

Playing with What-If Tax Scenarios

Should you sell the stock, even if it means taking the capital gains hit? Should you renounce all worldly goods to save on taxes? You can answer these and other questions by creating a second or third scenario with the Tax Planner. To do that, click the Alt 1 or Alt 2 button after you estimate your income taxes the first time. These buttons are near the upper-right corner of the Tax Planner screen. A dialog box asks if you want to copy the current scenario. Click Yes if you want to make the first scenario the starting point for the next one, or click No to start from scratch.

Now either tinker with the numbers in the Tax Planner dialog box or generate a new set of numbers. When you are done, you can click the Compare button to see how the different scenarios you created stack up:

Tax Scenario Comparisons

	Base Case	Alternate Case 1	Alternate Case 2
Filing Status	Married-Joint	Married-Joint	Married-Joint
Tax Year	1998	1998	1998
Adjusted Gross Income	166,908	175,383	92,926
Deductions and Exemptions	26,904	26,650	28,176
Taxable Income	140,004	148,733	64,750
Total Tax	37,177	39,461	12,625
Marginal, Avg. Tax Rates	21.5% 22.2%	31.9% 22.5%	28.0% 13.5%

OK   Help

ESTIMATING CAPITAL GAINS

Estimating the capital gains taxes on the sale of a security can be difficult, so Quicken offers the Capital Gains Estimator to help you with this difficult chore. In the Capital Gains Estimator, you tell Quicken the rate you are taxed, select one of the securities you own, enter how much you propose to sell your shares for, and find out how much you stand to profit and how much capital gains tax you have to pay on your profits.

Use the Capital Gains Estimator before you sell a security to see whether selling it is worthwhile, given the taxes you have to pay on the profits. To use the Capital Gains Estimator, either click the Capital Gains What-if hyperlink in the Tax Center or choose Features | Taxes | Estimate Capital Gains. You see the Capital Gains Estimator window shown in Figure 15.6. The securities you own appear in the bottom half of the window.

If this is the first time you have used the Estimator, click the Tax Rates button and choose the capital gains tax rates that apply to you. Your short-term capital gains tax rate is the same as your marginal tax rate. You can use the Tax Planner to see what your marginal tax rate is (see "Estimating How Much You Will Owe in Taxes" earlier in this chapter). Click the Tax Planner button and look beside Marginal, Avg. Rate in the Tax Planner window (see Figure 15.5).

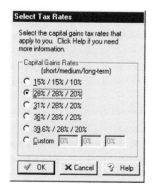

Select Tax Rates

Select the capital gains tax rates that apply to you. Click Help if you need more information.

Capital Gains Rates
(short/medium/long-term)
- ○ 15% / 15% / 10%
- ● 28% / 28% / 20%
- ○ 31% / 28% / 20%
- ○ 36% / 28% / 20%
- ○ 39.6% / 28% / 20%
- ○ Custom 0% 0% 0%

✓ OK   ✗ Cancel   ? Help

4. Note your profit, taxes, and net profit.

2. Click the Add button.

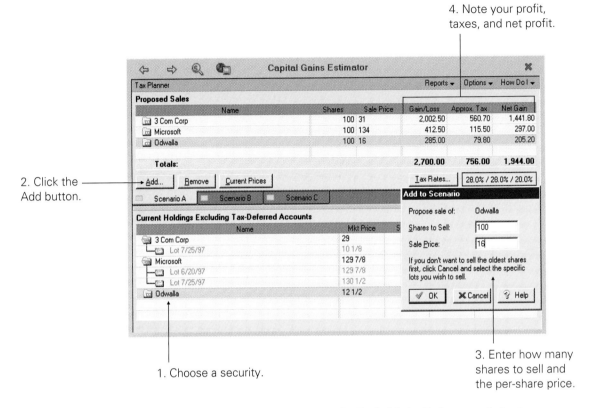

1. Choose a security.

3. Enter how many shares to sell and the per-share price.

Figure 15.6 Before you sell a security, use the Capital Gains Estimator to find out how much tax you have to pay on the profits.

Follow these steps to learn how much tax you have to pay on profits from the sale of a security:

1. Click a security on the bottom half of the screen.

2. Click the Add button.

3. In the Add to Scenario dialog box, enter how many shares you propose to sell, enter the sale price of those shares, and click OK. The top half of the window shows your profit, capital gains taxes on the profit, and your net profit.

Don't like what you see? Click the Scenario B or Scenario C button and start all over, but enter different figures in the Add to Scenario dialog box.

USING QUICKEN WITH TURBOTAX

TurboTax is a tax-preparation software package available from Intuit Corporation, the same company that makes Quicken. It's lucky for you that Quicken and TurboTax are made by the same folks, because it makes using TurboTax easier. As I write these words, Intuit plans to offer a discount on TurboTax to users of Quicken 99, although the details have yet to be made public.

Registered Quicken users can use TurboTax online by choosing Features | Taxes | TurboTax Online. Choose this command and you go on the Internet to the TurboTax Online site, where you answer questions about your income and expenses and let TurboTax do the work of preparing your income taxes. However, TurboTax Online is not for everyone. Only people whose tax situation is relatively simple can take advantage of the service.

To use TurboTax after you have installed the program on your computer, choose Features | Taxes | TurboTax. The TurboTax program opens onscreen. On the Import tab in TurboTax is a special command for importing data from Quicken. If you followed the instructions in this chapter under "Assigning Categories to Lines on Income Tax Forms," you will find it especially easy to import your Quicken data into TurboTax. You have already done the work of assigning categories to lines on tax forms.

Index

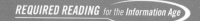